MW01343025

The Answer is in Your Handwriting!

VOLUME III:

Your Work, Your Career - Is It Right For You?

Cover design by Jonathan Perez.

ACKNOWLEDGEMENTS

I want, first, to acknowledge Dr. Paton, who in 1934 inspired me to later enter the medical profession. He had made a house call to my then-eighth-month pregnant mother, who was worried about giving birth to her seventh child. After he had examined her, I stood by. He listened compassionately while my mother wept, and I made up my mind then and there, at the age of eight, that I wanted to be a doctor like him (physician/psychologist). Though I did not achieve that dream, I did eventually become a medical lab technologist, and later, once financially secure, achieved another dream: becoming a graphologist. Nevertheless, I still often think of Dr. Paton, and he was in many ways, I realize now, a big inspiration for my "Dear Dena" columns and finally this book.

For thirty-odd years, I felt forced, on pain of poverty and starvation, to devote the bulk of my time to more practical and lucrative endeavors than handwriting analysis. I chose to make earning a living my priority, rather than graphology. And while I do not regret this decision, for I also enjoyed being in the medical field as well as real estate, I urge my readers never to abandon their passions for the sake of money alone. It is all too easy to neglect one's natural gifts and talents in life in the midst of career and family.

I wish to thank my technology guru Jonathan Perez, without whom I would be helpless, for his patient and kind attention to my many and varied technical problems, and especially for the beautifully rendered covers of each of the three volumes.

Many thanks also go to Steve Conifer for his patience with me, and his great professional help in editing and getting the book ready for the publisher.

I also wish to thank Larry Farwell for his kind and thoughtful critique of my skills as a graphologist, and in particular for his letter of recommendation, written almost thirty years ago, in which he amply praised the accuracy of my handwriting analyses.

Finally, I would like to acknowledge my daughter, Rena Smith, MFT, of Santa Barbara, whose emotional support and devotion to family and community inspired me throughout the writing of these books.

TABLE OF CONTENTS

PREFACE

Had I known graphology before my husband opened an electronics business alone, in 1967, we would not have been embezzled from almost to the point of bankruptcy. Upon studying the bookkeeper's deposits, accounts receivable and accounts payable, I found twenty-five ways she had stolen. We took her to court. The judge said she was guilty but he was not going to put a young mother of three in jail, and that was that.

I then went to a number of businesses, asking them if they had ever been embezzled from, and most said "yes." However, when I told them I was thinking of writing a book on embezzlement in small businesses (we hear a lot about embezzlement in the world of Big Business, but seldom in the world of smaller, usually family-operated concerns), they all begged me not to. Why? It would only teach others how to do it, they said. And they were ashamed and didn't want that sort of information "out there."

Just the other day I read in the Santa Barbara *News Press* about a police department employee of twenty-two years, made bookkeeper for the city's parking tickets, who had admitted to embezzling more than $100,000 over ten years. The crime would have been discovered much sooner had her boss or superior learned graphology.

After becoming a graphoanalyst in 1974, I found that my ex-husband's bookkeeper, Barbara Yanigihara, had all the graphological signs of an embezzler in her handwriting (which I had kept but subsequently lost). Incidentally, and perhaps somewhat ironically, a common warning sign that an employee may be inclined toward embezzlement is his or her being an excellent worker so dedicated that s/he will not take vacation or other leave (fearing an accounting in his or her absence).

So, we know how helpful graphology is in personnel selection. It is also exceptionally useful in vocational guidance, as many of the "Dear Dena's" and anecdotes in this volume will show. I have found it especially apt in helping young people to discover not only the kind of work they are best suited to, but also any emotional obstacles that might prevent them from successfully pursuing it.

INTRODUCTION

I first became interested in graphology when I was eighteen. Curious about the changes in my twenty-two-year-old sister's handwriting, I vowed to discover their meaning. It was not until after I was married with teenage children, however, that I finally took a course in graphology. It was through this course that I learned my sister had suffered from clinical depression. My personal belief is that her depression was exacerbated by her frustrated efforts to realize her passion in life: becoming an international journalist (very difficult for women in the 1930s). Her inability to support herself successfully added to her frustration. She met the love of her life and played the role society expected of her: a financially dependent housewife dedicated to her husband's happiness and career.

The conflict between the desire to do work one loves and the responsibility of supporting oneself is a common theme of "Dear Dena" writers. Graphology can be used as a tool to reveal not only psychological hindrances to success in personal relationships (explored in Volumes I & II), but also in one's work – where I believe it is best put to use.

This volume includes a collection of "Dear Dena's" requesting advice on choices of (and concerning) work, career paths, interpersonal relationships in the workplace, and the advantages as well as disadvantages of pursuing various vocations. I answer their "Dear Abby" type questions based on what I see in their handwriting, all the while teaching graphology by revealing the meanings of the strokes. Interspersed between "Dear Dena's" are bits of "grandmotherly wisdom" in the form of anecdotes on work and related subjects, which I hope the reader will at least find amusing or interesting, if not thought-provoking as well.

To help with the graphology learning process, each volume contains The Basics (in the Appendix), as well as a review of psychological traits in handwriting. By my "Dear Dena" method of teaching graphology, I hope to afford you, the reader, an easier and more enjoyable time learning it. You may also come to better understand both yourself and others, simply by examining and studying your own handwriting as well as theirs.

I act as sort of a "screener," dispensing initial advice to readers seeking career counseling. From just the strokes in one's handwriting (which, as explained in Volume I, is really brain-writing), I am able to infer basic personality traits indicating aptitude (or lack thereof) in a given field. Upon this basis, I am able to make a fairly reliable assessment of the writer's likelihood of success in the career of his choice and advise him accordingly.

CHAPTER ONE

Career Topics and Graphology

"Choose a job you love, and you will never have to work a day in your life."
- Confucius

"Frequently the man who thinks he is throwing away his career because he believes in something and acts on his belief, in the end makes his career."
- Eleanor Roosevelt

"What you believe has more power than what you dream or wish or hope for. You become what you believe."
- Oprah Winfrey

My "Dear Dena's" come from a wide range of people, responding to ads I place in some large-city classified ads, as well as from my newspaper and magazine columns. From this cross-section of people, I have found a few themes:

1) **Many have conflicts between obligations at work and obligations at home.** Often these conflicts involve disputes over the boundaries and duties of so-called "male/female roles," and can be resolved only by redefining those roles in the context of the particular relationship.

2) **A familiar dilemma to many of us, some "Dear Dena's" describe conflicts over pursuing one's passion or career of choice, on the one hand, and financial security on the other.**

Either way, there is a price to pay. Sometimes it involves postponing our dreams, sometimes living on little money. Human nature being what it is, we experience anxiety over "paying the price"; we do not do it *willingly*, of course, because we'd all prefer to "have our cake and eat it too." But we can find a kind of balance; it doesn't have to be "either-or." However, there will still be certain undesirable consequences. A career woman who marries and has children, for example, must make peace with doing less than her very best not only at work, but in her marriage, home life, and the care of her children, even if her husband tends to some of the domestic responsibilities. The same goes for the career man, but perhaps to a lesser degree.

3) **Some seem confident, and "want it all"** – work they love, money, a happy mate, good familial relations, and recreation. Without making compromises, they are bound to suffer anxiety.
4) **Some adults don't know what they want to be when they "grow up." Others have so many talents they have a hard time focusing on just one.**
5) **Some are in careers possibly unsuited to them,** spending lives on work they dislike.
6) **Surprisingly few are not seeking more money, but rather satisfaction at work.**
7) **Some are making their first real career decision.**

8) **Some wonder if they should leave their career and ask me what's best for them.**
9) **Some are changing careers in mid-life.**
10) **Some ask if it is the "right time" for change.**
11) **Others want to refocus the careers they are in.**
12) **A few are about employer/employee conflicts.**
13) **It seems that more women than men have very little confidence and self-esteem,** whether in career or personal relationships. Men, traditionally *expected* to make their mark in the world, are working, gaining confidence, and becommng more ambitious. Too many women, on the other hand, seem to be waiting to marry and live vicariously through their husbands. Their lack of confidence and low self-esteem are often evident in their handwriting. **Graphotherapeutics** (simple handwriting exercises taught in the book) can help people with low confidence and little self-esteem to set realistic goals and develop the determination to achieve them.
14) **Some have a career in mind, but don't have sufficient emotional maturity to achieve it,** due to conscious or unconscious fears and negative ways of handling them. Fortunately, handwriting reveals not only one's talents and intellect, but more importantly one's *emotional* "IQ," these days popularly known as one's "EQ." The immaturity found to be hindering one's career and/or personal life can often be lessened with therapy, including graphotherapeutics.
15) **Others have no motivation, longing for work with "passion." But passion is related to one's purpose in life, or why we're here on Earth – for what purpose?** My guess is that it's to discover and use our inborn talents in a **positive** way, contributing somehow to a better world. I

believe every talent or gift is unique and important, whether it's the discovery of a cure for cancer, or the gift of love from a retarded child. Everyone has something of value to give to mankind.

So, is the work you're doing right for you? Or are you a square peg in a round hole? Are you a would-be entertainer in a research lab, a slow and deliberate thinker in a high-pressure job, or a statistics expert who longs to write fiction?

Look at your handwriting. To begin with: what's your emotional make-up? Your dominant mental processes? Your imagination quotient?

Whether you're young, searching for your first job, or middle-aged or even a senior, refer to the "Dear Dena's" and the "Basic Graphology" (Appendix). You'll not only learn how to analyze handwriting, but you may also gradually discover what work you're best suited to, what you're unsuited to – and, most importantly, what obstacles may be preventing you from securing the kind of work you desire.

Specimen #1
(conflict regarding work, marriage, home life)

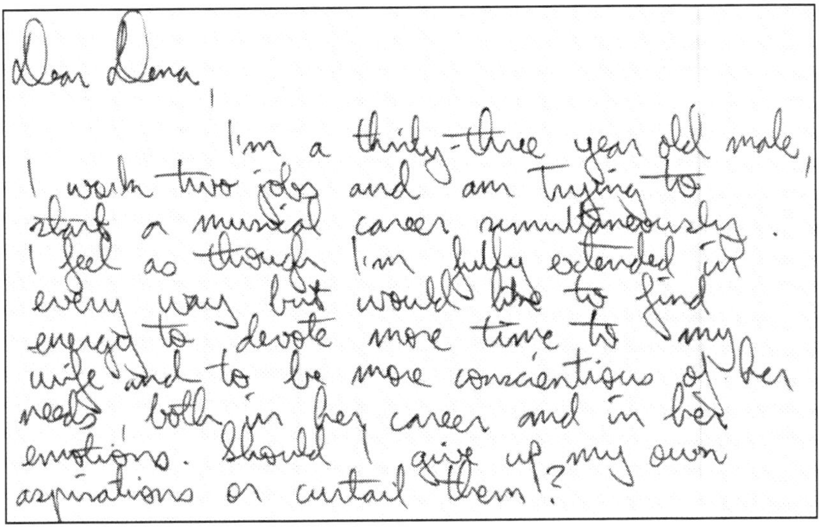
Dear Dena,
I'm a thirty-three year old male, I work two jobs and am trying to start a musical career simultaneously. I feel as though I'm fully extended in every way but would like to find energy to devote more time to my wife and to be more conscientious of her needs both in her career and in her emotions. Should I give up my own aspirations or curtail them?

Dear Dena,

I'm a thirty-three-year old male, I work two jobs and am trying to start a musical career simultaneously. I feel as though I am fully extended in every way but would like to find energy to devote more time to my wife and be more conscientious of her needs, both in her career and in her emotions. Should I give up my aspirations or curtail them?

Dear 33 year old male,

Your goal is realistic (t-bar high on stem), your determination strong (good down-strokes in "y" and "g"); you've analyzed (sharp angular "m" and "n") and planned this move. Though you use the traditional cursive capital "D," you see yourself as a creative person (simple stick "I"), a trait necessary for success in music or art—and which requires having your own space (larger than normal space between words), suggesting conflict. In addition, you fear risking your career (large space after "to" in second line), wondering if you have what it takes (very low t-bars in the key words "to start").

Lower loops of "g" and "y" which lean to the right but end to the left without a loop indicate unfinished projects or less than fulfilled material or sexual needs. The conflict is making you rather irritable (dashes for dots), sensitive to criticism (loops on "d" and "t," especially in the key word "start"), critical (inflexible beginning stroke on angular "m"), a bit moody (variable slant), and secretive (many right loops on "o").

Should you give up your aspirations? You have too much going for you to give them up entirely. Nor should you. You have a right to your dreams. Curtail them? It all depends on your priorities, how much you yearn to be with your wife, and how much your marriage means to you. At present you have too many irons in the fire (lower loops dangling into next line).

My advice? Look for balance in life. If you give a little and she gives a little, you and she could make time to smell the roses. Also, you don't "find" energy to devote time; you become motivated *about your priorities, and, lo and behold, the energy is there. Then both marriage and career prosper.*

Specimen #2
(conflict between work one loves and financial security)

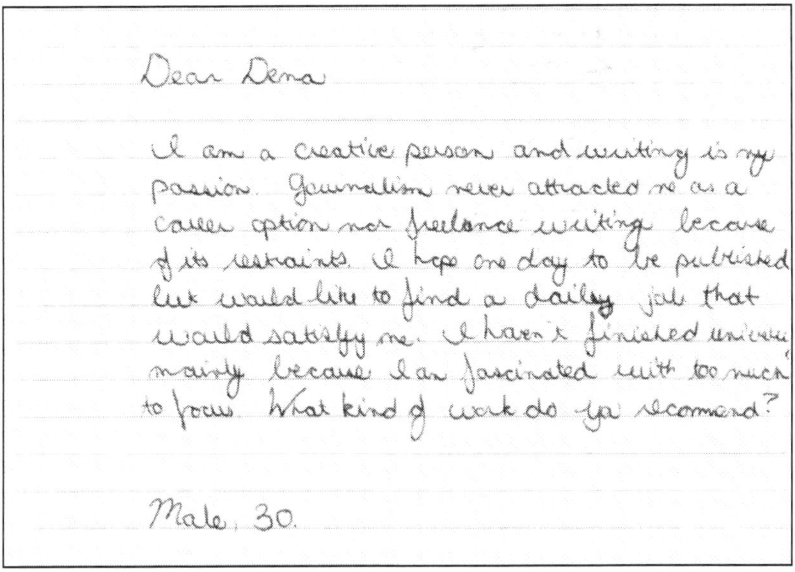
Dear Dena

I am a creative person and writing is my passion. Journalism never attracted me as a career option nor freelance writing because of its restraints. I hope one day to be published but would like to find a daily job that would satisfy me. I haven't finished universi mainly because I am fascinated with too much to focus. What kind of work do you recomend?

Male, 30.

Dear Dena,

I am a creative person and writing is my passion. Journalism never attracted me as a career option nor freelance writing because of its restraints. I hope one day to be published but would like to find a daily job that would satisfy me. I haven't finished university, mainly because I am fascinated with too much to focus. What kind of work do you recommend? – Male 30

Dear Male 30,

Your nature is warm and caring (rounded "m" and "n") and, except for some evasiveness at times ("a" in "am"), basically straightforward and honest (no loops on "a" and "o"). You are a philosophical seeker (pointed loop in "l") with some intuition (breaks between letters) and a good mind for writing (many fluency strokes, i.e., letters joined to the next). Some word endings droop even on the lined paper, so it seems you are battling a low-level depression, but you handle it; the next word is back on the line.

What kind of work do I recommend? I am sorry to say: none that would satisfy you; all work at some time or other has some restraints of one kind or another, and you show resentment (inflexible beginning strokes in the key words "its restraints").

This feeling could possibly have translated into repressed feelings (retraced "h") and weak goal-settings (very weak t-bar in key word "haven't). You're moody (variable slant), very independent-minded (short "t" and "d" stems), and very stubborn (wide wedge of "t" in "haven't"). However, your self-control and diplomacy (convex t-bar in "can't" and tapering of letters in the word) counteract those traits when dealing with people.

There is larger than usual space after "daily" and the word following is what one fears. In your case it is "job." Perhaps it is the "restraints" again. Look closely at the word "university." The t-bar is not only very light and low on the stem (lack of confidence), but slanting downward (you feel you must do it or learn it your way*). Perhaps "too much to focus on" is a rationalization (large left loop on "o" in "you").*

Now look at the word "that" (referring to a daily job). The t-bar is firm and strong but low on the stem of the "t," which has a wide wedge (stubbornness). This suggests you firmly believe that you will not find a job that satisfies you.

You know the saying: if you can't have what you love, then love what you have. I don't think it really matters what kind of work you choose. It's not your life's work; it's your financial support. It has benefits (e.g., money). So if you say to yourself (even though you don't care much for the job) that you choose it, *you* choose *to work at the job because it enables you to write and live, rather than* you have to work*—you'll find not only that it's no longer draining your energy, but freeing it for your writing, perhaps even giving you story ideas.*

Making Lemonade

I was a lab technologist in a noisy irritating environment doing routine hematology work that bored me. I yearned to be in the quiet bacteriology lab next door, doing work I was more interested in. My boss refused my request for transfer with "We need you here. If you don't like it, you can leave!"

I needed the job, so I was stuck. I decided I would have to find a way to block out the noise and commotion around me. I had to find something to focus intently on, concentrate on, so that I would be oblivious of the irritants. I decided to spend extra time in work not required of me in hematology, painstakingly viewing blood slides for pathological blood cells, especially immature cells of early leukemia. I became so engrossed in this, I no longer heard or felt the movement of people coming and going around me. When my boss finally allowed me to transfer, I almost didn't care.

So, as I advised the writer above, if you can't have what you love, then love what you have (if you've been given a lemon, as they say, make lemonade).

Specimen #3 (reduced 20%)
(wife/mother – conflict between career and home life)

Dear Dena:

Help! I'm a recent grad, and ~~alloco~~ although
I struggled really hard to get through
school as a mom and wife – commuting
long distances to finish my education,
I'm finding it difficult to muster
up the confidence to get out there
and do it! I've gotten a good job,
but not in the field of my study.
I've taken little steps ~~to~~ to obtaining
a business license so I can get
going in the right direction, but
finding it hard to commit the time
needed to get a business going &
work all hours without neglecting
my family. It wasn't easy to
justify less time with the family
to finish school, and finding
it even harder now. I'm dissatisfied
with the pace. Am I expecting too
much, am I stalling or just afraid?

– Estring

Note the large right margin showing fear of the future.

Dear Dena,

Help! I'm a recent grad, and although I sruggled really hard to get through school as a mom and wife---commuting long distances to finish my education, I'm finding it difficult to muster up the confidence to get out there and deo it! I've gotten a good job, but not in the field of my study. I've taken little steps like obtaining a business license so I can get going in the right direction, but finding it hard too commit the time needed to get a business going and work 40 hours without neglecting my family. It wasn't easy to justify less time with the family to finish school, aqnd finding it even harder now. I'm dissatisfied with the pacve. Am I expecting too much, am I stalling or just afraid? – Estring

Dear E-string,

Yes, you are expecting too much of yourself; you have high standards (height of t-stem) and feel you have not lived up to them (low t-bars on the stem). Yes, you are stalling with procrastination (t-ars to left of stem). And yes, you are afraid (very large right margin), showing fear of dealing with people and facing the future. Emotinal conflict is seen in the varying widths of both the right and the much narrower left margin, as well as the variable size of middle-zone letters in "distances."

You don't say what you studied or trained for, but your handwriting indicates you are very intelligent, with a sharp analytical mind (anagular "m" and "n"). With your large writing, right slant, fluency strokes (one letter joining the next), cultural interests (Greek "s"), and intuition (breaks between letters), you could work in one of the helping fields (medical, psychological, spiritual, etc.)—not directly, but rather behind the scenes, managing or running your own business or department. I say this because you are much too sensitive to criticism (large loop on "d") and, at times, stubbornly (wedge in t-stem in "recent") desire things done your own way (t-bars slanting down).

Communication with coworkers, employees, husband, and children could be better. You are too evasive (cover over or hook inside "a" or "o") or secretive (right loop on "a" or "o")—and you can be quite irritible (many dashes for dots).

Being "superwoman" is hard. To accomplish such a feat you have to first be kinder to yourself. Give yourself credit for the wonders you have already accomplished by graduating from college while a wife and mother. To continue as "superwoman" you must stay optimistic (risng lines) and learn to let things be imperfect. You must learn to cut corners for meals and housekeeping and delegate work to others, as you tend to your priorities—your career and being there for your husband and children. It might mean you work nights and weekends only—or perhaps you may have to temporarily postpone the career you studied for. It might mean that you have to attend to your physical and mental health first. However, I gather you are still a young woman, and time is on your side. Times have changed and women have equality—but then there's the real world where women's careers suffer or else their home lives suffer. It's an art to balance both.

Your main problem is lack of confidence and weak will in handling so much. Feeling discouraged (down-turned loop on "y" in "family" and "g" in "Estring"), you have the tendency to give up (low and concave t-bar in "without"). What's needed is more belief in yourself (heavier and higher t-bars). Practice making them, and you will see a slow but certain rise in confidence. Still, as "superwoman," things can get messy. So I say again, be kind to yourself.

Specimen #4

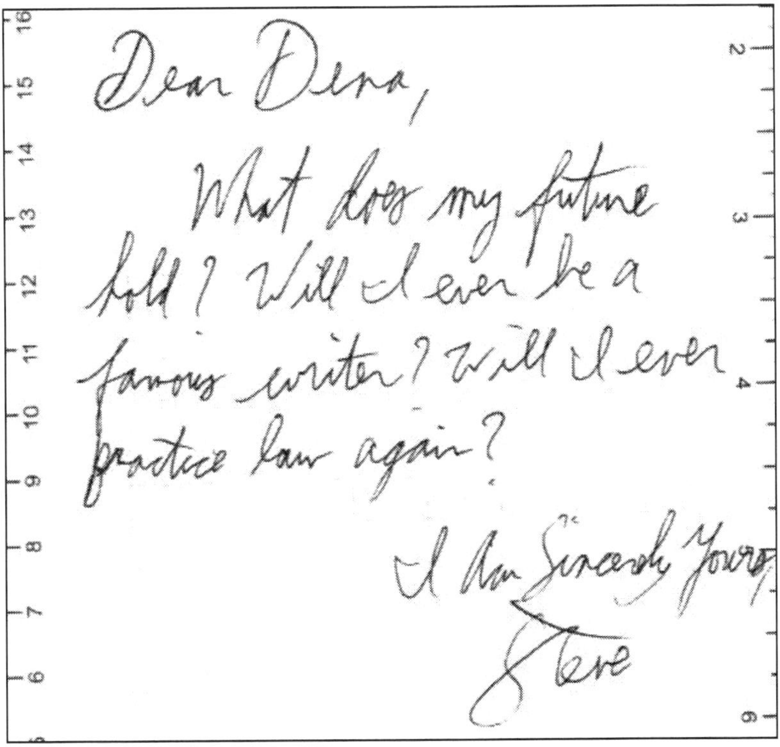
Dear Dena,
What does my future hold? Will I ever be a famous writer? Will I ever practice law again?
I Am Sincerely Yours,
Steve

Dear Dena,

What does my future hold? Will I ever be a famous writer? Will I ever practice law again? – I Am Sincerely Yours, Steve, 33

Dear Steve,

In answer to your questions, I am not a psychic. But from your handwriting, I can tell you where your talents lie and what may be hindering you in achievement of your goals. You are intelligent with both logical and analytical thinking processes (rounded and angular "m" and "n"). With your ability to concentrate (small middle-zone letters) you could be successful in long-range study in any profession. Your goals are realistic and your determination strong (height of t-bars on stem and down-strokes on "y" and "g"). You're versatile (variable baseline), diplomatic (tapering letters of words), and take pride in your work (height of t-stem).

You have artistic and creative talent (printed capitals), probably used in your work (thinking outside the box) as well as in your writing, where you have talent (figure eight "S" in "Steve"). Though you have great ambition as a writer (large beginning hook on the key word "writer"), you somehow do not see yourself predominantly as a writer (the capital "I" is the conventional "I," not the artistic capital "I"). So, you obviously have conflicts.

In the key words "practice law," *you not only messed up the "p" (emotional conflict about law) but you reversed it (rebelliousness). The "r" floats above the line and is retraced (deep emotional conflict), and the baseline of the word is up and down (moodiness). Emotional conflict is indicated in the variable size of the middle-zone letters from tiny to large, as well as variable space between letters. There is no dot over the "i" in "practice," although you place dots or dashes over other "i's"—meaning you do not like the constant detail involved in law practice. Furthermore, you want to do law your own way (down-slanting t-bar), so it would be hard for you to work under someone. The beginning stroke of "l" in "law" shows some resentment (almost inflexible beginning stroke). All in all, there seems to be a lot of conflict regarding the practice of law,* *making you indecisive about the future (feathery ending on the key word "future").*

Added to the above is your extreme *stubbornness (wedges in "t" in the key words "what," "future," "writer," and practice"), temper (beginning strokes on "what," "will," and "you"), and irritability (dashes for dots). Resentment strokes (inflexible beginning stroke of "e" in "Dear") begin below the line (from childhood) with a small hook (you hold onto it). Resentment is also seen in the inflexible beginning strokes of the "m" in "my" and the "i" in "will."*

Though you are very open-minded (wide "e"), you have strongly repressed some feelings (retraced "h" and retraced "m" in "my," and very narrow "a" in "what"). There is also rejection of someone close or a feeling of being rejected (lower loops of "f's" in "future" and "famous" turn left before the baseline). Sometimes you want to give up (slightly concave t-bar in the key words "what" and "future").

*It seems to me, overall, from your handwriting, that your conflict is about what you think you should be doing/**what you need to do to make a living—and what you really*** **want** ***to do.** You need to resolve your conflict and lessen the emotional turmoil. There need not be a conflict as long as you are **willing to pay the price either way**. My advice is to go with your dream, be willing to pay the price of less income (if that be the case)—and be happy. All the best!*

Specimen #5
(working long and hard, yet broke)

"Having more money doesn't make you happier. I have 50 million dollars but I'm just as happy as when I had 48 million."
- Arnold Schwarzenegger

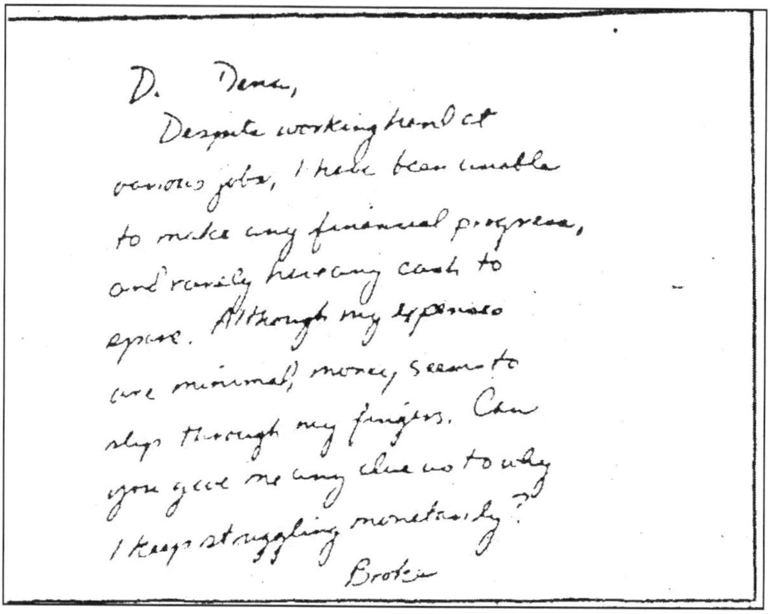
D. Dena,
Despite working hard at various jobs, I have been unable to make any financial progress, and rarely having any cash to spare. Although my expenses are minimal, money seems to slip through my fingers. Can you give me any clue as to why I keep struggling monetarily?
Broke

Dear Dena,

Despite working hard at various jobs I have been unable to make any financial progress, and rarely have any cash to spare. Although my expenses are minimal, money seems to slip through my fingers. Can you give me any clue as to why I keep struggling monetarily? – Broke

Dear Broke,

You're artistic and creative (printed capitals, especially capital "I") and intuitive (breaks between letters), work efficiently and well (fluency strokes) with people (slight right slant). Furthermore, you're intelligent (rounded and angular "m" and "n"), reliable, and dependable (spacing between letters, words, lines, rhythm). Your confidence is good (high and strong t-bars), as well as your determination (strong down-strokes on "y" and "g"). You don't say what kind of work you do, or how much education you have, but your handwriting shows you could be a professional in one of the helping fields such as teaching, psychology, medicine, social work, etc.

Depression is seen in the drooping of the word "progress". Perhaps you are in an occupation unsuited to you and unconsciously sabotaging yourself. You're afraid of the future and afraid to risk (very large right margin). You will "attract" money when you are willing to risk and possibly lose what little you now have—that is, when you fill in the wide right margin. As it is, you cling to what you know and try to conserve what you have (narrower left margin). You love simplicity (simple stick "I"); you're more concerned with who you are than what you have (no acquisitive hooks). You need work with meaning, work that is creative, not just a job. You need to express your talents in meaningful work—work you love. It would not only bring satisfaction, but eventually monetary rewards as well.

Specimen #6 (actual size)
(wants it all, and optimistic)

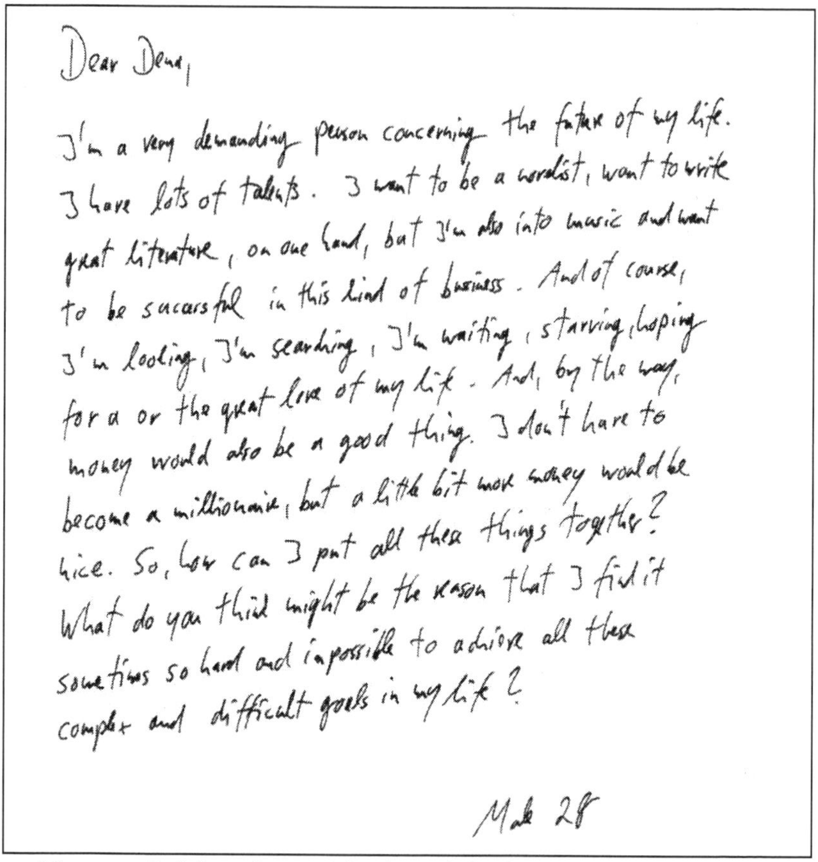
Dear Dena,
I'm a very demanding person concerning the future of my life.
I have lots of talents. I want to be a novelist, want to write
great literature, on one hand, but I'm also into music and want
to be successful in this kind of business. And of course,
I'm looking, I'm searching, I'm waiting, starving, hoping
for a or the great love of my life. And, by the way,
money would also be a good thing. I don't have to
become a millionaire, but a little bit more money would be
nice. So, how can I put all these things together?
What do you think might be the reason that I find it
sometimes so hard and impossible to achieve all these
complex and difficult goals in my life?
Mark 28

Narrow left border, widening right border.

Dear Dena,

I'm a very demanding person concerning the future of my life. I have lots of talents. I want to be a novelist, want to

write great literature, on one hand, but I'm also into music and want to be successful in this kind of business. And of course, I'm looking, I'm searching, I'm waiting, starving, hoping for the great love of my life. And by the way, money would be also a good thing. I don't have to become a millionaire, but a little bit more money would be nice. So, how can I put all those things together? What do you think might be the reason that I find it sometimes so hard and impossible to achieve all these complex and difficult goals in my life?
– Male 28

Dear Male 28,

First of all, I notice your "European" capital "I" and perfect spelling (unlike so many American writers), and wonder if your cultural background should be taken into account. Next, your tiny middle-zone writing tells me that you have the ability, with your strong analytical mind (angular "m" and "n"), to concentrate on long-range endeavors in any professional field, such as psychology or research. You are direct (no unnecessary beginning strokes), open, and honest (some open and no loops on "a" and "o").

Also evident are artistic and creative interests (simple capitals, Geek "r" and "s"), enhanced by an intuitive sense (breaks between letters) and fluency of thought (t-bar joining next letter). So I know you are intelligent and talented, as well as passionate (ink-heavy writing)—good for music and writing.

Furthermore, you set realistic goals (most t-bars high on stem) and your determination to carry them out is good (down-strokes on "g" and "y" firm and long); only rarely do you lose confidence in yourself (low t-bar in "the" in the sixth line).

So what might be in the way of your fully realizing all your dreams? As you say, you fear for your future (very wide right margin that gets even wider as you think about it).

Though you are basically optimistic (slightly rising lines), your optimism can drop quickly (drooping last letters in the key words "life," "write," "want," and "reason"), indicating **constant combating of low-level depression***—perhaps by using frequent self control (convex t-bars—twenty-four in total).*

Moodiness*, or emotional confusion, is also seen in the variable baseline and variable size of the middle-zone letters of certain words, e.g., "concerning" (some large, some tiny), as well as in the mixture of very large spacing with normal spacing between words. The largest spacing between words is at the beginning with "I'm a very demanding person concerning the future," followed by "to be successful in" and "to achieve all these complex and difficult goals" in the last line. Large spacing between words is indicative of a strong need for "space" to do one's thing, to* not always *be around people. So I would say it is a strong priority that would have to be taken into account in a relationship. However, as you can work well alone (no loop on "y") and are very selective of friends (narrow loop on "g"), it may not be a drawback.*

What is definitely a drawback in relationships and career *is your strong stubbornness (wedge between stem of "d"—ten in all), your desire at times to have things your own way, the tendency to be irritated (dashes for dots magnified by the small writing), and resentful (inflexible beginning stroke in "l" in key words "life," "love," and "literature")—as well as moody; your self-image changes with your moods. Your tiny fourth capital "I" becomes larger (self-esteem at a low ebb, gradually returns).*

However, you're still young; these drawbacks can be worked on while focusing on priorities. The rest will take care of itself in time. All in all, you have a lot to offer. All the best in working towards your goals!

I hope you readers are using "The Basics" in the Appendix when uncertain of the meaning of a stroke in the handwriting. To hasten the learning process, **a concise summary of "The Basics" follows:**

EMOTIONS

"The best and most beautiful things in the world cannot be seen or even touched. They must be felt with the heart."
- Helen Keller

1) **Slant**: Emotions dominate the personality. So look carefully at the slants. They can be anywhere from far right (highly responsive) to far left (withdrawn) or upright (poised) or a mixture. Then, depending on other traits, they may intensify or reduce the influence; the writer may or may not express certain traits.

2) **Pressure.** Light (emotions lightly felt and memories recalled but quickly relinquished). Heavy (passionate; emotions deep and memories long held)

MENTAL PROCESSES (particularly in the "m" and "n")

"Great minds discuss ideas; average minds discuss events: small minds discuss people."
- Eleanor Roosevelt

1) Angular writing – analytical, exploratory or investigative depending on height of stroke.

2) Rounded "m" and "n" at *base* (comprehensive) – the fastest thinking process of all.
3) Rounded "m" and "n" at *top* (logical or cumulative) – the slowest of all.
4) A fast thinking process does not necessarily denote greater intelligence, or a slow thinking process lesser intelligence.
5) Each mental process may be intensified by positive traits in the writing and reduced by negative ones.

IMAGINATION (Loops)

"If you can imagine it, you can achieve it. If you can dream it, you can become it."
- William Arthur Ward

1) Upper loops: abstract – philosophical, spiritual or theoretical concepts.
2) Lower loops: concrete, material (ideas for projects), or sexual. (Both upper and lower may be restricted, moderate, broad, or exaggerated in width.)
3) Middle zone loop "e": narrow- or broad-mindedness, depending on width.
4) Middle zone loops in "o" and "a": deceiving self or others; secrecy; communication.

Fears Regarding Career Choice and Defenses Used

"'Fearless' is living in spite of those things that scare you to death."
- Taylor Swift

1) T-bar to right of stem (anger), inflexible beginning stroke (resentment) – **Resisting.**
2) Low, weak, floating or concave t-bars (daydreaming, giving up, drugs) – **Escape.**
3) Horizontal word endings (caution), convex t-bars (self-control) – **Adjusting.**

ABILITY TO ACHIEVE ONE'S GOALS

"Twenty years from now you will be more disappointed by the things that you didn't do than by the ones you did do."
- Mark Twain

1) T-bars high and heavy on the stem, or low, weak, concave – **Confidence.**
2) Straight "y" and "g" down-strokes, or curved, short, turning left – **Determination.**
3) Capital the normal size of capitals, or tiny – **Self-esteem issues.**

INTEGRITY AND SOCIAL TRAITS

*"Integrity without knowledge is weak and useless;
knowledge without integrity is dangerous and dreadful."*
- Samuel Johnson

1) Left and right loops on "a" and "o," hooks in "a" and "o" – communication problems; possible dishonesty. (More details in separate chapter).
2) Slant, size of writing, pressure – extrovert; introvert; depth of feeling; fearfulness; daring.

CHAPTER TWO

Questioning the Rightness of Career Choice

"There are many paths to the top of the mountain, but the view is always the same."
- Chinese proverb

Specimen #7
(unsure of career change)

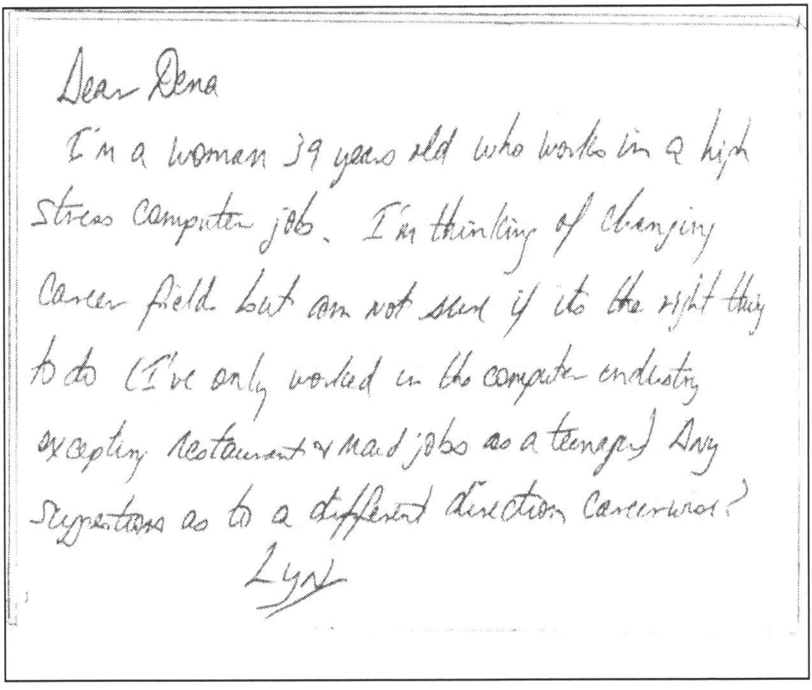
Dear Dena
I'm a woman 39 years old who works in a high stress computer job. I'm thinking of changing career field but am not sure if its the right thing to do (I've only worked in the computer industry excepting restaurant & maid jobs as a teenager) Any suggestions as to a different direction career wise?
Lyn

Dear Dena,

I'm a woman 39 years old who works in a high stress computer job. I'm thinking of changing career fields but am not sure if it's the right thing to do (I've only worked in the computer industry excepting restaurant & maid jobs as a teenager). Any suggestions as to a different direction career-wise? – Lynn

Dear Lynn,

Anything, as long as it entails using your intelligence; you have a keen concentrating mind (tiny middle-zone letters) with variable thinking processes, analytical and logical (rounded and angular "m" and "n") enhanced by intuition (breaks between letters) and directness (no beginning strokes). You have the ability to do long-range study, perhaps earn a master's degree or Ph.D., or conduct scholarly research in any field. However, I'm not sure you have the confidence for it (many low t-bars).

You don't say what your work actually entails, but you see yourself as creative (printed capital "I"). Perhaps your computer work is too routine, or managerial, and you need to have the freedom of being a computer consultant or programmer—or be entirely away from machines and work more with people, here you can express yourself (right slant).

However, you would have problems relating with people due to your secretiveness (large right loop on "o" and "a"); evasiveness (incomplete covering of "o"); insincere diplomacy (strong tapering of words); and depression (drooping key words "computer," "changing," and "industry").

You are more suited to research work (tiny writing), where interaction with others is limited, because of your emotional sensitivity (various sizes of middle-zone letters). You have a flair for writing (figure 8 "g") with cultural and literary interests (Greek "s"), which could be combined with computer work. Keeping a journal would help to develop this talent and perhaps also help you to see why you procrastinate (t-bar to left of stem) and are irritable (dashes for dots) to the point of losing temper (t-bar to right of stem).

Your sadness is handled well (you pick up the drooping words and go on), but you are avoiding the cause. Your high t-stems and low t-bars tell me you have high standards for yourself and feel guilty that you haven't lived up to them, feeling you should do more with your talents and abilities. Maybe what you need is a "position" rather than a "job," at least once you've gained some measure of confidence and belief in yourself.

Your exceptional intelligence and talents must not go to waste. Perhaps a good therapist could help sort out things for you. Meanwhile, make high and strong-bars thirty times for thirty nights before going to bed and see how it affects you. You will be impressing on your subconscious mind that you have the ability to set realistic goals with confidence. Good luck!

Specimen #8 (Zorah, female, no age)
[NOTE: The first page has been omitted for space considerations.]

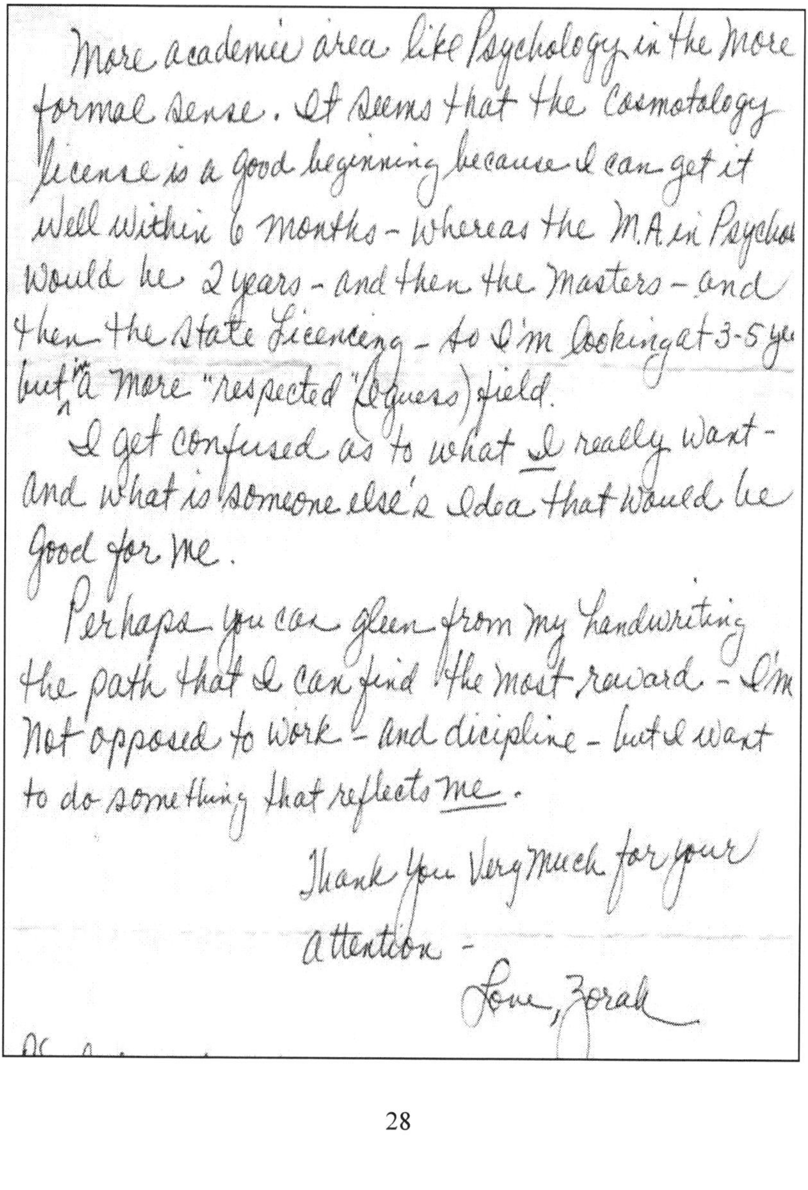

More academic area like Psychology in the more formal sense. It seems that the Cosmotology license is a good beginning because I can get it well within 6 months - whereas the M.A. in Psycho would be 2 years - and then the Masters - and then the State Licencing - so I'm looking at 3-5 ye but it's a more "respected" (I guess) field.

I get confused as to what I really want - and what is someone else's Idea that would be good for me.

Perhaps you can gleen from my handwriting the path that I can find the most reward - I'm not opposed to work - and dicipline - but I want to do something that reflects me.

Thank You Very much for your attention -

Love, Zorah

Dear Dena,

[I guess what my question is whether is it under-shooting my abilities. Should I try to push into a] more academic area like psychology in the more formal sense. It seems that the cosmotology [sic] license is a good beginning because I can get it well within 6 months – whereas the M.A. in Psychology would be 2 years – and then the Master's - and then the State Licencing [sic] - so I'm looking at 3-5 years, but in a more respected (I guess) field.

I get confused as to what I really want – and what is someone else's idea that would be good for me. Perhaps you can gleen [sic] from my handwriting the path that I can find the most reward. I'm not opposed to work – and discipline – but I want to do something that reflects me, Thank you very much for your attention – Love, Zorah

Dear Zorah,

It's pretty clear to me that unconsciously you know what you want and what's best for you at this time, but are looking for validation. You don't want to go the college route for an M.A. in psychology. Your large writing and right slant indicate you like people and would be good dealing directly with them, especially with your sense of humor (curved beginning strokes on "m" and "M"). You're intelligent (angular and rounded "m" and "n") and can handle college, but I don't think it is right for you at this time.

Sometimes you lack confidence and feel like giving up (low and concave t-bars in "that" in the second line and in "something"). You seem to be struggling with pessimism or low-grade depression; sometimes lines rise upwards, sometimes downwards. It is also evident in the downturned ending of the key word "Psychology," first line, but interestingly, not in the ending of the "y" in "Cosmotology." And you are not opposed to the discipline of college, but you are depressed at the thought of it (last few letters in "discipline" drop).

You have great imagination (large lower loops) and like to do things your own way (downturned t-bar in "what," "want," and "that"). The cosmetology will give you a chance to use your talents in the business. You are a very giving person (long finals to words) and are probably not appreciated for it. As a result, you may feel imposed upon (beginning inflexible stroke in "s" in "state" and "r" in "respected").

Back of your indecision (feathery endings to words), I believe is how you really feel about yourself. The tiny capital "I" in "I guess," and the still smaller one in "I want," indicate a feeling of low self-worth. So I think the choice of cosmetology is the right one at this time. It will give you a chance to see what you can do, and the experience will be great for bolstering your confidence and self-esteem. You may even, some years into the future, go for that M.A. in Psychology.

Specimen #9
(no motivation)

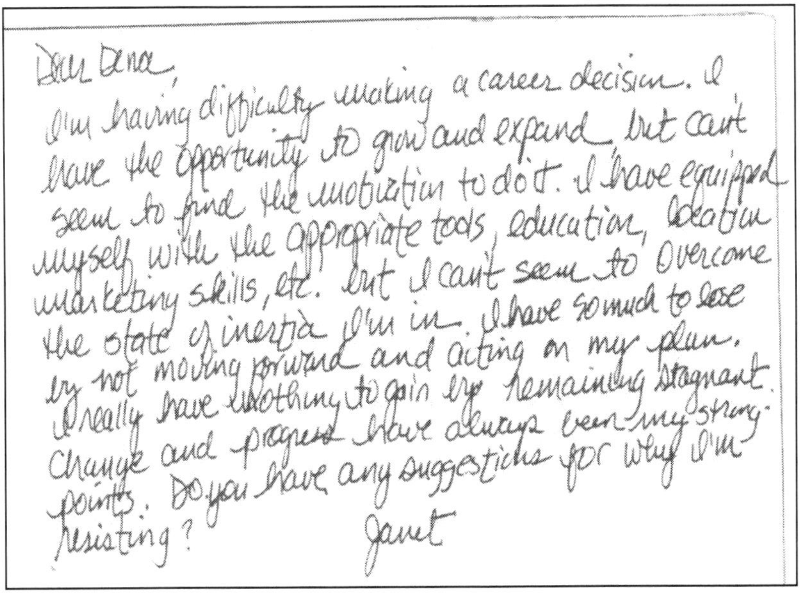

Dear Dena,
I'm having difficulty making a career decision. I
have the opportunity to grow and expand but can't
seem to find the motivation to do it. I have equipped
myself with the appropriate tools, education, location
marketing skills, etc. but I can't seem to overcome
the state of inertia I'm in. I have so much to lose
by not moving forward and acting on my plan.
I really have nothing to gain by remaining stagnant.
Change and progress have always been my strong-
points. Do you have any suggestions for why I'm
resisting?
Janet

"Nothing great was ever achieved without enthusiasm."
- Ralph Waldo Emerson

"To succeed, you need to find something to hold on to, something to motivate you, something to inspire you."
- Tony Dorset

Dear Dena,

I'm having difficulty making a career decision. I have the opportunity to grow and expand but can't seem to find the motivation to do it. I have equipped myself with the appropriate tools, education, location, marketing skills, etc. but can't seem to overcome the state of inertia I'm in. I have so much to lose by not moving forward and acting on my plan. I really have nothing to gain by remaining stagnant. Change and progress have always been my strong points. Do you have any suggestions for why I'm resisting? – Janet

Dear Janet,

Perhaps it's because, deep down, it's not the career you really want to be in. Could that be? You don't say how old you are, or what career you are now in, but you are very bright (angular and inverted "m" and "n"), creative (heavy writing, simple printed capitals), intuitive (breaks between letters), and have cultural interests (Greek "s" and "e"). Perhaps your feeling of responsibility (loop on capital "I") has caused you to choose a "practical" career you know you can do, but in which your heart is lacking. You are showing some lack of perspective (very little space between lines) and as a predominantly creative person, the marketing skills of selling yourself may not be your cup of tea. So perhaps that's why you don't follow through with ideas or projects (incomplete lower loops), making you irritable (dashes for dots), and somewhat frustrated (drooping word "education").

Despite your quick intelligent mind, training, creative talents, and basic optimism (rising lines), you seem to doubt your capabilities at times (low t-bars especially in the key word "can't"). Is it regarding the career change or in personal relationships? I don't know.

But the strong caution you show (straight word endings in key words "decision," "expand," "inertia," "plan," and "stagnant") tell me you have misgivings, doubts, about going forward. If so, perhaps you should re-assess what you really want to do with your life. Perhaps it's to pursue what you are emotionally driven to do, which might not be what you have talent for or are trained for.

Yes, I always recommend that clients follow their hearts rather than their heads (or, in other words, pursue their passions rather than those skills which are merely marketable, even if the former are not likely to prove lucrative). But sometimes fate steps in. Below is the "Dear Dena" of a girl who was a gymnast and in one split-second maneuver became a quadriplegic. Being an artist was not her original choice; her passion was being a gymnast. Quite courageously, she chose to nurture the artistic talent she already had, and made it her new career.

Though her "Dear Dena" is written with pen in mouth, I am able to analyze for personality and character traits, despite the tremors. This convincingly proves the thesis, I think, of all three volumes in the *Handwriting* series: so-called "handwriting" is not really handwriting at all; it's *brain*-writing.

Note her response to my analysis of the specimen which follows.

Specimen #10 (reduced 20%)
(Cindi, female 50, paraplegic mouth artist)*

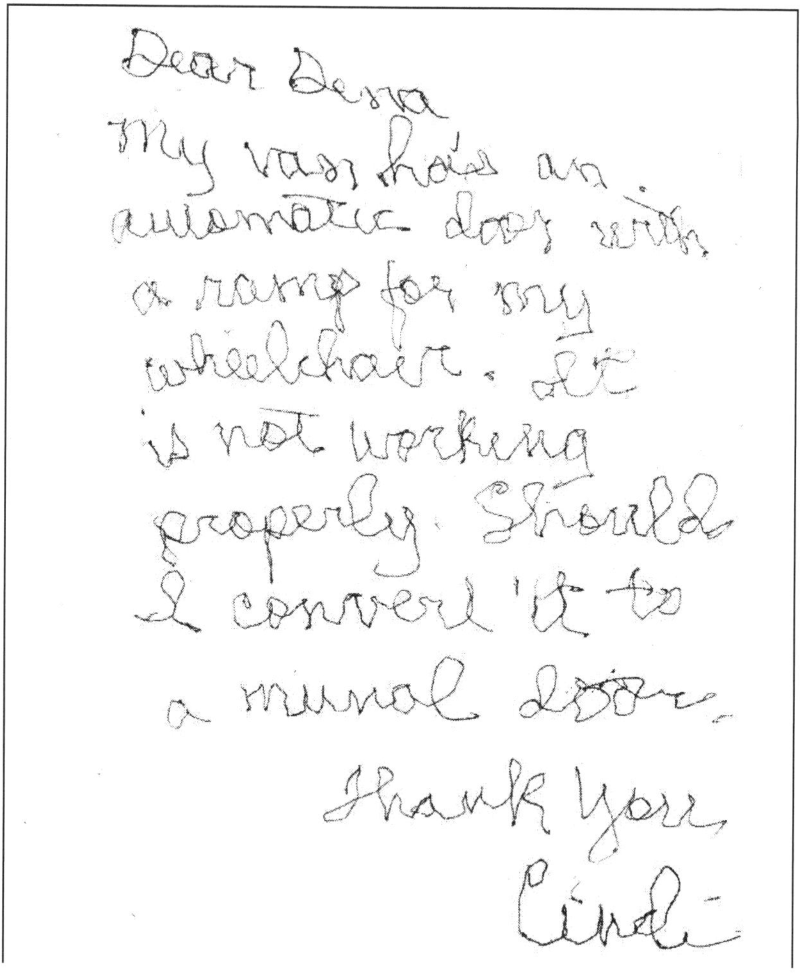
Dear Dena
My van has an
automatic door with
a ramp for my
wheelchair. It
is not working
properly. Should
I convert it to
a manual door.
Thank you,
Cindi

***View a photo of Cindi as she paints, on p. 1 of Volume I in the *Handwriting* series.**

Dear Dena,

My van has an automatic door with a ramp for my wheelchair. It is not working properly. Should I convert it to a manual door. Thank you, Cindi

Dear Cindi,

You are very warm and caring (rounded "m" and "n"), intelligent (angular as well as rounded "m" and "n"), dependable (regular slant and spacing) and responsible (loop on "l"). Though reticent (mostly closed "a" and "o"), you can work well with people (slight right slant, large writing). However, about some issues you are very secretive (large right loop on "o" in "automatic," "door," "working," "properly," convert," and "you"). You have your own well-developed philosophy (large looped "l") and you're open-minded (wide "e") to others' beliefs.

You have artistic ability (printed capitals) with an aesthetic sense (spacing on page) and keen manual dexterity (all "r's" are flat-topped)—especially helpful for painting or playing a musical instrument.

I know that you paint holding the brush in your mouth, and that you are already a distinguished artist. So I am surprised to see that the writing shows a conflict between the artistic side of you and the traditional (traditional capitals, especially capital "I"); you do not make your capital "I" as an artist would.

Regarding the door. I would be very surprised if you decided to convert the door to manual. You're a fighter; you must have what you want and need (downturned t-bars in "automatic," "with," and "not"). You can be defiant about it (large buckle on "k" in "thank"), and angry (temper tic on "M" in "My" and "T" in "Thank"), especially in reaction to criticism (large loop on "d" in "should," "door," and "Cindi"). But you have self-control over these feelings (convex t-bar on "it" and mostly vertical slant).

Don't let this setback get you down (sudden drooping of "Dear Dena"). Stick to your guns. I admire your courage. You will find a way to get the door repaired rather than have it converted.

This being my very first analysis of a "mouth-writing," I asked for Cindi's response:

Dena,

That was certainly fun reading your analysis of my writing even though some things letters, slants, spacing, and crossing of t's and dotting of i's have been affected because I write with my mouth it seems pretty accurate especially in terms of my stubbornness, creativity and reaction to criticism. I thoroughly enjoyed your comment about the artist and my letter "r." I also found it interesting that my traditional letter "I" means something. I do feel artistic and creative but sometimes feel that I am not a true "artist" because that was not my goal or dream in life and sometimes feel I am not eccentric like most artists ha ha but my boyfriend and family members say that I am! Anyway thanks again it was really fun.

Gratefully,
Cindi

Specimen #11
(mid-life career change)

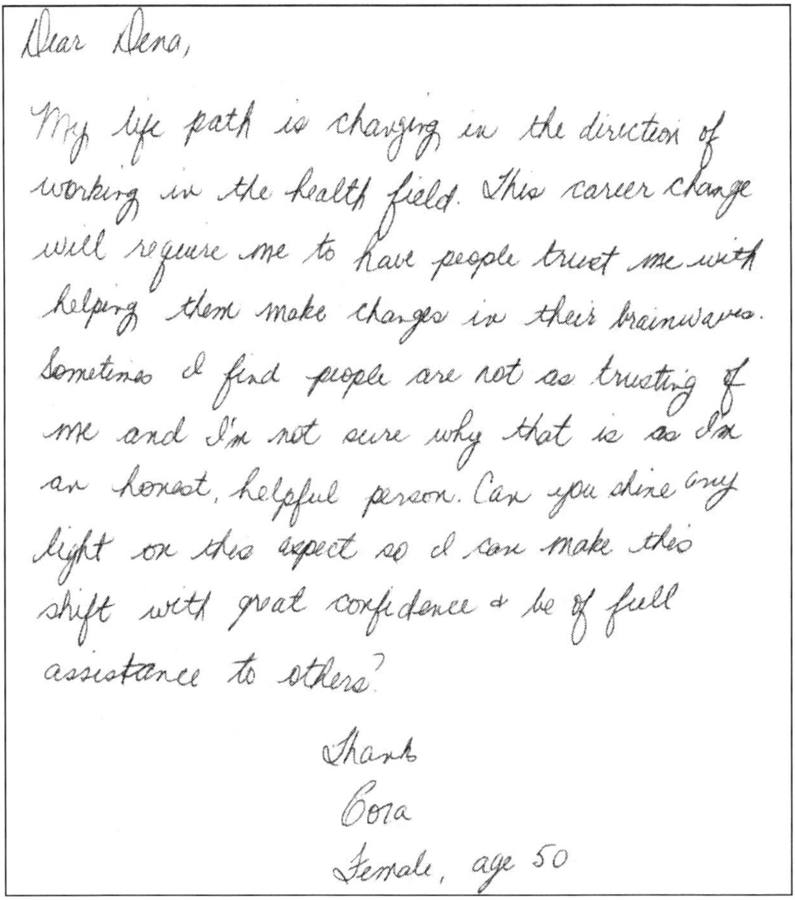
Dear Dena,

My life path is changing in the direction of working in the health field. This career change will require me to have people trust me with helping them make changes in their brainwaves. Sometimes I find people are not as trusting of me and I'm not sure why that is as I'm an honest, helpful person. Can you shine any light on this aspect so I can make this shift with great confidence & be of full assistance to others?

Thanks
Cora
Female, age 50

Dear Dena,

My life path is changing in the direction of working in the health field. This career change will require me to have people trust me with helping them make changes in their brainwaves. Sometimes I find people are not as trusting of me and I'm not sure why that is as I'm an honest helpful person. Can you shine any light on this aspect so I can make this shift with great confidence and be of full assistance to others. Thanks Cora, Female age 50.

Dear female 50,

I can see why you have chosen to work in one of the helping fields: you like people (moderately sized writing, right slant); you're dependable (good rhythm and spacing), loyal (dots over "I"), and willing to take on responsibilities (loop on capital "I"). You have important qualities necessary to be your own boss, or some kind of therapist; you're independent (short "t" stem) with deep-seated determination (good down-strokes on "y" and "g") and strong ambition to get ahead, to succeed (many beginning hooks to words).

Furthermore, you are warm and caring (rounded "m" and "n") and very giving of yourself and your time (generous word endings). People who give so much of themselves and also "give in" to others at times (rounded "s") are not always appreciated, and are sometimes taken for granted, which can result in resentment (inflexible beginning stroke to "me" in third line and "can" in eighth line). However, you are not overly sensitive, and can take criticism with poise and dignity (retraced t-stem), even while being self-conscious about something (last hump on "m" in "me," sixth line).

Why are people not as trusting of you? *Perhaps it's because they sense your sadness and depression, revealed in the drooping of key words "direction," "working," "health field," "trust," "trusting," "helpful," "confidence," "assistance," and* *"others." You want to be optimistic (upwards slant of "female, age 50"), but you're constantly battling pessimism.*

Also, perhaps they feel a contradiction between your non-traditional career and your traditional and conservative side (traditional capitals and retraced "m" and "h".) Perhaps they also sense that at times you have weak confidence (low and weak t-bar in the key words "trusting" and "great"), and a feeling of hopelessness (very downturned endings in "g" in key words "changing," "working," and "helping"). Or perhaps they lack trust, sensing your strong irritability (t-bars to the right), secretiveness (right loop on "a" and "o"), and evasiveness (partly closed "a" and "o), indicated at times.

Could it be that you fear for the success of this "shift"? What you fear is the word following a large space; after "this" it is "shift." Perhaps you have not been completely honest with yourself and have rationalized going into this field (large left loop in "a" and "o")—best seen with magnification. ***Perhaps you need to reevaluate why you chose this particular work.***

Battling depression (many drooping words) saps energy and doesn't help in a new venture. You need to get at the cause in order to confidently assist others. You have to strongly believe in yourself and your work so that it inspires your clients and establishes trust. However, your confidence and willpower waver. What can help is practicing, before going to bed, making t-bars high and strong on the stem thirty times each night for thirty nights. You will experience a gradual strengthening of clarity of purpose and confidence.

CHAPTER THREE

Is Now the Right Time to Change?

"The world stands aside to let anyone pass who knows where he is going."
- Jordon

"We make a living by what we get, but we make a life by what we give."
- Winston Churchill

Specimen #12

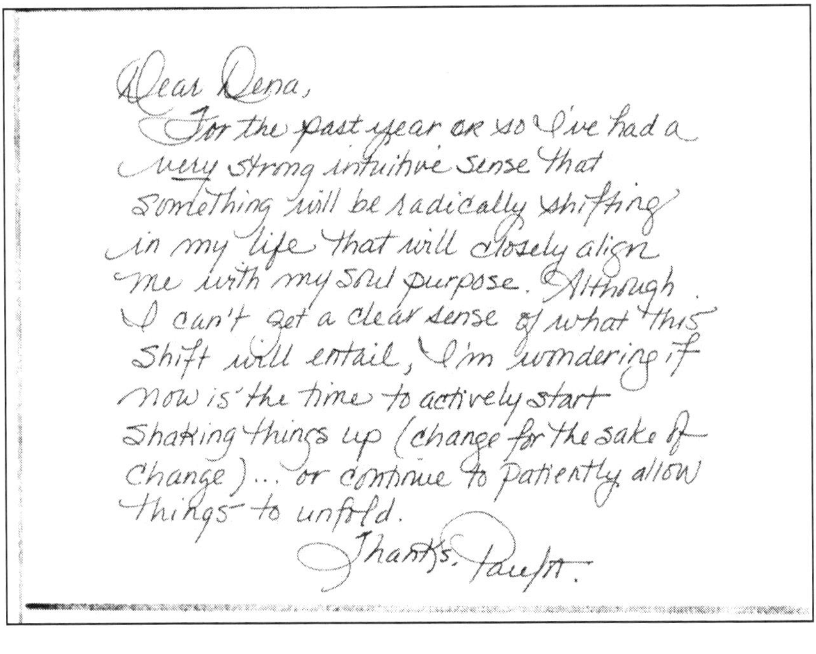
Dear Dena,
For the past year or so I've had a very strong intuitive sense that something will be radically shifting in my life that will closely align me with my soul purpose. Although I can't get a clear sense of what this shift will entail, I'm wondering if now is the time to actively start shaking things up (change for the sake of change)... or continue to patiently allow things to unfold.
Thanks. Paula.

Dear Dena,

For the past year or so I've had a very strong intuitive sense that something will be radically shifting in my life that will closely align me with my soul purpose. Although I can't get a clear sense of what this shift will entail, I'm wondering if now is the time to actively start shaking things up (change for the sake of change)... or continue to patiently allow things to unfold. – Thanks, Paula

Dear Paula,

Your strong intuitive sense (many breaks between letters), together with your fluency of thought (letters joined to the next) and strong determination (straight down-strokes on "y" and "g"), make you an efficient worker who is dependable (good rhythm, straight baseline, balance on page) as well as loyal (dot over "i"). Being open and honest (no loops in "a" or "o") and warm-hearted (rounded "m"), you would work well with people (right slant, fairly large writing).

Though you have a very strong desire to achieve (very large hooked beginning stroke in "very," "in," and "me," and large capital "P"), you are still a bit fearful of change. What you fear is the word after the large space after "that," and it is "something." As you say, you don't have a clear sense of what it entails. Also, the word after the large space following the word "start" is "shaking." Again, your unconscious tells you that you are not quite ready for shaking things up.

For one thing, your confidence needs some bolstering (low t-bars in the key words "can't," "what," and "shift"). You have a tendency to procrastinate (t-bar to left of stem), leaving projects unfinished (incomplete loops on "g").

Furthermore, there is still a longing or a holding on to something from the past ("g's" ending to the left, as well as hooks on endings of "e's" in "life" and "time," and the "g" in "shifting"), with a feeling that there is nothing much you can do about it (downturned ending of "y's" in "year," "radically," and "patiently").

Caution is also indicated by the endings on "align" and "of" (third-to-last line). My advice is to take it easy for now, be patient, and do some writing, for which I think you have talent with so many fluency strokes and cultural interests (Greek "r," printed "s," figure 8 "g"). And with more confidence things will unfold at the right time.

Specimen #13

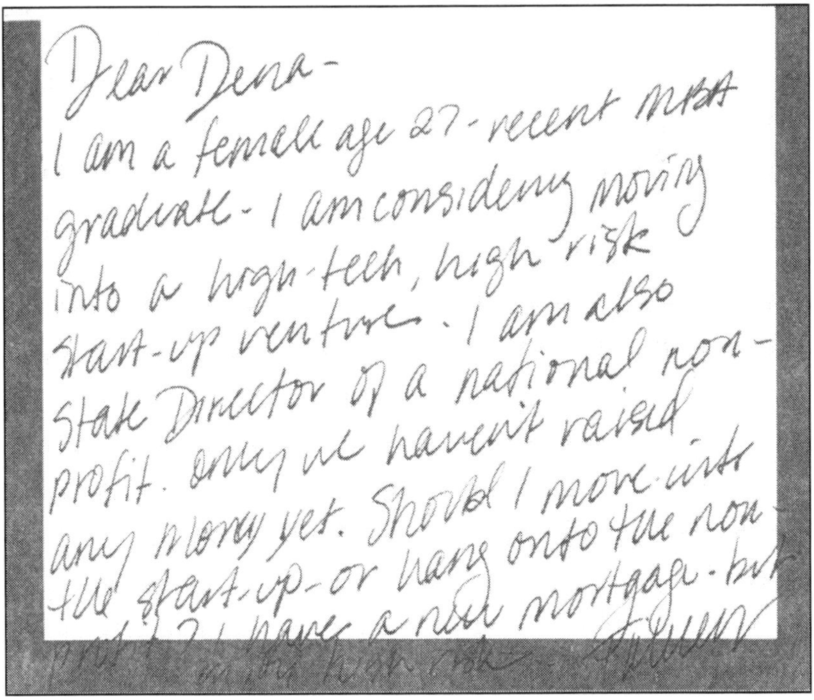

Dear Dena-
I am a female age 27 - recent MBA
graduate - I am considering moving
into a high-tech, high risk
start-up venture. I am also
State Director of a national non-
profit. only we haven't raised
any money yet. Should I move into
the start-up - or hang onto the non-
[illegible] I have a new mortgage - but
[illegible]

Dear Dena,

I am a female age 27 - recent MBA graduate. I am considering moving into a high-tech, high risk start-up venture. I am also State Director of a national non-profit. Only we haven't raised any money yet. Should I move into the start-up, or hang onto the non-profit? I have a new mortgage—but enjoy high risk.

Dear MBA Graduate,

You have a dynamic personality (large letters, right slant, speed), a sharp analytical mind (angular "m" and "n",) creativity (simple "I"), initiative ("t" in "recent"), intuition (breaks between letters), ability to shift focus easily (fluency strokes, such as t-bars joining next letter, and figure 8 "g"), and if need be, you can be aggressive (final ending in your name), all traits supporting an aptitude for business. Nevertheless, you doubt yourself at times (very low t-bar in key word "profit").

Should you move into the start-up? The answer is in your own unconscious. The word "moving" simply falls, depressed. Next, look at the large space after "risk." The next word is what you fear—start-up venture. You feel a strong need to be cautious (hook on straight long ending in key word "venture").

You worry about not raising money (space after "raised"), but you would worry still more should you go into a risky business. I think you should stay where you are for a while. There will be other opportunities. Your unconscious says wait, be cautious—the time's not right

Specimen #14

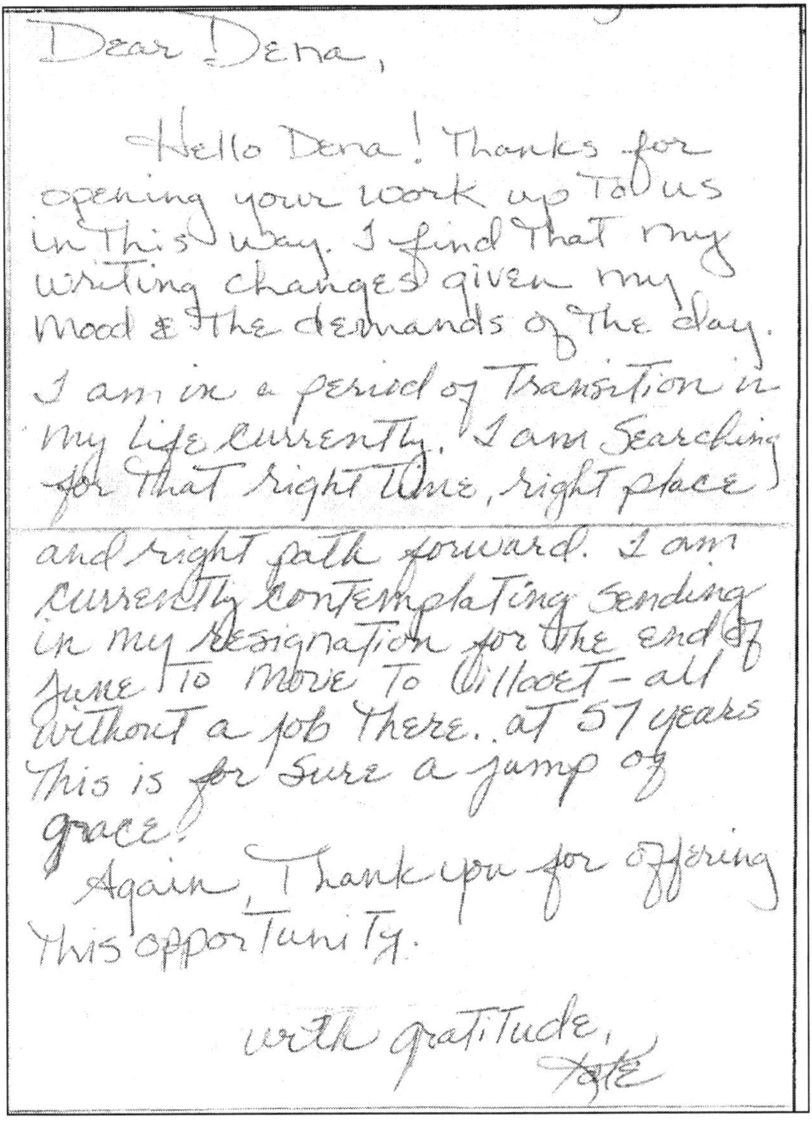
Dear Dena,

Hello Dena! Thanks for opening your work up to us in this way. I find that my writing changes given my mood & the demands of the day.

I am in a period of transition in my life currently. I am searching for that right time, right place and right path forward. I am currently contemplating sending in my resignation for the end of June to move to Willaoet - all without a job there.. at 57 years this is for sure a jump of grace!

Again, Thank you for offering this opportunity.

With gratitude,

Kate

Dear Dena,

Hello Dena! Thanks for opening your work up to us in this way. I find that my writing changes given my mood and the demands of the day. I am in a period of transition in my life currently. I am searching for that right time, right place and right path forward. I am currently contemplating sending in my resignation for the end of June to move to Lillooett—all without a job there... at 57 years. This is for sure a jump of grace! Again, thank you for offering this opportunity. With gratitude, Kate.

Dear Kate,

The first thing I notice is, of course, the change in slant and wavy baseline—your moods change quickly. The first part is predominantly upward—objective mood, business-like, stating a fact. The next part is right-slanted (opening up emotionally to people, being responsive). The last sentence is upright again (a business-like ending for a letter). Finally, it slants again to the right when you speak from your heart, openly and honestly (no loops or hooks in "a" or "o").

You don't say what your work is, but you certainly have ability in the artistic and cultural areas (printed capitals, Greek "e" and "s"), but you could also run a business or organization—perhaps one connected with cultural endeavors; you're intelligent with an analytical and investigative mind (angular and rounded "m" and "n"), intuitive (breaks between letters), diplomatic (tapering letters), decisive (firm word endings), and persistent when necessary (lasso loop in "A"). However, you also have a tendency to take on too many projects at once (lower loops dangling into line below).

If you already made the move, you have what it takes: enthusiasm, strong confidence, and the willpower to set long-range goals (strong, long, high on stem t-bars), as well as deep-

seated determination to see them through to fruition (long down-strokes on "g" and "y"). However, your moodiness and sensitivity to criticism (loop on "d") can create difficulties in relationships and holding a job; you resent someone or something (inflexible beginning stroke on the "c" in "currently" and "contemplating") and have rejected someone close, or feel rejected by someone close (lower loop of the "f" in "find" ends far left). There is a temper tic on the capital "I," which means you see yourself as having a temper, and the "I" varies in size with your mood, becoming smaller when you feel bad about your shortcomings. Perhaps some medical help in stabilizing your moods is called for. Something to look into. All the best.

CHAPTER FOUR

Can't Commit, Can't Focus, or is Unsuited

Specimen #15
(can't commit to any career)

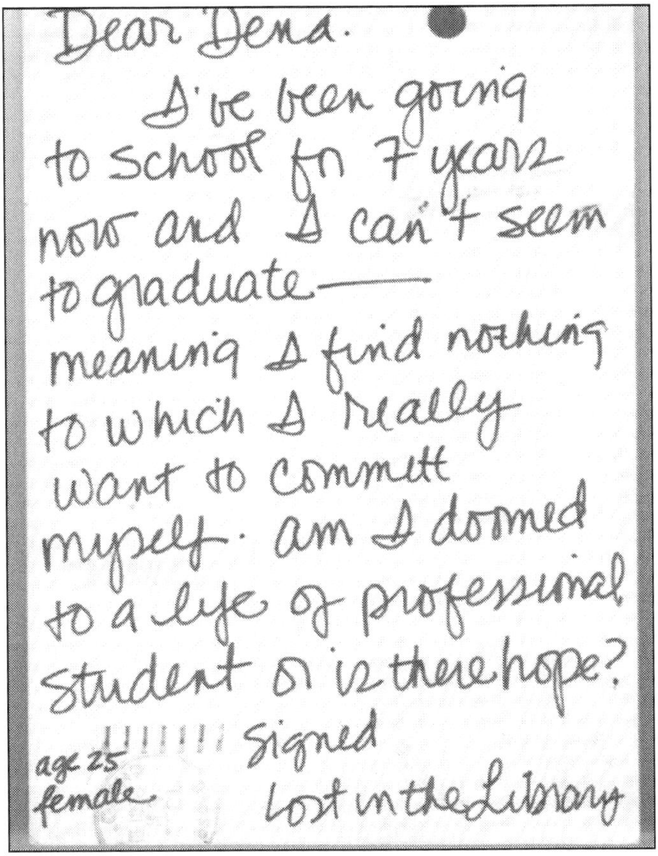

Dear Dena.

I've been going to school for 7 years now and I can't seem to graduate— meaning I find nothing to which I really want to committ myself. am I doomed to a life of professional student or is there hope?

!!!!!!! Signed

Lost in the Library

age 25
female

Dear Dena,

I've been going to school for 7 years now and I can't seem to graduate — meaning I find nothing to which I really want to commit myself. Am I doomed to a life of professional student or is there hope? – Signed Lost in the Library, age 25 female.

Dear female 25,

You have deep feelings, passion (very heavy writing)—good for expressing your artistic and cultural leanings (some printed capitals, Greek "s," flat-top "r," and fluency strokes in "f"). With your intelligence (angular and rounded "m" and "n") and intuitive sense, there is nothing you can't do, should you choose.

Are you doomed to be a professional student? With unlimited money and your independent nature (short "t" and "d")—you could be, unless you do something about it.

The word after the large space following "commit" is what or who you fear, and it is "myself." The capital "I" is made with a beginning inflexible stroke which indicates a feeling of being imposed upon, being unappreciated, and resentment. The final stroke cuts through the bottom of the "I," like a knife—and this resentment stroke is only in the capital "I." In other words, you are your own worst enemy.

You have strong determination (good down-strokes on "g" and "y"), but as you say, you haven't found what would make you set higher goals than the day-to-day ones (low t-bars in "can't,""want," and "commit"). You show a lack of confidence in setting goals for the future (low t-bar in last "t" in "student").

My suggestion is to think back to when you were eight or nine and people asked you what you were going to be when you grew up. Another help is to note when the time seems to fly while doing something or being interested in something.

That's what you should "commit" to, work towards, what you will be happiest and most productive doing. Writing and lecturing on a passionate subject is what comes to my mind and may or may not be what you have been studying. Of course, if you do not have unlimited money, you would have to find a way to support yourself until you become successful at it. But it can be done. You have the intelligence and talent.

Specimen #16
(hard time focusing)

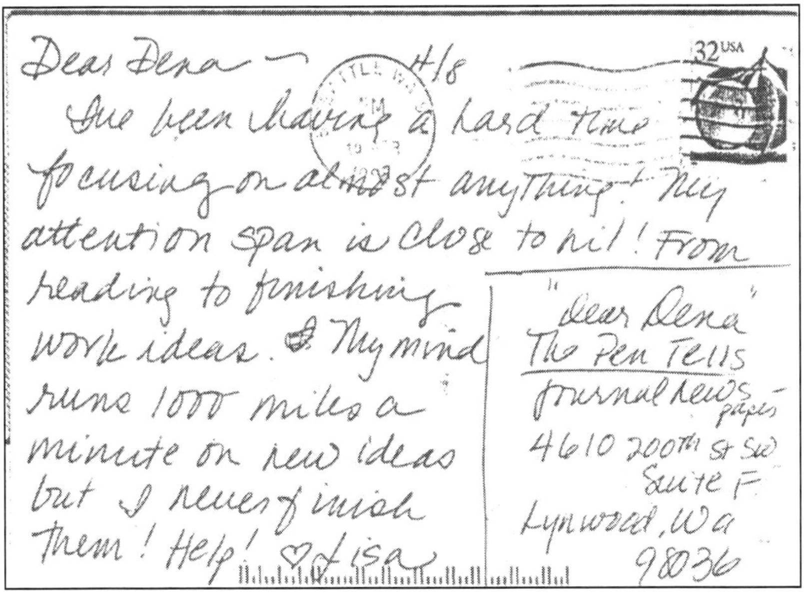
Dear Dena — 4/18
I've been having a hard time focusing on almost anything. My attention span is close to nil! From reading to finishing work ideas. My mind runs 1000 miles a minute on new ideas but I never finish them! Help! ♡ Lisa

"Dear Dena"
The Pen Tells
Journal newspapers
4610 200th St SW
Suite F
Lynwood, Wa
98036

Dear Dena,

I've been having a hard time focusing on almost anything. My attention span is close to nil! From reading to finishing work ideas my mind runs 1000 miles a minute on new ideas but I never finish them! Help! – Lisa

Dear Lisa,

Perhaps your artistic and cultural interests (printed capitals and printed "s") conflict with other responsibilities (loop on "I")? You have talent for writing that needs expression and development (unfinished figure 8 "g's" in "reading" and "finishing")—enhanced by your intuition (breaks between letters) and fluency of thought (one letter joined to the next).

You rationalize leaving projects unfinished (large left loop on "a" and "o" in key words "having" and "hard"). More likely it's your sharp analytical and investigative mind that censures your creative work, resulting in loss of confidence at times (low t-bar in "almost," "but," and "minute")—a feeling of not being able to live up to your own standards (short t-stem) and abilities.

By not finishing projects (incomplete lower loops) you're sabotaging yourself (sliced loop in "I" in "I've"). It's obviously getting you down (down-turned endings on "g" in key words "focusing" and "finishing," and slight drooping of words and lines). However, you're a reliable person (rhythm and slant) with a sense of humor (beginning stroke on "m" in "my"); you'll complete your projects in time. You're sharp, intelligent, witty, talented. Just take one project at a time. Practice making strong and firm downstrokes to the "y" (determination). You can do it. One day at a time. Little by little.

Specimen #17
(too many talents to focus)

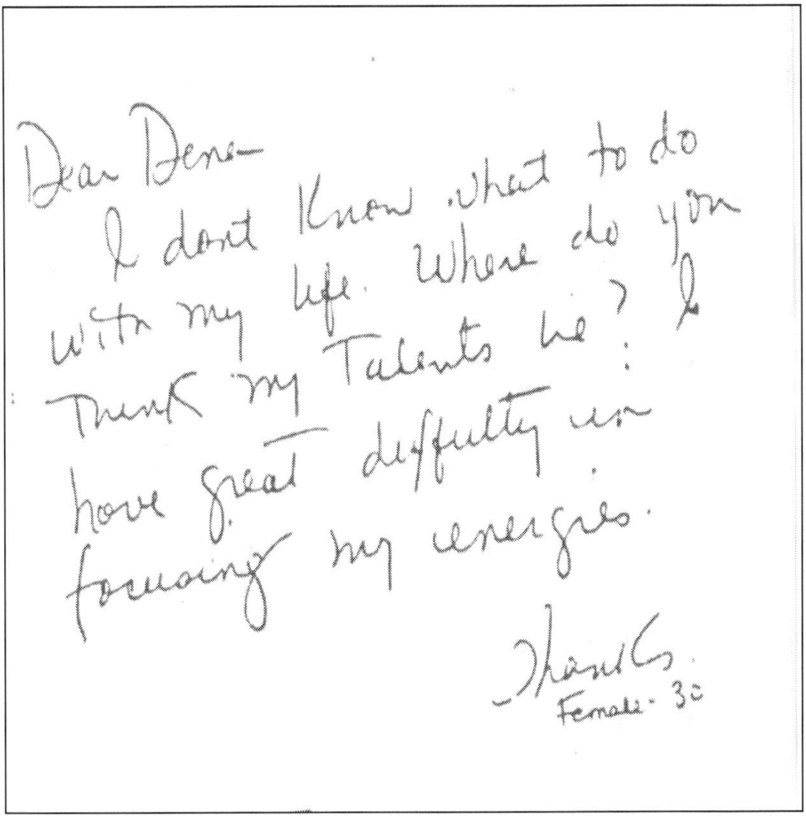
Dear Dena—
I dont Know what to do with my life. Where do you think my Talents lie? I have great difficulty in focusing my energies.

Thanks
Female - 30

Dear Dena,

I don't know what to do with my life. Where do you think my talents lie? I have great difficulty in focusing my energies. – Thanks, Female 30

Dear Female 30,

You have difficulty because no matter what you do, you do it well (fluency strokes of one letter joining the next), with your analytical mind (angular "m" and "n") and ability to concentrate on long-range study (small middle-zone letters). You could be successful in any field you choose with your confidence (high t-bars), determination (good down-strokes on "y"), and enthusiasm (long t-bars).

You have strong creative talents in writing and art (figure 8 "g," printed capitals) aided by intuition (breaks between letters), suggesting journalism or photography as good career choices. But you could also go for the professions of psychology, sociology or the medical field.

However, you do have a tendency to procrastinate (t-bars to left of stem), daydream (t-bar floating above stem), and be too easily influenced by others' opinions (rounded "s"). You then may rationalize why you can't do this or that (large left loop in the "a" in "thanks").

So what should you focus on? I would choose the field of endeavor where the time flies by when you're immersed in it—even if it isn't the one you have the most talent in; I believe it's more important to do the work you like or are emotionally driven to do. Perhaps this will help you narrow it down. Good luck!

Of those seeking career counseling, some have a dominant trait, making choosing a career easy. Others with talents for *various* occupations may become confused and unable to decide on a vocation, having so many to choose from. At this point I feel I have to emphasize how lucky we Americans have always been. *We have choice!* We may not know what we are best suited to – but by God, we have *choice!*

In Appreciation

"If the only prayer you ever say
is thank you, that will be enough."
- Meister Eckhart

Lilly

It took a few moments for me to realize I was under "house arrest." *This* was my welcome to East Berlin? The minute I had arrived I had been questioned on why I had come, who did I want to see, and why?

It was 1983. By chance my arrival date was May 1st – May Day, and all the Communist regalia were out in full force. I was a naïve American. A month earlier in Warsaw, at an International Genocide Convention attended by research professionals from all over the world, I had met an East Berlin historian and researcher of the Second World War. I wanted from him some pertinent Holocaust information, so while the authorities checked out why an ordinary housewife wanted to see this man, they placed me and a girl called Lilly in a hotel with adjoining rooms.

Thus I had free room and board and a delightful eighteen-year-old to accompany me wherever I went. She spoke almost perfect English, and was my *constant* companion. At breakfast, lunch, and dinner we talked; while shopping we talked; after a movie we talked; while sightseeing we talked. She was wary at first. However, it was soon obvious that we liked each other. I understood she was there to feel me out, but there was nothing to report. I had no connections with any anti-communist group.

When she asked what I did, what I'm doing now, I told her: I write about the Holocaust, I've helped run an electronics business, I've worked as a bookkeeper and invested in real estate. I'm a graphoanalyst, and had a newspaper column on it. Before that, I babbled on, I was a medical laboratory technologist for many years doing bacteriology, chemistry, histology, parasitology and hematology in hospitals and clinics. Before that I was a hospital medical secretary, a doctor's assistant, and X-ray technician.

She was quiet. I studied her now more closely. She seemed tired for her age… or was it sadness? Yet she was decidedly pretty – blond, cute figure, and blue eyes that lit up with the rare smile.

"Speaking of careers," I said, "How did you get to be an interpreter?"

She sighed. "When I was sixteen," she said, "they tested me and asked if I liked it, and *that was it*." She paused, looking down. "Now I can be nothing else for the rest of my life. Why? Because money was spent training me."

Like I said, I was a naïve American and not very perceptive. I just didn't "get" it. The next day we again went sightseeing. She took me to the usual tourist attractions (which usually bore me), but thanks to her congenial company, I had a great time.

"What's your religion," she asked suddenly, as we were leaving a "museum" church, purposely kept so that the government could watch who frequented it.

"Jewish," I said, "but not Orthodox." I went on to tell her that actually my religious beliefs were quite simple. She looked wistfully at me, but I still didn't see the connection. Then she drew me into an alley and pulled out a cross from her bosom.

"I'm a Christian," she said. "A *secret* Christian. We meet in guarded rooms in each other's homes." Her eyes were moist. She looked like she was about to cry. The thought crossed my mind that perhaps this was an act put on to "trick" me, to find out who I *"really"* was. But I glanced at her again and I knew she was sincere. She was confiding in me, trusting me.

I said nothing in response. She, too, was silent. We retraced our steps in the alley, and entered the street. She turned and looked at me. "Where are you going," she asked, "after you leave here?"

"Who knows?" I said with a laugh. "South America, Australia. I haven't been there yet. I've been to Russia and Poland, Yugoslavia and Hungary – Austria, Italy, France, England, Canada…." I rambled on. "Mexico, Hong Kong, Thailand, Singapore and Malaysia. Got to see China – I'm saving that trip. I've been to Israel, and a lot of the United States and Canada." And again I didn't see it. I didn't realize it was the straw that broke the camel's back.

"You certainly know how to *hurt* a person!" she said coldly.

"What do you mean?" I said, shocked. "What did I say? What did I do? I didn't mean to hurt you. Tell me."

"You know, you know what you're doing," she answered angrily.

"Please, please tell me," I beseeched her. "I won't do it again."

"Look where we stand," she said. "Now look over there," she said, pointing to about twenty feet away.

OK, I thought, I'd seen the Wall all along as we were sightseeing. What did it have to do with this?

"You," she said, her voice rising, "first you tell me of all the careers you can freely sample, and then you tell me of all the exotic places in the world you've been to, and I can't even go behind that wall. Don't you see? I'm in a prison!"

I apologized profusely, and she became friendly once more. That afternoon I was given permission to see the person I wanted to see. He was curt and cold. He would send me the information I needed. I left, knowing that he never would. Still, I didn't realize the dangerous position my being there put him in.

We didn't talk much. I made sure I had my pass. It was time to go through the border and time to say good-bye. In the darkness of night no one could see us. We hugged each other and wiped away our tears. I didn't ask for her last name, address, or phone number. I knew better now.

"Someday, someday," I said, "it will be different." And we parted.

Specimen #18
(in a career possibly unsuited to her)

Dear Dena

I am going back to school for a Career Change. I've been a forester, a baker & I am now striving to be a health care assistant. I feel like I really want to do this but I am afraid that I won't be able to handle the not so nice parts of the job.

I am investing a lot of time & money into this. How can I be sure I am doing the right thing?

Jenn

Female 29 years

Dear Dena,

I am going back to school for a career change. I've been a forester, a baker, and I am now striving to be a health care assistant. I feel like I really want to do this but I am afraid that I won't be able to handle the not so nice parts of the job. I am investing a lot of time and money into this. How can I be sure I am doing the right thing? – Jenn, Female 29 years

Dear Jenn,

You're intelligent (angular and rounded "m" and n") and can work efficiently (fluency stroke on "k"). But more importantly, you are a warm, kind, open, and honest person (rounded "m" and "n," no loops on "a" or "o," medium-sized writing, mostly right slant)—so I can see why you have chosen to go into the health care field. However, there are signs of conflict.

There are variable spaces between the words "but I am afraid I won't be able" and "be sure I am." It's indicative of a need for your own space. Could it be because you are self-conscious about something (last hump of "m" higher), as well as independent-minded (short "t" stems in "that" and "right")? A forester away from people or a baker working at night seems to fit the bill.

Furthermore, though you use diplomacy (tapering of words, e.g., in "assistant" and "investing"), you stubbornly (wedge in "t" in "right") like to do things your own way (many t-bars slanting down with feathery end), making it difficult for you to work with people.

Other possible hindrances to your success and happiness in the new field are the following: you procrastinate (many t-bars left of stem), sometimes give up when the going gets rough (concave t-bars in "want," "the," and "right"), and have a tendency toward depression (falling key words such as "career," "feel," "won't," and "into").

With weak willpower (light and weak t-bars) in setting your goals, and weak determination (curved down-strokes on "g" and "y") to carry out your goals, the chances of success and happiness in your new venture are not great.

That is, unless you raise your confidence and belief in yourself, which is at present quite low (low t-bars in key words "that," "want," "right," and "lot")—and come to terms with the "not so nice parts of the job" (perhaps working with bodily excretions and ornery patients), or the responsibilities that go with it which you would rather not take on (narrow loop in "l"). You may decide that the positive aspects (financial security for your later years) outweigh the negative. ***But it seems that with your traits you are unsuited to this particular field.***

However, if you're already in the course, my advice is to use your stubbornness (wedge in "t" in "that") to complete it, even if you want to quit and do other work. If nothing else it could discipline you, and even come in handy someday, when you may feel differently.

CHAPTER FIVE

No Passion? – Refocus Your Career

Specimen #19

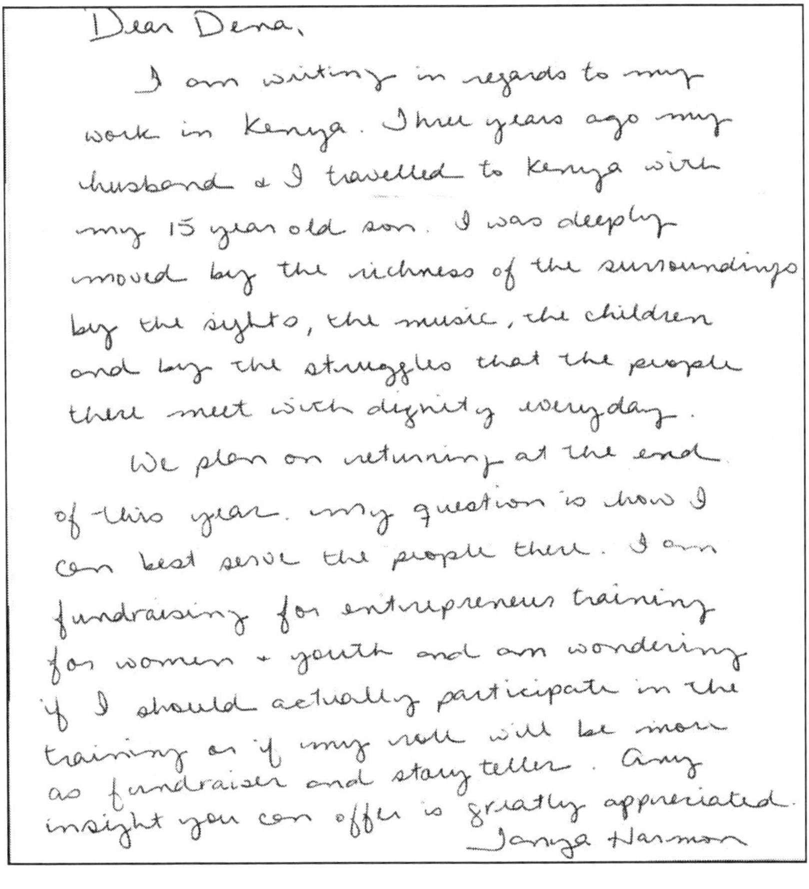

Dear Dena,

I am writing in regards to my work in Kenya. Three years ago my husband & I travelled to Kenya with my 15 year old son. I was deeply moved by the richness of the surroundings by the sights, the music, the children and by the struggles that the people there meet with dignity everyday.

We plan on returning at the end of this year. my question is how I can best serve the people there. I am fundraising for entrepreneurs training for women + youth and am wondering if I should actually participate in the training or if my role will be more as fundraiser and story teller. Any insight you can offer is greatly appreciated.

Tanya Harmon

Dear Dena,

I am writing in regards to my work in Kenya. Three years ago my husband and I travelled to Kenya with my 15 year old son. I was deeply moved by the richness of the surroundings, by the sights, the music, the children, and by the struggles that the people there meet with such dignity every day.

We plan on returning at the end of this year. My question is how I can best serve the people there. I am fundraising for entrepreneurs training for women & youth and am wondering if I should actually participate in the training or if my role will be more as fundraiser and storyteller. Any insight you can offer is greatly appreciated—Tanya

Dear Tanya,

In my opinion, rather than train, and finally become an entrepreneur (which I understand to be the business of making a profit), you should do what gives you emotional satisfaction, which I think is writing and communicating (figure 8 "g"). You have artistic and creative interests (simple printed capitals, except in the capital "I" and capital "T" of your name), which tells me you have a conflict about using those creative talents in a serious way.

There are things standing in the way of your being successful as an entrepreneur, as well as a creative writer or artist: procrastination (t-bar to left of stem), a tendency to give up (some weak concave t-bars), and wavering determination (down-strokes on "y" slightly curved).

On the other hand, your stubbornness (wedge in "d" and "t"), temper (t-bar to right of stem), and anger (temper tic on the first upstroke that joins the down-stroke in capital "I") could be useful in writing, bringing passion to it. However, you do take responsibility for your temper (loops on other "l's").

Becoming an entrepreneur, I believe, is for you a way of rationalizing (many large left loops in "a") why you don't write about your experiences in Kenya and why you are beginning to lose faith in achieving your dreams (endings on "y's" beginning to turn down).

There is much to being a fundraiser (a type of entrepreneurial business) and much to being a good storyteller (whether on stage or writing). I just think you would be more emotionally satisfied with concentration on writing and giving talks.

An Awareness

About fifty years ago, I attended a week at Idyllwild School of Music in California. There I sampled various pursuits: drama, painting, jewelry making, and sculpturing. My teacher, a woman in her sixties, was amazed at the "head" I quickly sculpted.

"It's not too late," she exclaimed. "You're only in your thirties – you can still be a great sculptress. I'll send you to a great teacher I know. To-morrow we'll fire the "head."

Instead of being pleased, I felt strangely sad. I couldn't understand it. Next day, instead of going to "Sculpting," I attended a class in Drama. On the last day of the week, just before leaving, I stopped by the Sculpting class. Still determined to see me use my talents, she gave me the name of a sculpting teacher in Los Angeles, and a place with a kiln to fire my head. "Good luck," she said warmly. "Let me know how you do."

Well somehow, I conveniently lost the paper, and for the next thirty-five years, the sculpture, with the top of the head separate for firing, has been neatly in a box under my bed, in every house we moved to.

Awareness came slowly. One day, I realized why I didn't fire the head. I simply didn't want to be a sculptress. Forget the talent. I had a *need* – a desire to be a psychologist. That was my secret passion. But I used my talent at money-making instead; it was more practical and urgent at the time. Now, as a graphoanalyst doing career counseling, I tell my client to follow the "passion" rather than the talent. Of course there can be "success" with a developed talent, but the feeling of *fulfillment* comes from doing what you feel *compelled* to do for some reason.

Specimen #20

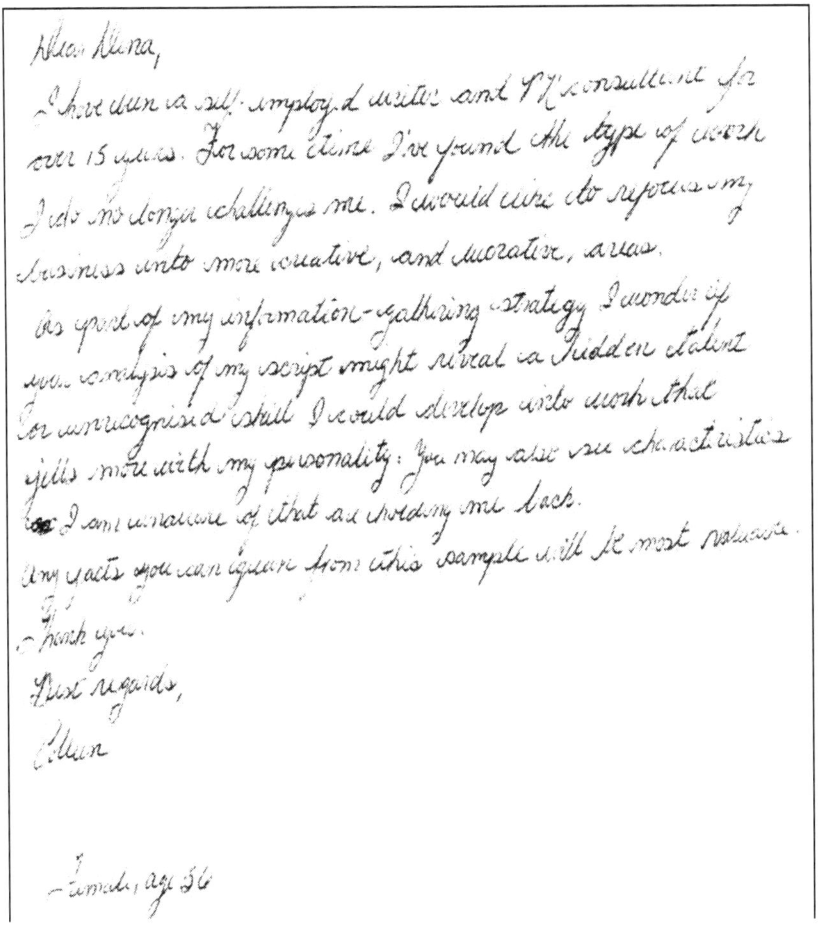
Dear Dena,
I have been a self-employed writer and PR consultant for over 15 years. For some time I've found the type of work I do no longer challenges me. I would like to refocus my business into more creative, and lucrative, areas.
As part of my information-gathering strategy I wonder if your analysis of my script might reveal a hidden talent or unrecognized skill I could develop into work that fits more with my personality. You may also see characteristics I am unaware of that are holding me back.
Any facts you can glean from this sample will be most valuable.
Thank you.
Best regards,
Ellen

—female, age 36

Dear Dena,

I have been a self-employed writer and PR consultant for over 15 years. For some time I've found the type of work I do no longer challenges me. I would like to refocus my business into more creative and lucrative areas. As part of my information gathering strategy I wonder if your analysis of my script might reveal a hidden talent or unrecognized skill I could develop into work that jells more with my personality. You may also see characteristics I am unaware of that are holding me back. Any facts you can glean from this sample will be most valuable. – Thank you, Best regards, Colleen – Female, age 56

Dear Colleen,

If you want to refocus your business to be more lucrative and at the same time more creative, you are asking a lot. You would be lucky to find them together. Chicken sexing is lucrative but not very creative. You are very meticulous in everything you do, and you're very good with detail—but I know you wouldn't want to be a chicken sexer. What comes to mind that you might do are:

Writing ads for products of large corporations (lots of money).
All forms of editing for writers.
Researching for writers.
Indexing for authors.
Librarian assistant.
Forgery expert.
Writing children's books – demand for them, so easier to publish.
Writing romance novels – demand for them, so easier to publish.

Not Connected to Writing:
Working with anthropologists or archaeologists.

Restoring paintings, photography retouching, etc.
Working in a museum.
Working in a kindergarten.
Working as a certified public accountant.
Any work that requires a great deal of patience and accuracy, as well as loyalty.

You'd be good with children, and you could undertake any of the above suggestions because you have ambition (many beginning hooks to words), fairly strong willpower and realistic goal-setting (t-bars mostly high and firm), as well as deep-seated determination (firm down-strokes on "y" and "g").

However, you are not suited to any business that requires a lot of risk (you are too careful), nor one that requires being "on stage" selling yourself. You prefer to work behind the scenes, whether for yourself or others. So this rules out some careers.

You're good with your hands (flat-topped "r"). Are you an artist? You also have an aesthetic sense (balance on the page). What kind of writing do you do? You like people (right slant) but you're a little self-conscious (last hump on "m" higher), and quite selective of friends (small loop on "y").

Specimen #21

Dear Vera,

I am a recent graduate with a BA in communication studies
There are many ways I can use my degree but my goals
have recently changed. One day I would like to be financially
free, the best way to achieve this is to invest & work for myself.
This may take some time to accomplish so in the mean time I may
have to work for someone else. I have student loans and other
monthly payments that are more important than future financial goal.
Therefore I need to find a balance and decide what I want to do
for a career, working for someone else. I love working with people,
I could never work in an office. I also enjoy the outdoors, were
and working with children. Finding a job that would include
one of my passions would be ideal! That is until I am in the
position to work for myself, to invest and create a passive
income. I want this in order to spend time with my future
family and to continue my travels. What type of career do
you think would suit me best?

Ashley

Dear Dena,

I am a recent graduate with a BA in communication studies. There are many ways I can use my degree but my goals have recently changed. One day I would like to be financially free, the best way to achieve this is to invest & work for myself. This may take some time to accomplish so in the meantime I may have to work for someone else. I have student loans and other monthly payments that are more important than future financial goals. Therefore I need to find a balance and decide what I want to do for a career, working for someone else. I love working with people. I could never work in an office. I also enjoy the outdoors, wine and working with children. Finding a job that would include one of my passions would be ideal. That is, until I am in the position to work for myself, to invest and to create a passive income. I want this in order to spend time with my future family and to continue my travels. What type of career do you think would suit me best? –Ashley, age 23.

Dear Ashley,

You have artistic and creative talents with manual dexterity not always utilized (printed capitals, flat-topped "r"). You're kind and caring (rounded "m" and "n"), but not very demonstrative (mostly upward slant). Rather than argue, you show poise and dignity (retraced "t," upright slant)—suppressing some feelings (squeezed-together letters of "Dear Dena") and repressing other feelings (retraced "m" and "n").

You work slowly and carefully (slow writing, dot over "i"), with little ambition for long-range goals (no beginning hooks on words), for you dislike a lot of responsibility (extremely narrow loop in capital "I") and are rather passive in nature (slow, rounded writing, and no strokes of initiative or strong drive); you tend to wait to be acted upon—to react, rather than be the actor in your life.

A clue may be in the tiny left margin that narrows to nothing (the past has a hold on you and you cannot or will not let it go). What it is I cannot tell from the handwriting. But it has left you with feelings of inadequacy (very low and weak t-bars) and pessimism regarding work and finances (downturned lines beginning with "have recently changed".) As a result, you procrastinate in deciding what to do (twelve t-bars to the left of stem, especially in "want to"), setting only day-to-day goals, rationalizing (left loop on "o" and "a") that it is because you are independent-minded (short "t" and "d" stems) and must do your own thing.

What kind of career would suit you best? A career requires ability to focus on long-range goals and work. You lack the necessary belief in yourself for persistent study, working towards a distant goal—unless you change. But finding a job that would include one of your passions is possible and attainable. However, your choices are limited because of your desire not to work in an office, and your lack of self-confidence.

You could work well with small children's art projects, as a nursery or kindergarten assistant; a camp counselor for young children, taking them on outdoor excursions, etc.; a children's photographer; working in a resort taking care of guests' children and organizing programs for them; a children's helper on a cruise ship; or work for a travel company finding special off-the-beaten-track trips. You could also work outdoors for a winery. These all involve your passions and could be exciting and rewarding.

However, it doesn't matter what kind of work you do or in what capacity; ***belief in yourself is crucial.*** *Perhaps behind your lack of confidence is a tape playing negative self-talk from the past. You need to replace it with a new one, one with a belief in yourself, so that no matter what you do—job, career,* *marriage, whatever—you will be successful and happy. I know this is easier said than done.*

Meanwhile, Graphotherapeutics can help. Every night for thirty nights, place t-bars high and firm on the stem, together with straight (not curved) down-strokes on "y" and "g." This will tell your brain that you can confidently set realistic goals with the necessary determination to achieve them. All the best!

Specimen #22
(refocus to teaching human nature in sales?)

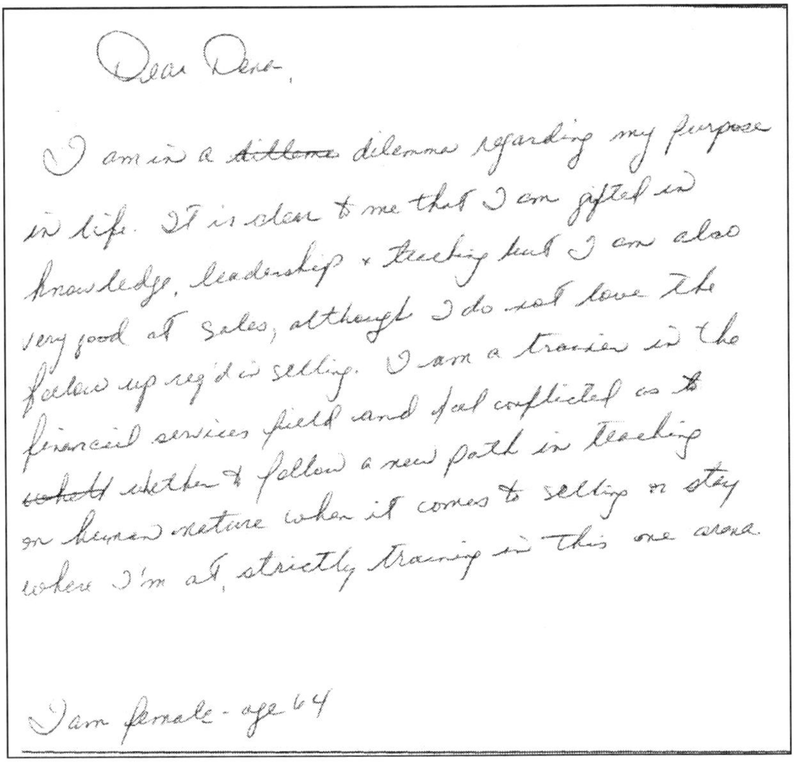
Dear Dena,

I am in a ~~ditlome~~ dilemma regarding my purpose in life. It is clear to me that I am gifted in knowledge, leadership + teaching but I am also very good at sales, although I do not love the follow up req'd in selling. I am a trainer in the financial services field and feel conflicted as to ~~whet~~ whether to follow a new path in teaching on human nature when it comes to selling or stay where I'm at, strictly training in this one area.

I am female - age 64

Dear Dena,

I am in a dillema (sic) regarding my purpose in life. It is clear to me that I am gifted in knowledge, leadership and teaching but I am also very good at sales, although I do not love the follow up req'd in selling. I am a trainer in the financial services field and feel conflicted as to whether to follow a new path in teaching on human nature when it comes to selling or stay where I'm at, strictly training in this one arena. – I am female - age 64

Dear female 64,

Though you have the talent for the area you are presently in (small to medium-sized writing; fluency strokes, i.e., letters joined to next; high and strong t-bars; straight and firm down-strokes on "y")—the new path will give you more emotional satisfaction with the opportunity to express your true self and visions for the future (t-bars floating above stem). You could be more demonstrative (many far right slant letters) of your real feelings. As it is, you are quite secretive (large right loop in "o" in follow" and "not love"); evasive (covered "a" in "arena"), and not 100% truthful (hook in "o" in "although")—traits good in selling.

Your independent spirit (short "t's" in "that" and "path," short "d" in "do"), desire to do things your own particular way (down-turned t-bars in "to," "the," and "stay"), and acute sensitivity to criticism all tell me you would be happier being completely your own boss (if you are not already). You have what it takes: enthusiasm (long t-bars), as well as realistic goal-setting and determination to achieve your goals (good t-bars and down-strokes on "y"). However, you cling to the security of what you have (tiny left margin), fearing risk and showing conflict and lack of belief in yourself, though you know you have what it takes for any endeavor you choose.

I say this because you write a normal-sized capital "I" in the first line regarding your purpose in life and in the last "I" ("I am a female"), but when you talk about your present position as trainer, the capital "I" becomes tiny—not once, but five times, meaning you see yourself as not very important or influential in your work or as not realizing your full potential there. Note the capital "I" before "am gifted," "am also very good with sales," "do not love the follow-up," "am a trainer," and finally the "I" in "where I'm at."

In the fifth line you show self-consciousness (last lump on "m"), temper (t-bar to right), and a sudden depression (drooping of last letters in key word "trainer")—despite your basic optimism (slightly rising lines), there is also resentment or the feeling of not being appreciated (inflexible beginning stroke on "a" in "am"), and in the beginning stroke of "regarding," "clear," "my," "not," "love," and the key word "training."

Therefore, I feel you'd be happier following the new path of teaching human nature in the selling field; you'd feel more fulfilled as you learned more about yourself and others. Also, I feel that understanding your own irritableness (dashes for dots), acute sensitivity to criticism of your ideas (loop on "t") as well as what you do (loop on "d"), occasional procrastination (t-bar to left of stem), and temper (t-bar to right of stem in "trainer") could make you a more understanding teacher or supervisor of teachers. Furthermore, you have writing talent (figure 8 "g") for books, seminars, CD's, as well as selling talent, to apply to the subject you teach.

Specimen #23 (reduced 30 %)

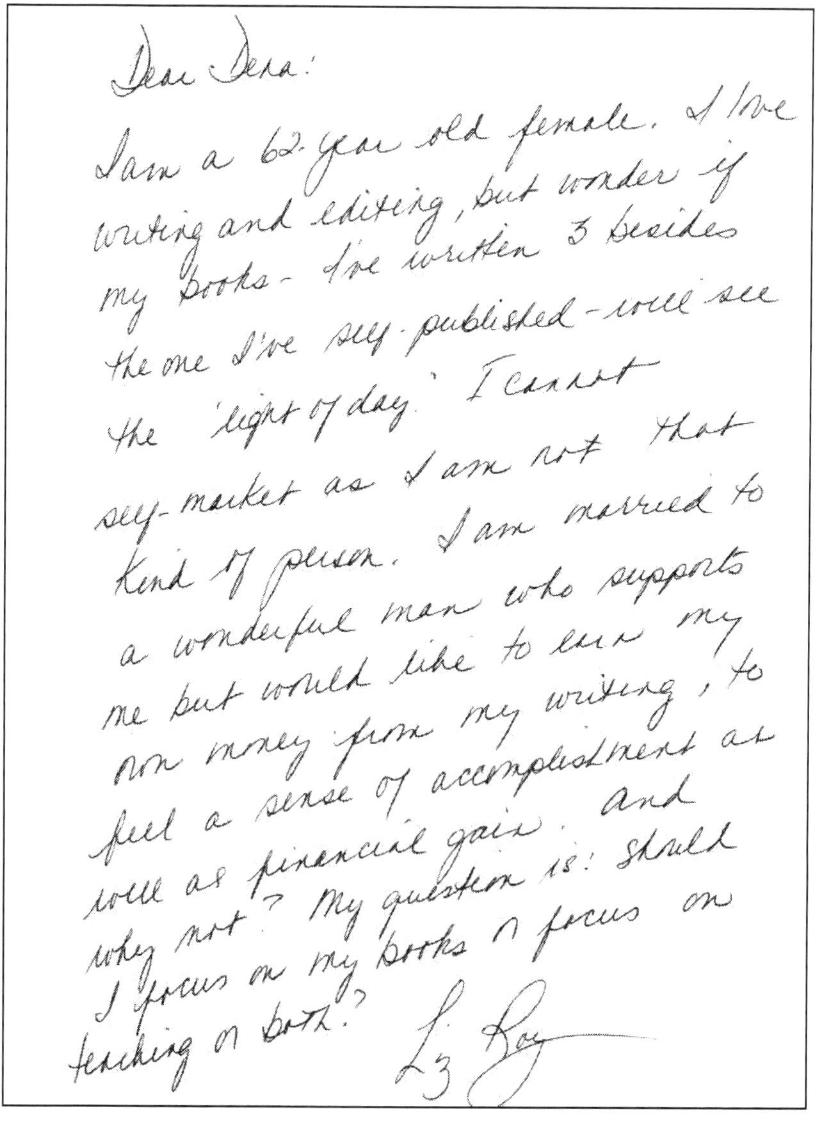
Dear Dera:
I am a 62-year old female. I love
writing and editing, but wonder if
my books - I've written 3 besides
the one I've self-published - will see
the 'light of day.' I cannot
self-market as I am not that
kind of person. I am married to
a wonderful man who supports
me but would like to earn my
own money from my writing, to
feel a sense of accomplishment as
well as financial gain. and
why not? My question is: should
I focus on my books or focus on
teaching or both?
Liz Roy

Dear Dena,

I am a 62-year old female. I love writing and editing, but wonder if my books—I've written 3 besides the one I've self-published—will ever see the "light of day." I cannot self-market as I am not that kind of person. I am married to a wonderful man who supports me but would like to earn my own money from my writing, to feel a sense of accomplishment as well as financial gain. And why not? My question is: should I focus on my books or focus on teaching or both? – Liz Roy

Dear Liz,

The large size and right slant of your writing tell me you are a "people person," meaning friends and family are important to you, and you would be good in any of the helping fields (teaching, medical, psychology, or social work, for example). You're generous (long word endings), dependable, reliable (rhythm and spacing). You have initiative (ending on "t") and work efficiently (fluency stroke of t-bar joining the next). Furthermore, you're artistic and creative (printed capitals, spacing, aesthetic sense), with writing ability (many fluency strokes), cultural interests (Greek "s"), and optimism (slightly rising lines).

Your left margin is irregular, sometimes veering to the right and sometimes to the left. This demonstrates a conflict between taking risks with the new, the unfamiliar, the future (towards the right)—or sticking with the known, safe, and familiar (towards the left). You fear self-marketing; the handwriting corroborates it: the word after the large space after "cannot" is your fear ("self-market").

***The sentence "I cannot self-market as I am not that kind of person" reveals a great deal.** You begin with a large artistic and creative "I" (the only one in your letter) and then use the traditional "I" as if saying you're an artist, not a business-*

woman). The drooping of the word "person" indicates pessimism at the thought of self-marketing, and the unnecessary down-slanting cross on the "t" in "not" shows doubt that it could be done your way or to your satisfaction. The endings on "n" in "cannot" and "m" in "am" evince a desire to achieve, and the irregular spacing between words show a desire to have one's own space. The slight drooping of the last letters of the key word "married" also shows some pessimism. The very narrow "a" and "o," together with the retraced "n" in "cannot" and the retraced "h" in "that," suggest repressed feelings.

The left loops in "a" in "market," "as," and "that," along with the "o" in "person," reveal rationalizing about marketing. The "k" in "market" and "kind" show defiance. The inflexible beginning stroke to "o" in "of" starting below the line indicates resentment carried over from childhood. Left loops on "a" and "o" (best seen magnified) mean rationalizing or fooling yourself.

However, most importantly, the inflexible beginning stroke of the second capital "I" in the sentence shows resentment (as the basis of your personality) at the cause of who you are—it defines you, so to speak, because it is in the "I" which represents you. It is also seen in other parts of the letter (e.g., inflexible beginning stroke in the "w" in "why" and the "n" in "not," as well as in the "s" in "supports" beginning below the line, clearly reveal the resentment carried over from childhood).

You want to be more independent financially, but the anger (t-bar to right of stem in "supports") and resentment (first stroke on "s"" in "supports") that comes from being dependent in that way is not helpful. However, you have what it takes to accomplish your goals—a lot of initiative (endings on "t") and determination (long and straight down-strokes on "y" and "g"). Your handwriting shows teaching, speaking before audiences, or promoting a cause or product to fit well with your dominant traits (large size, right slant). With today's technology promoting books, and some help, I think you could do both.

Specimen #24 (reduced 33%)
(needing refocus)

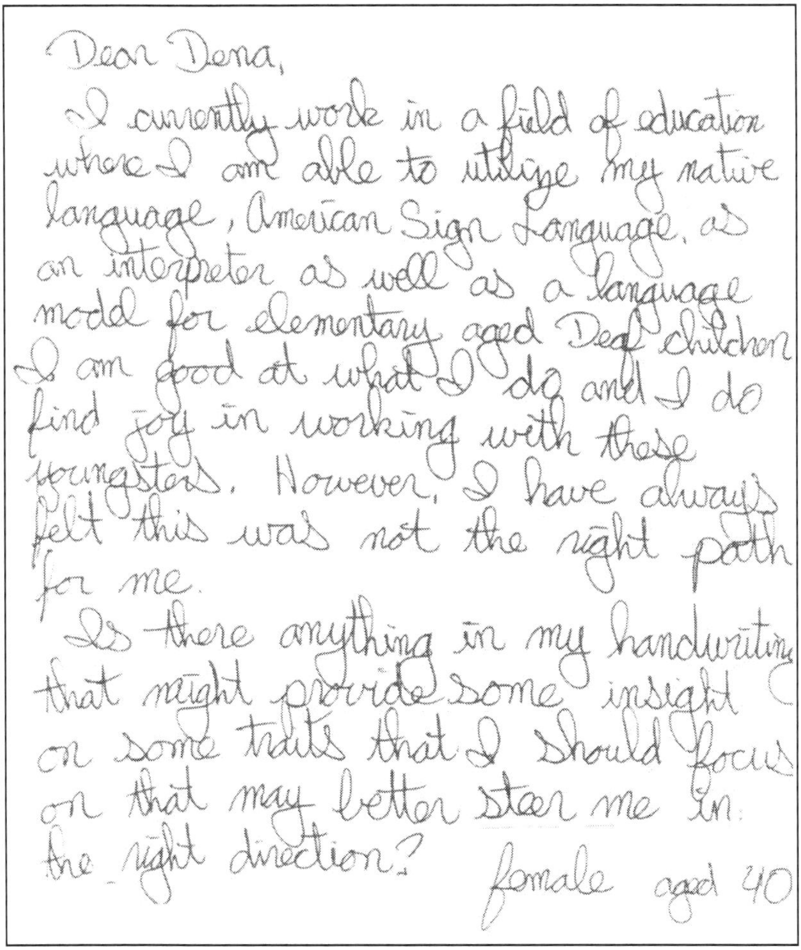

Dear Dena,

I currently work in a field of education where I am able to utilize my native language, American Sign Language, as an interpreter as well as a language model for elementary aged Deaf children. I am good at what I do and I do find joy in working with these youngsters. However, I have always felt this was not the right path for me.

Is there anything in my handwriting that might provide some insight on some traits that I should focus on that may better steer me in the right direction?

female aged 40

Dear Dena,

I currently work in a field of education where I am able to utilize my native language, American Sign Language, as an interpreter as well as a language model for elementary aged Deaf children. I am good at what I do, and I do find joy in working with these youngsters. However, I have always felt this was not the right path for me. Is there anything in my handwriting that might provide some insight on some traits that I should focus on that may better steer me in the right direction? – female aged 40

Dear female 40,

The very large writing tells me you are very aware of the people and things around you without getting too emotional (mostly upward slant). However, while good for your work, it can be very irritating for you (long dashes for dots) when you can't turn it off. Furthermore, the t-bars in "at" and "what" indicate you feel you haven't lived up to your own standards or expectations (large distance from t-bar to tip of stem), causing some depression (slightly down-slanting lines).

So what other work could you be happy in? You have many imaginative creative ideas (large lower loops) and you're good with your hands (rounded "r" in "interpreter"), with a likely aptitude for making things. You're open-minded and open philosophically and spiritually (wide upper loops), basically honest (no loops or hooks in "a" or "o"), with a strong sense of responsibility (large loop on "I").

With your passion (heavy pressure) and enthusiasm (long t-bars), I think you would make a great seminar leader of teenage children or adults, a motivational speaker for large groups, or whatever. You need to be onstage (large writing) where, with your background, you can inspire growing minds.

However, you would have to improve your self-image (low t-bars in "at," "what," "felt," "not," "insight," and "right"); stop the tendency to give up when the going gets rough (concave t-bars in "what," "felt," "traits," "right," and "direction"); stop procrastinating (t-bar to left of stem in "might" and "right"); and get over your self-consciousness (last humps on "m's," especially in "me").

You're already holding onto some resentment about the children (hook on the beginning inflexible stroke to "children"), so it looks like it's time for change. I think being before a larger-than-classroom audience would also loosen suppressed feelings (little space between letters in key words "education" and "interpreter") as well as bring out repressed feelings (retraced "m"). It would give you more confidence and self-esteem (higher t-bars on the stem), though you've had what it takes all along.

I asked female age 40 to respond to the reply I gave her. She wrote the following:

Dena,

Thank you so very much for your analysis of my writing. I smiled as I read it and felt connected to what you had to say.

I have thought about stage storytelling in American Sign Language as well as public speaking in regards to Deafness. In a very positive and truthful manner I agree I need to work on self image confidence and I <u>will</u> just "give up" if I feel like a situation is at odds to how I feel and what I believe. I do need to work on that! :)

I loved this insight and feel that everything you said was spot on

What is really neat is that I had some of these same ideas already deep down inside. It was very satisfying to see that come out in your analysis. Thank you, Dena!

Dena,

Thank you so much for your analysis of my writing. I smiled as I read it and felt connected to what you had to say. I have thought about stage storytelling in American Sign Language as well as public speaking in regards to Deafness. In a very positive and truthful manner I agree I need to work on self image, confidence and I will just give up if I feel like a situation is at odds to how I feel and what I believe. I do need to work on that!

I loved this insight and feel that everything you said was spot on. What is really neat is that I had some of these same ideas already deep down inside. It was very satisfying to see that come out in your analysis. Thank you, Dena.

CHAPTER SIX

Career Counseling Using Graphology

The usual Vocational Guidance tests do not in themselves take into account the emotional burdens or experiences creating a passion for, or aversion to, a certain way of life or vocation. Graphology, on the other hand, reveals personality and emotional blocks to achieving your goals, as well as strengths which could help one to overcome limitations indicated in career tests.

Analyzing Handwriting at a College Career Counseling Center

Teacher and career counselor Larry Farwell understood this and asked me to analyze the handwriting of his students in his Career and Personal Development class in Santa Barbara Community College, California.

They were **day and evening students, all ages, from various backgrounds.** All had already completed the many tests given by the vocational guidance department for personality and aptitude. Their tests had been scored, they had been told what work they were best suited to, but many were still uncertain. Now they were gathered in a huge lecture room – to have their handwriting analyzed.

College Blackboard "Quickies"

I stood before the group, gave a brief little introduction to handwriting analysis, and then asked a volunteer for a "quickie" at the blackboard. I don't believe it's really necessary to go into a lot of detail; a good graphoanalyst instantly sees the most important aspect of the writing, the heart of it - in other words, what must be seen and understood in choosing your career path. I believe it comes from an understanding of your basic nature, being true to yourself and working towards your goal, little by little, whether financially, emotionally or educationally.

SBCC

Santa Barbara Community College District / Santa Barbara City College
721 Cliff Drive, Santa Barbara, California 93109 / (805) 965-0581

March 1, 1984

Carolyn Kenny
Santa Barbara Creative Arts Health Center
924 Anacapa Street Suite 4E
Santa Barbara, Ca 93101

Dear Carolyn,

Dena Blatt, graphoanalyst, is interested in working with your group and requestd that I contact you regarding her skills and abilities. I am a counselor and teacher at Santa Barbara City College. I teach "Career/Life Planning and Decision Making" (Personal Development 10) and work as a life planning counselor for students and non-students at life change points. I have known Dena for the three years that she has been guest lecturing to my classes on graphoanalysis and graphotheraputics.

My classes average 27 students, between 18 and 72 years of age, of all racial and religious backgrounds, of all economic standings - all questioning who and what they are and will be, all at watersheds of graduation, divorce, re-entry, retirement, health, values. The class focuses on healthy choices, healthy lifestyles, self-motivation and responsibility. Dena Blatt has made significant contributions to the growth and health of over 150 students attending this class over the last three years.

Dena's ability to 'see' a person, their characteristics, strengths, traits, and paths from a sample of their handwriting is outstanding. I have not seen Dena make an incorrect analysis of a person's interests, career goals, personality or health. Much of this personal information is delicate to communicate in a class setting and Dena's skills with people allow her to touch and teach in such a way that we all learn and yet feel safe.

The students are always very inpressed by Dena. The class opens with much scepticism and closes with everyone asking her to remain or asking if they can bring their mothers, friends or spouses. Dena is there to help, heal and teach and does all three well. Her knowledge of graphotheraputics allows her to influence health and behavior as well as interpret them.

I hope that you will allow Dena to contribute to your group, and hence the community. Dena is a highly trained professional of exceptional ability. Please call upon me if I can be of assistance in this or any area.

All the best,

Larry Farwell

Larry Farwell
Counselor/Teacher
Counseling Department

Two students in the class stood out to me. One was an eighteen or nineteen-year-old girl, who couldn't decide on her major. I could see by her handwriting that she had no real long-range goals, but had a warm heart and interest in daily living. I told her she would make a wonderful wife and mother, and if that suited her more than a career, there was nothing wrong with it. She broke down and cried then and there, and said that she was only going to college to please her parents. What she wanted most was to marry a good man and have a baby.

The other that stayed in my memory was the blackboard writing of a young Asian girl. I was surprised at the intellect and emotional maturity in the handwriting of so young a person. I told her she should definitely stay on for extended studies, for she was Ph.D. material in at least *some* profession, whether it be law, medicine. "I intend to be an attorney," she said with a smile.

The Importance of Focusing on What You *Do* Want (and Not on What You *Don't* Want):

I like what Deepak Chopra has to say in one of his blogs. He emphasizes there is power in focused intention: if you intend (believe) with strong emotion that you will receive what you think you need or want, then you will. The power is lost when you're desperate, confused, frustrated, feel ambivalent, indecisive, or have hidden agendas or mixed motives. **When intentions are unclear, he says, you send confused messages:**

1) You don't really know what you want or are indecisive (e.g. please parents or self?).

2) You think you don't deserve to get what you want (low self-esteem).
3) You're skeptical of receiving the desired result (science versus paranormal).
4) You have mixed motives (e.g. you think you are doing it for family but it's actually for self).
5) You have inner conflict (e.g. working for a company you view as immoral).

Specimen #25
(that first real career decision)

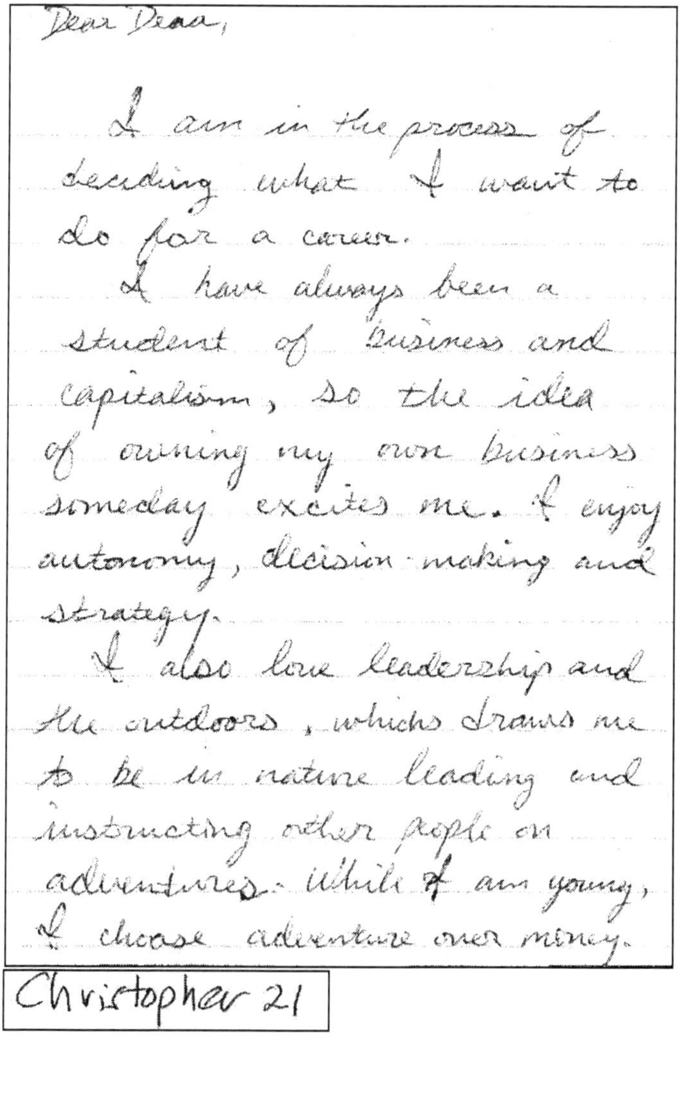

Dear Dean,

I am in the process of deciding what I want to do for a career.

I have always been a student of business and capitalism, so the idea of owning my own business someday excites me. I enjoy autonomy, decision-making and strategy.

I also love leadership and the outdoors, which draws me to be in nature leading and instructing other people on adventures. While I am young, I choose adventure over money.

Christopher 21

Dear Dena,

I am in the process of deciding what I want to do for a career. I have always been a student of business and capitalism, so the idea of owning my own business someday excites me. I enjoy autonomy, decision-making, and strategizing.

I also love leadership and the outdoors, which draws me to be in nature, leading and instructing other people on adventures. While I am young I choose adventure and freedom over money. – Christopher 21

Dear Christopher,

Well, you certainly have a mind that is independent (short t-stem), analytical (angular "m"), efficient (fluency strokes of joining one letter to the next), intuitive (breaks between letters), objective (some upright slant), yet able to relate well with people (mostly right slant), as well as determined (fairly good down-stokes on "y" and "g")—the mind necessary for business—but, like you say, you are undecided on where to focus your determination (light, weak t-bars).

Also, being a little sensitive to criticism (loop on "d"), very irritable at times (dashes for dots), stubborn (wedge in "t"), and sometimes wanting your way (downturned t-bar in printed "student," "autonomy," and "instructing"), you would be happy being your own boss.

You have strong manual dexterity (flat-topped "r"), so you would be good in certain outdoor sports. Your cultural interests ("Greek "d") and artistic abilities (simple printed capitals) would make you a good photographer or painter of the outdoors.

What is lacking for business (or any career), however, is the setting of near-future goals; your goals are for realistic day-to-day life (light t-bar on short stem), where you do not have to leave your comfort zone and demand more of yourself.

Could it be that you (understandably for your age) lack some confidence (very low t-bar in cursive "strategy" and "adventures")? With more experience that would come.

As for choosing a career: you are clear that you like business and the outdoors; why not simply combine the two? How about getting experience in an outdoor resort—learning it from the ground up—studying what makes it successful, and when you know the business well and have saved enough money, buy or start your own resort or adventure company. This takes years and a lot of work, but you are young. With more experience and confidence ***you've definitely got what it takes!***

Specimen #26

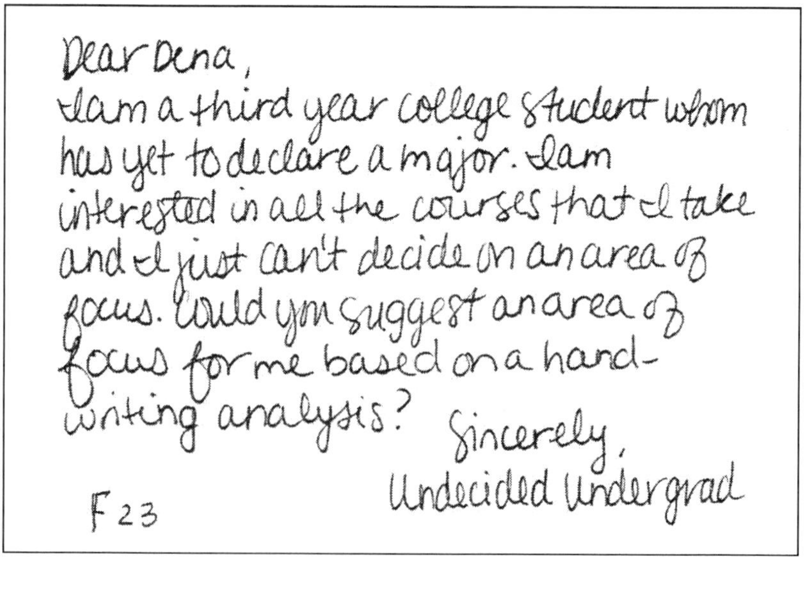
Dear Dena,
I am a third year college student whom has yet to declare a major. I am interested in all the courses that I take and I just can't decide on an area of focus. Could you suggest an area of focus for me based on a hand-writing analysis?
Sincerely,
Undecided Undergrad
F 23

Dear Dena,

I am a third year college student whom (sic) has yet to declare a major. I am interested in all the courses that I take and I just can't decide on an area of focus. Could you suggest an area of focus for me based on handwriting analysis? Sincerely, Undecided Undergrad age 23 female.

Dear Undecided Undergrad,

You have artistic and creative abilities (aesthetic sense, heavy pressure, balance on page) conflicting with traditional values (traditional capital "I"). Your cultural interests (Greek "r" and "s") could be utilized in literature, English, and photo-journalism. Being warm and caring (rounded "m" and "n"), you could also work well with children.

You say you are interested in all the courses, but you hesitate (large space) after "I am," showing fear or doubt, before writing "interested."

Your very low t-bars, especially in the key word "can't," tell me you don't have enough self-confidence, and as a result have not set higher standards (short t-stems). You need time to get to know yourself better. Perhaps you really don't want a career that takes years to pursue. Perhaps you would rather be a happy housewife, using your artistic and creative talents in the interior decorating of a home, putting your warmth and caring to use with children at home or at a nursery or kindergarten, which would also draw on your talents with arts and crafts.

But finish college. Perhaps psychology courses will give you some insights and time to make the right decision. Good luck!

Specimen #27

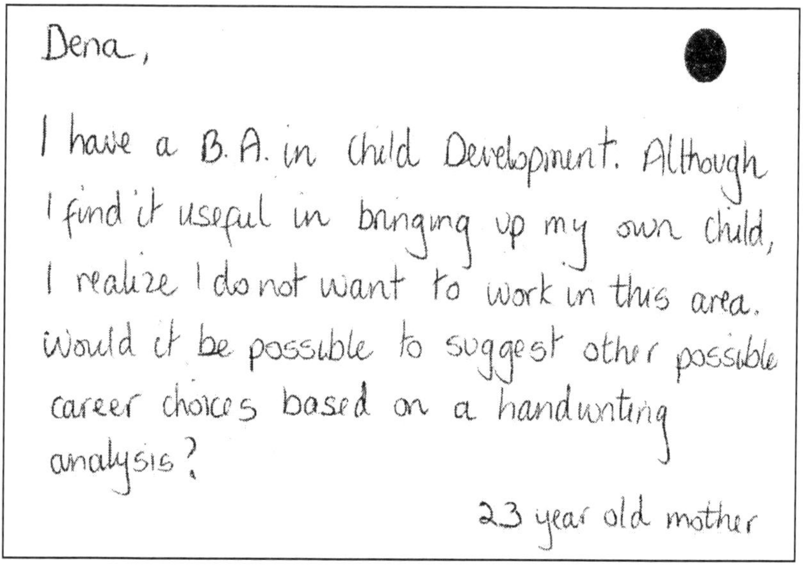
Dena,

I have a B.A. in Child Development. Although I find it useful in bringing up my own child, I realize I do not want to work in this area. Would it be possible to suggest other possible career choices based on a handwriting analysis?

23 year old mother

Dear Dena,

I have a B.A. in Child Development. Although I find it useful in bringing up my own child, I realize I don't want to work in this area. Would it be possible to suggest other possible career choices based on a handwriting analysis. – 23 year old mother

Dear 23 year old mother,

You have a hang-up on something from the past (all down-strokes on "y" and "g" turn left and do not make a loop returning to the right, towards people and the future). Also, the slant is vertical (you're not very responsive), suggesting that working directly and closely with other people may not be what you want.

Therefore, the work I suggest for you would perhaps be the following: art therapy, photography, arts and crafts for children, architecture, interior design, manager of an art gallery or bookstore, or writing about child development.

Specimen #28
(career decision later in life)

"Whenever you're in conflict with someone, there is one factor that can make the difference between damaging your relationship and deepening it. That factor is attitude."
- Timothy Bentley

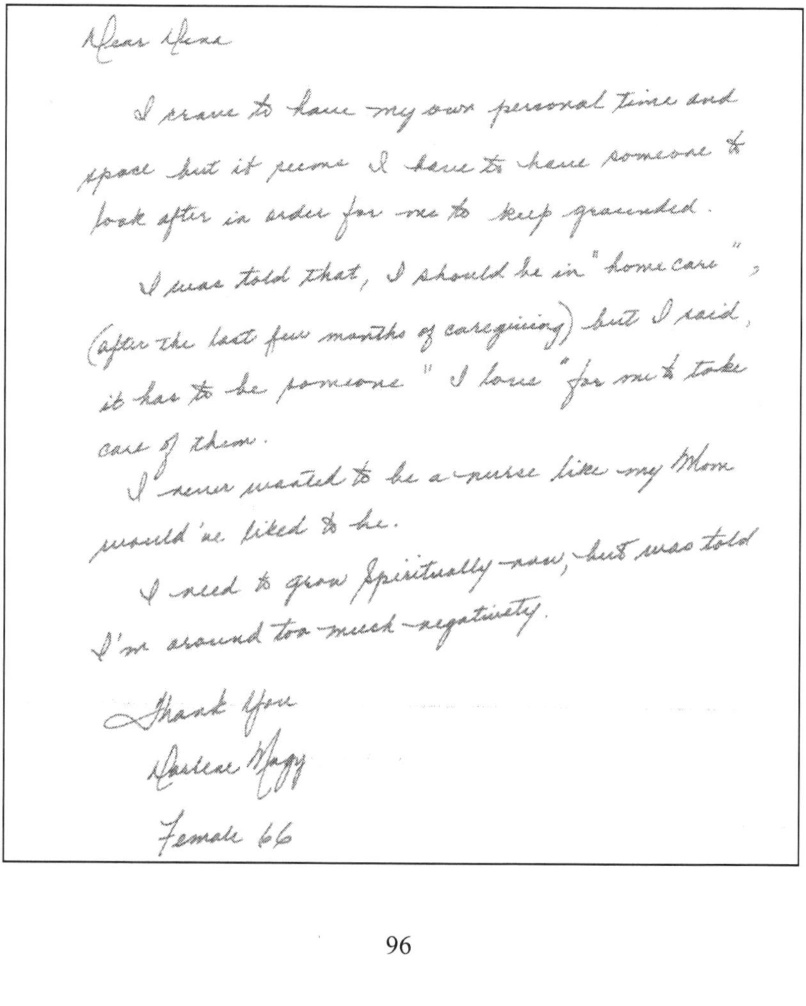
Dear Dena

I crave to have my own personal time and space but it seems I have to have someone to look after in order for me to keep grounded.

I was told that, I should be in "home care", (after the last few months of caregiving) but I said, it has to be someone " I love "for me to take care of them.

I never wanted to be a nurse like my Mom would've liked to be.

I need to grow Spiritually now, but was told I'm around too much negativity.

Thank You
Darlene Nagy
Female 66

Dear Dena,

I crave to have my own personal time and space but it seems I have to have someone to look after in order for me to keep grounded. I was told that, I should be in "home care", (after the last few months of care-giving) but I said it has to be someone "I love" for me to take care of them. I never wanted to be a nurse like my Mom would've liked to be. I need to grow spiritually now, but was told I'm around too much negativity. – Thank you, Darlene Nagy, Female 66

Dear Darlene,

I wonder why a person with your obvious education and maturity (small well-spelled writing, balanced upper, lower, and middle zones), intelligence (analytical and investigative mind with angular and rounded "m" and "n"), confidence and determination (high t-bars and straight down-strokes on "y" and "g"), as well as dependability and reliability (balance and rhythm on page, spacing between letters, words, and lines)—high school teacher, psychologist, medical researcher, or some kind of administrator, perhaps, in your younger years?—I wonder why you are so emotionally up and down (wavy baseline) that you have to have someone to look after to "keep grounded." Is it because of your spiritual search (pointed "l" and pointed "I") or something else?

If I understand you correctly, the work is also to pay for food and a roof over your head. However, you have free will; you don't have to do anything. Note that the words "have to" fall suddenly at the thought. By saying instead that you choose to do it for the pay-off (room and board or whatever), work becomes lighter, easier, less unpleasant. You may even hear about and appreciate the full, interesting lives your patients have had.

But unless you change your attitude about it, I would advise you against working with "home care" patients. There are so many other kinds of work you could do. At the present time you are not suited for "nursing" anybody. A patient would sense your resentment or ***"chip on the shoulder" (a feeling of having been imposed upon and not appreciated),*** *which shows itself in thirty inflexible beginning strokes—most noticeably in the words "crave," "time," "space," "someone," "love," "would've," and "spiritually," which all begin below the line—meaning the resentment, common in generous and giving people like you (long endings to words), has been carried over from childhood. Also, feelings of having been rejected or rejecting someone close (lower loop on "f" in "for" in sixth line swings left below the baseline), with some defiance (buckle on "k") and anger (temper tic "T" in "Thank"), only lessen emotional stability.*

Could the fact that you capitalized "Mom" (strong influence) with a temper tic (anger towards your mother?)—and the last hump of the "m" (curved, making a large acquisitive hook)—have something to do with your resentment? Note the "M" in Magy (your middle name) is different, showing a sense of humor (curved beginning stroke), strong resentment, strong stubbornness (wide wedge), spiritual searching (high pointed last hump), and strong determination (long, straight down-stroke with ending hook). But what is most important is the resentment stroke you drew across it. You are sabotaging yourself, getting yourself into unrewarding situations—in other words, you are your own worst enemy.

You have procrastinated (t-bar to left of stem) on fulfilling your dreams (t-bar floating above stem), vacillating between optimism (rising lines) and pessimism ("I love" drops suddenly), and between enthusiastic confidence (high, long t-

bars) and a tendency to give up (concave t-bar in "time" and "it").

For your psychological and spiritual health, you need to learn compassion (for your mother? or whoever) so that you can forgive and let go of resentment; you can then go on, using freed energy to do what you love to do, want to do, instead of what you think you "have to" do, or "ought to" do.

Today's Young Generation

Handwriting, generations ago, was done in cursive with a right slant (showing more responsiveness of feeling). Today many young people are more apt to print with a vertical slant (showing more cool-headedness and objectivity), while those who only block-print are reluctant to show their feelings, being more comfortable communicating with electronic technology.

During the political activism of the 1960s and '70s, Generation X, reacting to the thriftiness of the previous generation, had to learn to handle finances. Now both they and Generation Y must find ways to adjust to the exponentially fast growth of technology, the abundance and ease of attaining knowledge often necessary to secure and maintain employment. They also must adjust to the ever-changing "male/female" roles and their resulting expectations of the modern world, and ponder over the many choices available in career and relationships. So, how are today's young people, seeking work in a recession (or even quasi-depression) with almost record-high unemployment levels, expected to thrive or even survive? What has changed, and what has remained the same?

Time magazine called them "The Me, Me, Me Generation," coddled by parents. Now, as they go job-seeking in the "real world," many have low self-esteem, wondering why they can't find or keep a job. As I see it, from an employer's standpoint nothing has changed. Employers are still desperately looking for honest, skilled, reliable workers, and are having a hard time finding them, whether the economy is good or bad. The rule remains: if you really want to get ahead, be willing to start at the "bottom" (if necessary), show initiative, and be willing to give more of yourself than expected.

It's Called Initiative – The Kid Named Matt

I still remember the kid who came into our electronics store, years ago in 1974. "I'm looking for work," he said, with a big confident smile. My husband, seeing how young he was, dismissed him. But I admire a boy with initiative. "Wait," I said, "come back. How old are you?"

"Fourteen."

"Can you sweep the floor and put away some boxes?"

To make a long story short, he came in each day after school, helping out in various ways, while watching and learning about inventory, sales, and electronic repairs. The money he made with raises he was putting away for college, and finally that day came. The feeling was not one of loss, but of mutual appreciation and caring.

From my "Dear Dena's" it seems that, despite "Women's Lib" and laws giving "equal rights" to women, there are still many women who long for the "good old days," when men were expected to take care of them; they were satisfied living vicariously through their husbands. Today, too many men, I feel, are also longing for when "they had it good," their women extensions of themselves and "belonging" to them. Thus, both these sorts of men and women are today experiencing a somewhat historically ironic conflict: the men like the fact that the women take some of the financial burden off them, and the women like the idea of their being free to work if they so choose. At the same time, however, they both want to "have their cake and eat it too": women have now seen how hard it is to support a family, and men have learned that homemaking and caretaking of children does not come with a manual, is not at all easy, and can be hard on the nerves.

Then and Now

I come from that older era, when men were male chauvinists and proud of it. You didn't dare ask such a man to help with the housework or children. You could work outside the home if you never told anyone. And you didn't; it would be a humiliation for the man, "allowing" his wife to work, and thus showing he was a failure in supporting the family.

There are women who find it easy to make a living, and men who find it easier and more rewarding to stay home and be "househusband." If that's the case it's a good match. But if a woman is successful at work and making money and the man is still a chauvinist? The woman has to be superwoman, working both outside and in the home, making sure her husband has a clean home, good meals, and the children well behaved (or there is hell to pay). Women would ask in wonder, "You mean your husband *lets* you work?!" He "let" me as long as I managed to do it all. But it didn't make him happy; on the contrary, he felt emasculated (I was accused of trying to wear the pants). Not many men can stand the loss of ego. Though he understood my working was necessary (we both had no money and he had to learn a new language, as well as a new trade, business, or profession), he could not help being jealous and resentful of me ("side-effects" some working women may experience).

Not only did I have to contend with unequal rights at home, but unequal rights in the workplace, as well. I received 60% of a man's wage for the same work; there was no *paid* maternity leave, and when I asked to work again six weeks after giving birth in 1959, I was told that women lab technologists were no longer working in the hospital; they had all been replaced by men. When I asked the male head technologist why, he said that they had to get rid of them so men could be paid what they felt was fair for the work.

Sometimes I worked days, sometimes nights (secretly nursing the baby brought to me during a break; there was no such thing back then as "child-care" or "day care" for employees' little ones). Four years later, after a year of employment in a large clinic in Beverly Hills, California, I was made its head technologist. My female coworkers laughed at me and the outlandish idea of a woman "head." Female patients would yell at me with "You should be at home with your children!" Women were told to stay home and give the jobs to the men who were supporting families.

I didn't know then that my boss, a pathologist and head of the laboratory, had broken two "laws." He had knowingly hired a pregnant woman, and then even given her a raise and promoted her to "head" technologist. After giving birth to my second child over a weekend, I took the six weeks at home my boss promised me. But when I returned he told me he had been forced by the clinic not to allow me to come back. When I found it hard to believe, he brought me to the secretary of the clinic, a woman.

I asked if it was true. "Yes," she said coldly. "You can't come back." "Why?" I asked. "Because," she said, "the doctors will not respect a woman as head of the lab. Besides,[another crime?] you're still of child-bearing age." Then she simply dismissed me, apparently in disgust. So it seems that women themselves, as much as men, were holding women back.

CHAPTER SEVEN

Intellectual, Psychological and Biological Considerations on Hiring Personnel

"Ability may get you to the top, but it takes character to keep you there."
- James Wooden

"Try not to become a man of success, but rather a man of value."
- Albert Einstein

Intellectual

We may operate in any or all of the three thinking processes below:

1) **Logical**: rounded "m" and "n"; careful, slower type of thinking – can also be that of a genius (Thomas Edison).

2) **Analytical and Investigative**: deep, sharp, angular "m" and "n" with almost vertical slant – a very sharp, critical, and cool mind.

3) **Comprehensive:** deep garland shape ("m" and "n" made like "u"); fast, perceptive thinkers, quick to understand people and situations, but can be impulsive.

High Intelligence and Low Intelligence

A person with a high IQ may have one or a combination of the above traits, and all are magnified in those with tiny writing, such as that of the genius Albert Einstein. I leave the subject of low IQ to books on that specialty, not having enough expertise to comment intelligently on it.

Intellectual "IQ" vs Emotional "EQ"

It seems the best combination for success and happiness in life is an average IQ together with a lot of plain common sense and integrity. This is called a high *emotional* "IQ," or what is more popularly known today as "EQ" ("Emotional Quotient").

High EQ (Emotional Maturity with Integrity)

What would this "good" handwriting look like? There would be rhythm, an even baseline, and regular spacing between lines, words, and letters (dependability, reliability). There would be no loops or hooks in "a" or "o" (some form of dishonesty). There would be consistent left and right margins (no fear of the past or the future), and some positive traits: initiative, generosity, open-mindedness, honesty, optimism, patience, kindness, a good mind, confidence (realistic goals and standards, and determination to carry out those goals and meet those standards).

It would also show a noted absence of most negative traits such as: anger, temper, stubbornness, verbal or physical aggression, jealousy, resentment, irritability, hyper-sensitivity to criticism, criticalness, moodiness, blaming self, hurting of self or others, domineeringness, selfishness, stinginess, callousness, vanity, impulsiveness or over-cautiousness, suppressions and repressions of feelings, procrastination, indecision, narrow-mindedness, depression, defensiveness, rationalizing, secrecy and deceit – and, of course, low self-confidence, low self-respect – all from *fears*, of every type.

Biological Indications

Work or Careers for those with Dyslexia (poor visual-motor integration problem) attention deficit disorder and hyperactivity). Dyslexics and those with ADD/HD would naturally have learning problems and have difficulty relating at home and at work. For good detailed information on the subject, an excellent website is Bright Solutions for Dyslexia, Inc

The above disorders are neurobiological and can be mild to severe, separate or combined. Some indications of dyslexia and perhaps also AD/HD are: slow illegible writing. tight pencil grip, many misspellings; unusual placing on page (sentences all in one particular section); often no margins, words spaced too closely or far apart; difficulty learning cursive, especially with making the capital letter; reversing or changing certain letters. They can be very intelligent, but have trouble learning as taught in regular classrooms, and may be thought of as having low intellect. They may have additional emotional problems because of this, if their ADHD is not recognized and taken into account.

Example #1: Dyslexia

Example #2: Dyslexia

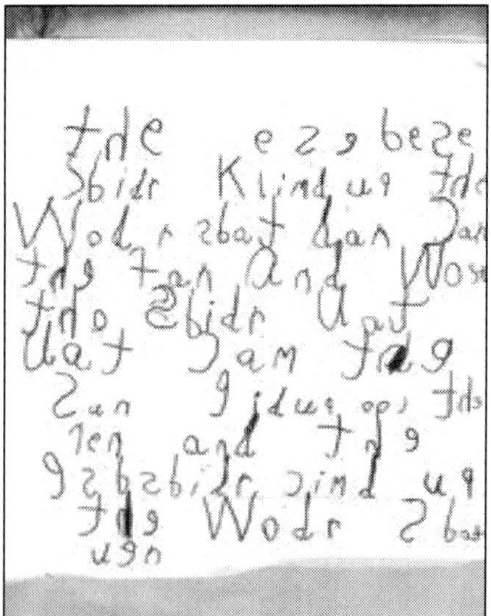

Notice misspellings of common words like "wat" for "want", "hav" for "have", and "b" for "be." This is a very common tendency of dyslexic children. Also notice the many reversed b's and d's, the inconsistent spacing between words and the letters within words, the way he ignores the margins, the mixing of capital and lower-case letters, the unusual formation of some of the letters, the way letters like little "g" always float above the horizontal line instead of going below the line, and the lack of punctuation. These errors are all classic signs of dysgraphia and also represent typical handwriting errors that dyslexic students make.

– OAK BRIDGE DYSLEXIA TUTORING
[http://www.oakdyslexiatutoring.com/homeschooling-dyslexic-children/dyslexia-writing-sample-2.html]

Biological and Psychological: Depression

There can also be problems with people suffering from depression. They may cope so well you would not notice anything abnormal in the workplace. Below is the cursive handwriting of a young person coping but needing help with depression, especially because of the lines drawn through the first name as if crossing it out. Note how words which dip are lifted up as long as possible.

Specimen #29

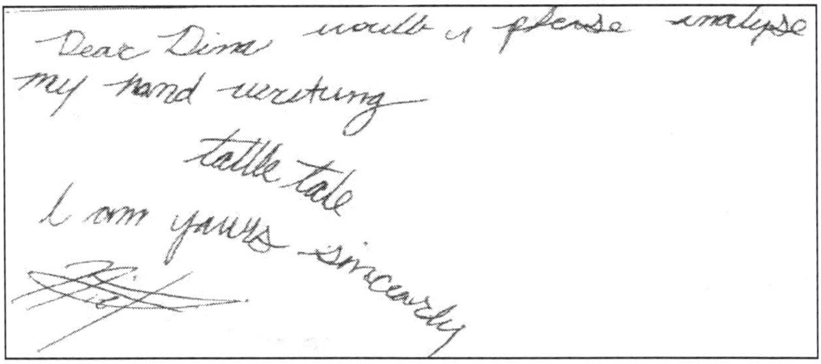

CHAPTER EIGHT

Low Confidence, Low Self-Esteem, and Graphotherapeutics

The Difference Between Confidence and Self-esteem

Confidence comes from experience and training, and results in trusting one's ability to handle life's situations, whether in work or relationships.

Self-esteem is the manner in which one measures oneself compared to others or one's own standards – **whether or not confidence is present.** For example, one may have confidence at work but little self-esteem in relationships, or have no confidence at work because it is something he or she has never done before, and yet nevertheless enjoy a healthy self-image. Conversely, bullies may camouflage their low self-esteem with what appears outwardly to be confidence.

People with high self-esteem like themselves, respect themselves, and see themselves favorably regarding looks, personality, and self-worth. Those with low self-esteem long to be different. All these traits can be seen in handwriting, arising from conscious or unconscious, positive or negative thoughts and *beliefs*. The following are some examples of poor confidence and low self-esteem.

Specimen #30
(woman, working part-time, living at home)

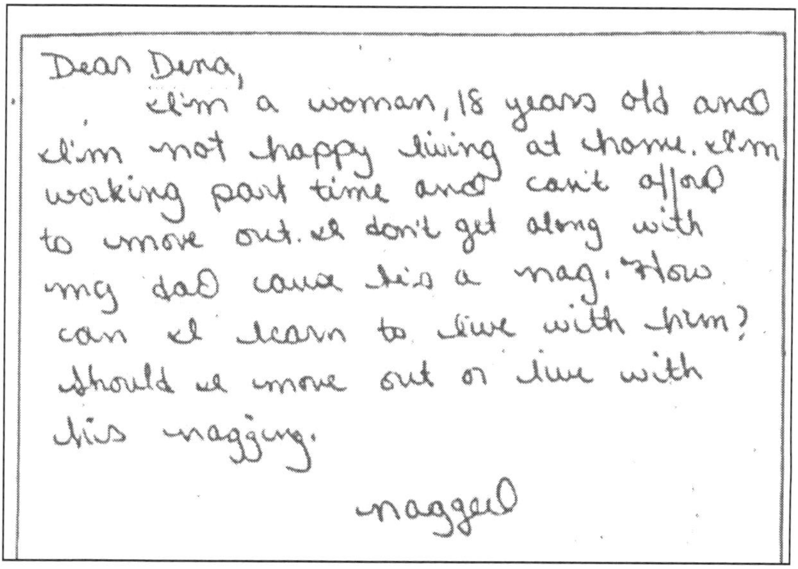
Dear Dena,
I'm a woman, 18 years old and
I'm not happy living at home. I'm
working part time and can't afford
to move out. I don't get along with
my dad cause he's a nag. How
can I learn to live with him?
Should I move out or live with
his nagging.
Nagged

Dear Dena,

I'm a woman, 18 years old and I'm not happy living at home. I'm working part time and can't afford to move out. I don't get along with my dad 'cause he's a nag. How can I learn to live with him? Should I move out or live with his nagging? – Nagged

Dear Nagged,

Apparently your dad is expecting behavior from you which you are unable or unwilling, at present, to show. While you are a kind and warm-hearted girl (rounded "m"), somewhat artistic and creative (simple printed capital), and have manual dexterity (flat-topped "r"), there is much in your handwriting that shows you are not ready to be on your own.

Your dangerously low t-bars in the key words "don't," "can't," and "out" tell me you have very low confidence or little belief in yourself, and the large loop on "d" means you are much too sensitive to criticism or nagging—causing you to react defensively. With your strong desire for love or a loving home (initial hooks), there is the danger that, if you leave now, you could enter a hasty marriage or relationship. You are certainly not ready or mature enough for such responsibilities.

Your last capital "I" is even tinier than the others (very low self-esteem). So, on an unconscious level you know *you are not ready to leave and must learn to live with his nagging or behave in such a way that he will not nag. Since you cannot change your father, only yourself, you could begin by proving to yourself and to him, while still at home, that you can hold a full-time job successfully for at least six months and have gained some measure of confidence and security. Only then should you leave.*

You might then have to learn to handle the nagging and criticism of an employer—for procrastinating (t-bars to the left). Keep working on this problem. A counselor could be of help. Good luck!

Specimen #31
(her work is not her passion)

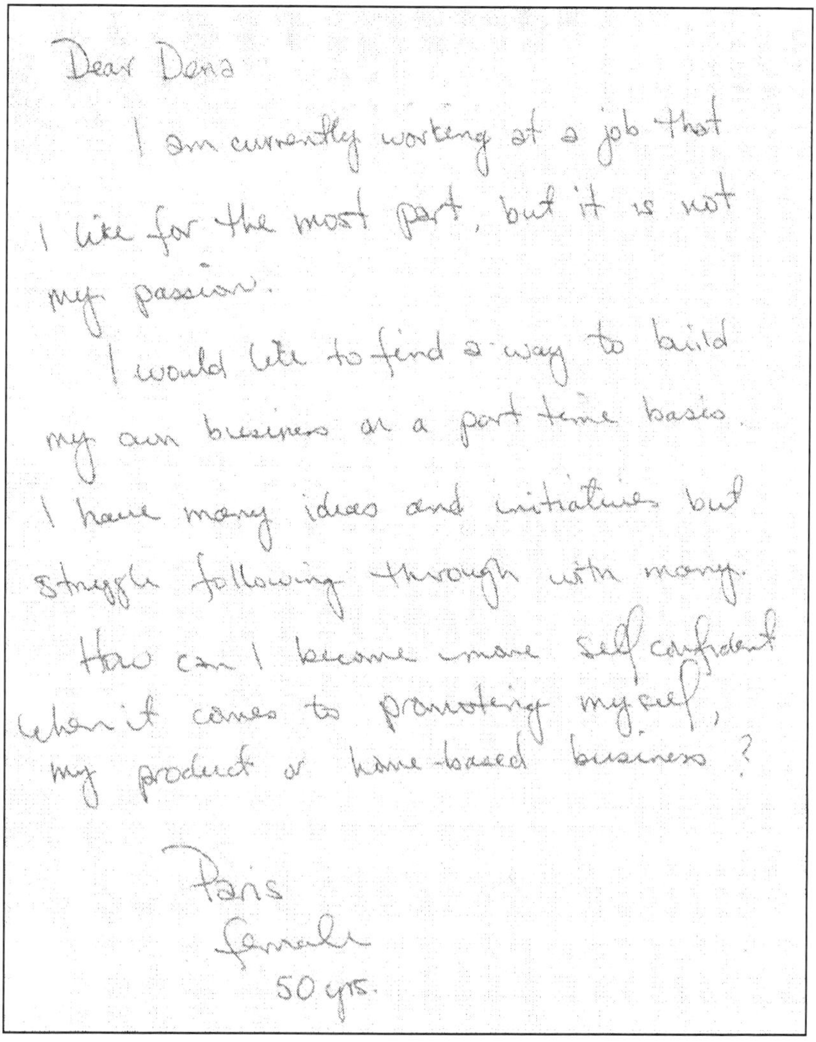

Dear Dena

I am currently working at a job that I like for the most part, but it is not my passion.

I would like to find a way to build my own business on a part time basis. I have many ideas and initiatives but struggle following through with many.

How can I become more self confident when it comes to promoting myself, my product or home-based business?

Paris
female
50 yrs.

Dear Dena,

I am currently working at a job that I like for the most part, but it is not my passion. I would like to find a way to build my own business on a part time basis. I have many ideas and initiatives but struggle following through with many. How can I become more self confident when it comes to promoting myself, my product or home-based business? – Paris, female 50 yrs.

Dear female 50,

You see yourself as a very creative person (very simple capital "I") and you are; you're artistic (printed capitals), intuitive (breaks between letters), and you have cultural interests, especially writing (figure 8 "g" in "struggle" and Greek "r," printed "s"). You work smoothly and well (many fluency strokes of letters joined to the next).

You certainly have many ideas—both abstract (large loop in "f" in "myself") and concrete (large loop in "y"). However, you seem to sabotage bringing them into fruition (endings on "y" turn downward—a little pessimism regarding readiness?). What seems to be the fly in the ointment is one dominant trait: an over-sensitivity to what others think of your ideas—a fear of criticism (large loops in "t's," especially in the key word "self-confident"). There is also your shyness and fear of getting hurt emotionally (left slant of "I"), and, as you say, your inability to materialize your ideas (no lower loop on "f" in "myself").

Working for someone you often have to give in to other people (rounded final "s"). But by 50 you pretty much need to have things done your way, the way that works for you (downturned t-bars, especially in "self-confident"), so it's understandable that you would want to work for yourself, at least part-time. At the same time there is fear of change.

In addition, your tiny writing (ability to concentrate) and bright analytical and logical mind (rounded and angular "m" and "n") make you a good researcher; you'd work well at home, in your own space.

However, promoting a business requires an extremely confident and extroverted nature. You're not emotionally very demonstrative (mostly left-to-upward slant of letters), even seeking more "alone space" (spacing between words, at first fairly normal but gradually becoming wider than normal).

Perhaps the answer is to get someone else to do the promoting while you create the product. If this is not feasible financially, you would have to learn to become more outgoing, more willing to risk getting your feelings hurt, and being unappreciated. You would have to become more thick-skinned, more trusting, more confident. How? You have the talent and the determination (good down-strokes on "y") but lack the confidence (low t-bars except for the one in "initiative").

What can help is practicing making high and strong t-bars (placing higher goals than the practical) showing more belief in yourself. Do this at night before going to bed so that it can work into your unconscious and soon you will feel a difference. Good luck!

Specimen #32
(Reiki worker lacking confidence and self-esteem)

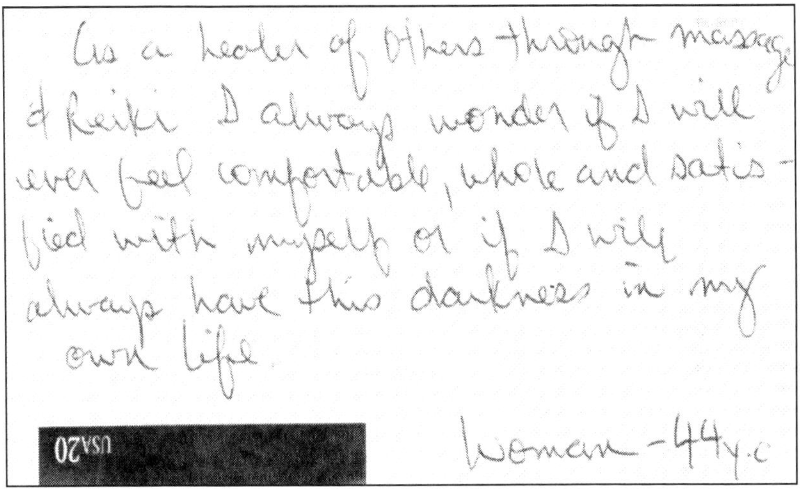
As a healer of others through massage
& Reiki I always wonder if I will
ever feel comfortable, whole and satisfied with myself or if I will
always have this darkness in my
own life

Woman - 44 y.o

Dear Dena,

As a healer of others through massage and reiki, I always wonder if I will ever feel comfortable, whole and satisfied with myself or if I will always have this darkness in my own life. – Woman 44 y.o.

Dear female 44,

What you fear is the word that follows the large space after the second "will"—and it is "always". But circumstances and people do change. Life is nothing but change. You are a spiritual seeker; you see yourself as one in the sharp pointed capital "I". And you know that the answers are within you, not outside. In Reiki you give of yourself (the only word that has a generous ending), where you feel helpful and appreciated. In your personal life, however, you fear being hurt emotionally (left-slanting letters). But why the fear? You're a sharp, intelligent woman (angular "m" and "n"), intuitive (breaks between letters), direct and to the point (no beginning strokes), objective, not overtly emotional but friendly (medium-size writing, with upward and slight right slant). You have the ability to do whatever you want.

However, you are hindered by a lack of belief in yourself (extremely low and weak t-bar in the key word "satisfied"), resulting in weak determination (curved down-strokes on "y" and "g"), procrastination (t-bar to left of stem), and a tendency to give up (low and weak concave t-bar in "with") when depressed (drooping key word "always" in the second line, and the drooping "will" in the fourth line).

There is a large distance between the t-bar and the top of the stem in "satisfied," meaning you feel you have not lived up to your expectations of yourself; the greater the distance, the more you feel bad about yourself. This is how you see yourself and feel about yourself, **not how others see you**. *If this were someone else would you be as hard on that person as you are on yourself?*

What I recommend is Graphotherapeutics. All you have to do is write a small cursive "t" with a strong and high t-bar. This will tell your brain that you are confident, you feel good about yourself, and have realistic goals. Next make a small cursive "g" with a strong and straight down-stroke. This will give you determination to carry out your goals. Do these thirty times a night for thirty nights. At first it will seem strange, but in time you will feel your self-esteem rising. With confidence in one's abilities, a strong realistic goal, and determination to carry it out, everything else will fall into place.

Specimen #33
(the missing traits for making money from hobbies)

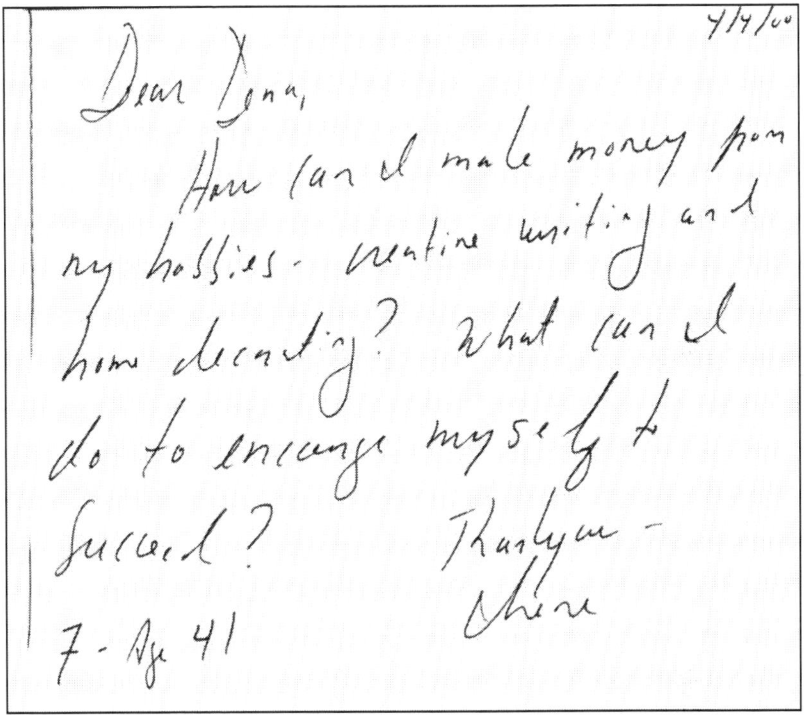
4/4/00

Dear Dena,

How can I make money from my hobbies - creative writing and home decorating? What can I do to encourage myself to succeed?

Thank you -
[illegible]

F - Age 41

Dear Dena,

How can I make money from my hobbies—creative writing and home decorating? What can I do to encourage myself to succeed? Thank you – F - Age 41

Dear Female 41 (I can't make out your name),

You have the talents necessary for writing and decorating—artistic and creative ability (simple capitals); an aesthetic sense (balance and spacing); cultural interests (printed "s"); fluency of thought (figure 8 "g")—all enhanced by a great imagination (huge lower loops in the key words "writing" and "decorating"); and strong intuition (many breaks between letters). Your openness and honesty (open, not looped "o" and "a"), as well as your diplomacy (tapering words), are added positives.

So what's missing here? What's wrong? It's your t-bars. They're very low and weak (low self-worth), and concave (tendency to give up). The wide distance from t-bar to top of stem in "to" tell me you feel you haven't lived up to your own high standards (tall t-stem). You have great determination but with your weak willpower (very light t-bar) you set only day-to-day goals (low t-bars), reflecting your lack of confidence.

What can you do? You can either lower your standards or raise your belief in yourself. Or do both. A good therapist could help. Your t-bars are much too low and weak for such an intelligent (angular and rounded "m" and "n") and obviously talented woman of your age. Your personality and character are reflected unconsciously in your handwriting. Graphotherapeutics, consciously changing one's handwriting, does the reverse. It affects your personality and character in subtle unconscious but powerful ways. As I am not a psychiatrist able to discern and treat deeper issues, I use only the letters "t" and "g" which cannot hurt but only help.

So here it is. Every night just before going to bed, make strong and high t-bars across the stem (you are setting your goal because you believe in yourself) and next to it make a strong down-stroke on a "y" like the one you made in the key word "money" (you are determined to carry out your goal). You could also make a loop on the "y" (imagination on how to make money), but be sure to bring the loop all the way back to the baseline (making ideas realistic) unlike the loops in "writing" and "decorating."

Repeat the "t" and "y" thirty times a night for a month. At first it'll seem strange. Keep doing it and soon you will feel stronger, more assertive, and confident. Good luck!

Trying to Win or Keep a Parent's Love

We all try to win our parents' love at some time or other. I regularly receive "Dear Dena's" involving conflict between the kind of work the writers would prefer to do and the kind their parents wish for them. The following "Dear Dena," however, is from the parent's point of view.

Specimen #34

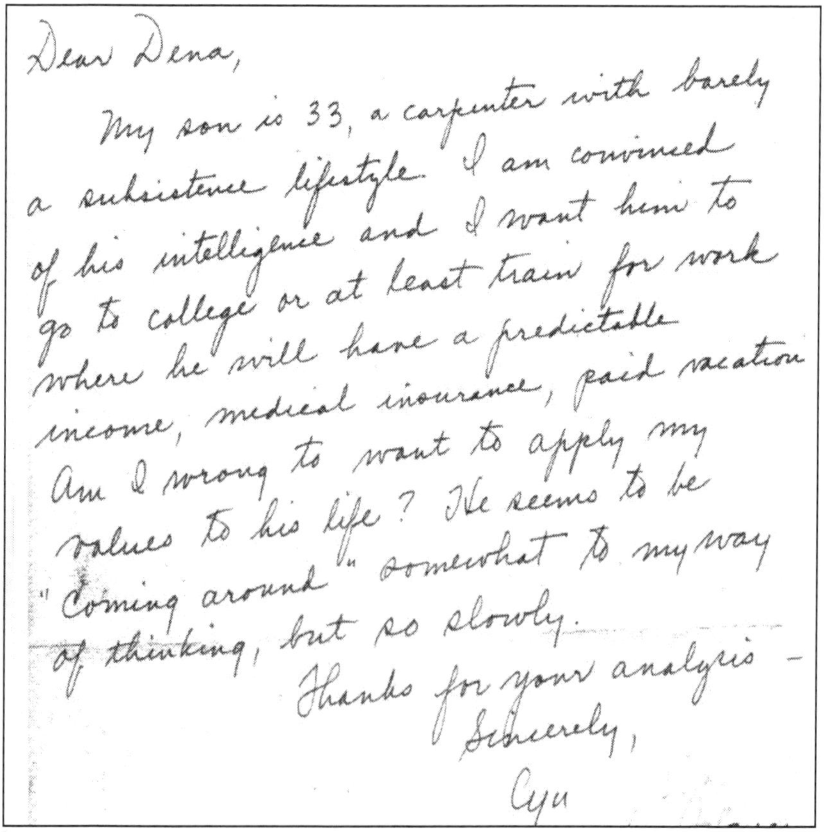
Dear Dena,
My son is 33, a carpenter with barely
a subsistence lifestyle. I am convinced
of his intelligence and I want him to
go to college or at least train for work
where he will have a predictable
income, medical insurance, paid vacation
Am I wrong to want to apply my
values to his life? He seems to be
"Coming around" somewhat to my way
of thinking, but so slowly.
Thanks for your analysis –
Sincerely,
Cyn

Dear Dena,

My son is 33, a carpenter with barely a subsistence lifestyle. I am convinced of his intelligence and I want him to go to college or at least train for work where he will have a predictable income, medical insurance, paid vacations. Am I wrong to want to apply my values to his life? He seems to be "coming around" somewhat to my way of thinking, but so slowly. Thanks for your analysis. – Sincerely, Cyn

Dear Cyn,

Your handwriting gives the overall impression of an accomplished person, an achiever with definite goals and determination (strong and high t-bars with firm and long down-strokes on "y" and "g"). You have a sharp analytical mind as well (angular "m" and "n") with a balanced perspective on life (even spacing between lines, words, letters, slant, size of writing). You like people (medium-sized writing, right slant), you're generous (long curved word endings), and you could work well in any one of the helping professions (psychology, sociology, medical, or educational).

Of course you're not wrong in wanting to apply your values to his life. What is wrong is resenting (inflexible beginning strokes in the key words "son," "lifestyle," "intelligence," "least train," "work," "income," and "want"), as well as feeling anger (temper tic on "M" in "My" and "H" in "He") towards him for not having your values. What is wrong is expecting him to be happy in applying your values. If by age 33 he hasn't wanted to go to college, there must be good reasons—reasons that must be taken into account.

Those reasons could possibly be any of the following:

1) *He's intelligent and he's dyslexic, learns differently, and so fears college.*

2) *He's intelligent, unsure of what career direction to take, and is taking time.*
3) *He's intelligent, but wants more time for creative work and enjoyment of life.*
4) *He's intelligent, believes in himself, and knows he will be well-off in future.*
5) *He's intelligent, but plans to have no family, home, children's college fees, etc.*
6) *He's intelligent, but has a different worldview, and is rebellious.*
7) *He's intelligent, doesn't like guarantees in life, and is comfortable taking risks.*
8) *He's intelligent, but has emotional or psychological issues.*
9) *He's intelligent, but also has good manual dexterity, enjoys using it, and is happy.*
10) *He's intelligent, but believes he cannot live up to your expectations.*
11) *He's intelligent, but lacks the confidence to seek higher carpentry qualifications*
12) *He's intelligent, confident as a carpenter, but has little self-esteem.*
13) *He's intelligent and thinks he will be subsidized by you or the government.*
14) *He is not intelligent and thinks he will always be healthy and live forever.*
15) *He is not intelligent and is doing the best he can.*

Without his handwriting, this is the best I can do for insight into your situation with your son. However, as you know, you cannot change another person, only yourself. So my unasked-for advice is: just let him be.

Graphotherapy is **graphotherapeutics** practiced by a therapist who is also a graphologist using his or her training in handwriting analysis (sometimes together with music or other aids) to help patients change their various negative traits into positive ones, which they achieve simply by having the patients change their handwriting. It has proven especially successful with dyslexic children.

Regarding work: those who are having trouble keeping a job, for instance, could change those aspects of their handwriting which suggest a tendency to give up or oversensitivity to criticism, and transform their anger and resentment in the workplace into more productive traits.

However, because graphotherapeutics is such a powerful influence on the writer, the therapist must be aware of the possibility of changes – changes the therapist may not be able to adequately handle alone or from a distance. Therefore, I use only one very simple exercise: before retiring, the writer places, thirty times a night for thirty nights, a strong and high t-bar (realistic and confident goal-setting) and a long, firm down-stroke on “g” (determination to achieve the goal or dream desired.) These two strokes cannot hurt or confuse the writer; they can only strengthen one’s resolve to achieve, thus improving his or her sense of self-worth.

Specimen #35

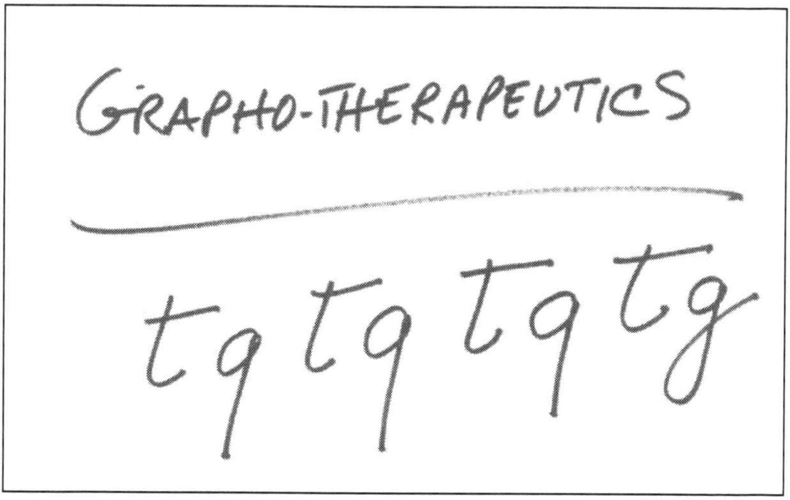

Breaking the Self-fulfilling Prophecy
The Importance of *Looking and Acting Confident!*

In 1950 I lost three lab tech jobs in seven months. I couldn't understand it. I had just come from Canada and had worked successfully in a hospital. Why was I having such trouble here in the States? Why was my superior constantly checking my work? With each "pink slip" I lost more and more of the confidence I had had to begin with. It was a self-fulfilling prophecy.

The fourth position, however, changed my life. As usual I was fired. But this time I asked why. And my pathologist employer said: "I can't afford to have a technologist whom the patients don't trust. You act like you have no confidence in yourself. So how do you expect others to?"

I decided then and there that I would have to fake the confidence I had lost, if I was to keep a job.

From Make-Believe Confidence to Initiative

I figured, as long as I had to appear to have a lot of self-confidence, I may as well show it by choosing the very job *I wanted*, in the location *I desired*. It was St. Vincent's Hospital, not far from where I lived. But they had no ads in the paper looking for lab techs. I knew the procedure was to send in my application to "Personnel," then wait. And I knew it would come to nothing. But what did I have to lose? I went to the hospital in person, with my application and resume in hand, and asked for the pathologist.

Surprised and a little annoyed, the female pathologist answered that they were not presently looking for lab techs, reminding me the correct procedure was to go to Personnel. I apologized. "But as long as I'm here," I said, with a warm smile, "could you please take my application?" She took it, I thanked her, and I left.

Two weeks later, she called me and offered me a job in the lab. Apparently I had made a good impression with my initiative.

They say you may be as brave as you make believe you are. So at work I put on an act. Like the song in *The King and I*: "I whistle a happy tune so no one will know I'm afraid, for when I fool the people I fear I fool myself as well!"

So I walked and talked as if I had confidence, and soon it was real. It worked. I wasn't fired. In fact, I worked there for seven years. So thank you, Dr. Meany, you rotten S.O.B. If not for you in 1950, there's no telling how or where I'd be.

Postscript

At St. Vincent's, kind co-workers quickly put me straight: work done slowly and carefully (like I did in Canada) was not appreciated in the U.S., where time equaled money.

CHAPTER NINE

Fears Regarding Choice of Career

"Life is fear versus trust! Fear brings us less of what we hate and none of what we love. Trust brings us some of what we hate and everything that we love!"
- Brian Stuart Germain

How we handle our fears boils down to what we *believe to be true* about life. **Arising from what we believe and fear are negative thoughts, which can be surmised from your handwriting.**

So look at your handwriting:

1) Are your t-bars high, and also low (conflicting goal-setting and confidence)?
2) Light in pressure, concave and weak (a tendency to give up)?
3) Do the slant and baseline strongly vary (changeable emotions)?
4) Down-strokes on "g" and "y" short, curved (weak determination to carry out goals)?

The above traits can reduce your chances of success – that is, your "prayer" may not be realized.

Your thoughts, therefore, are powerful. Watch your thoughts! However, only when there is *strong emotion and feeling* accompanying the thoughts do they enter the unconscious, and become *beliefs*.

A belief is a thought you accept as true. And you have free will to either accept or reject it. Furthermore, what you believe you draw to you—*as well as what you fear*.

So your beliefs, your fears, can rob you of confidence and a healthy self-esteem in your career.

Specimen #36

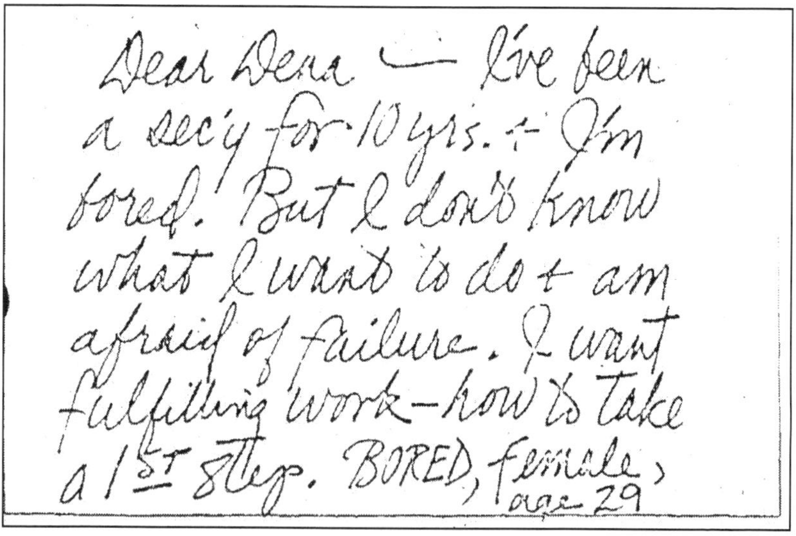
Dear Dena — I've been a sec'y for 10 yrs. + I'm bored! But I don't know what I want to do + am afraid of failure. I want fulfilling work—how to take a 1st step. BORED, female, age 29

Dear Dena,

I've been a secretary for ten years and I'm bored. But I don't know what I want to do and am afraid of failure. I want fulfilling work, how to take the first step. – BORED, female, age 29

Dear Bored,

First of all, stop blaming and "whipping" yourself (ending of word joins t-bar on "don't" and "to" crossing right to left) for not having achieved more. You are an excellent worker (high and strong t-bars with strong down-strokes on "y" and "g"). You're intelligent (analytical and logical thinking processes). You like working with people (large writing, right slant); you're dependable, (rhythm, spacing between words, letters, and lines). And I agree—secretarial work is not challenging enough for your capabilities.

You need a position, or career that will use your desire for responsibility (large loop in capital "I"), diplomacy (tapering words), dynamic nature (large, heavy pressure, right slant writing), directness (no beginning strokes), and decisiveness (firm word endings).

You could manage a small business, organization, or committee. However, your sensitivity to criticism (large loop on "d" in "bored") dampens your spirit with thoughts of failure and fear of the future (wide right margin), so that you cling to the security of your present job (less wide left margin gradually narrows).

For emotional satisfaction you should be in something like communication, advertising, drama, politics, writing—especially if it's something you ardently believe in (heavy pen pressure). You've got what it takes to be successful in these areas, though naturally your first step may be to study, or start in a job low on the ladder. However, if you think 29 is too old to start anew, ten years will pass and you'll find yourself saying that 39 is too old. And neither is. So stop regretting and start living!

Specimen #37

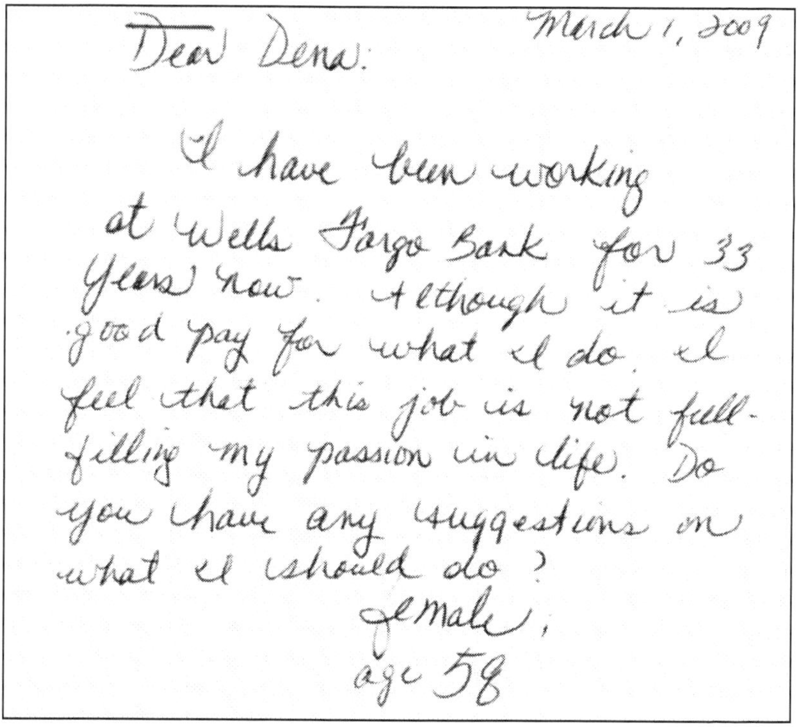
March 1, 2009

Dear Dena:

I have been working at Wells Fargo Bank for 33 years now. Although it is good pay for what I do. I feel that this job is not full-filling my passion in life. Do you have any suggestions on what I should do?

female, age 58

Dear Dena,

I have been working at Wells Fargo for 33 years now. Although it is good pay for what I do, I feel that this job is not fullfilling (sic) my passion in life. Do you have any suggestions on what I should do? – female, age 58

Dear female 58,

There are many things you could do. But I always advise people to go where their passion is. Do you know what it is or were you just using a figure of speech? Because there isn't much passion in your writing. Ambition? Yes (beginning hooks). Passion? No (no heavy pressure writing, no heavy t-bars.)

You are versatile—you can work well with people or alone (right slant medium-sized writing) and are intelligent (good sharp thinking processes in "m" and "n.") However, there are some traits that would hinder you in changing to another field. You have a tendency to procrastinate (t-bar left of stem in "what"). And when you ask about possible changes, you have little confidence in yourself (very low and weak t-bar in "suggestions" and last "I" becomes smaller.)

I don't see you changing your career at this stage. The gradually veering of your left margin to the very left tells me you are clinging to what you have, to security, what you know and what is familiar—despite your vague unhappiness (first line slants down markedly as you write about the bank, and also as you write the word "female," which tells me that you also perceive being female as having something to do with your freedom to make changes at your age—"58" is written larger than normal—albeit probably wholly unconsciously).

Your desire to have a nice home, material things for yourself and family (many large beginning hooks to words), also tells me you would be unwise to quit your well-paying position after 33 years. Better to do something on the side that brings you satisfaction.

The simple printed capitals in "Dear Dena" show artistic ability. Arts and crafts would be good. Another would be writing—you show signs of ability in the figure eight "g." Perhaps in these two endeavors you may finally get the attention you yearn for and deserve (long upward word endings in "Dear," "Dena," and "female")—and you may no longer feel a vague sense of hopelessness (downturned loops in "y").

Specimen #38

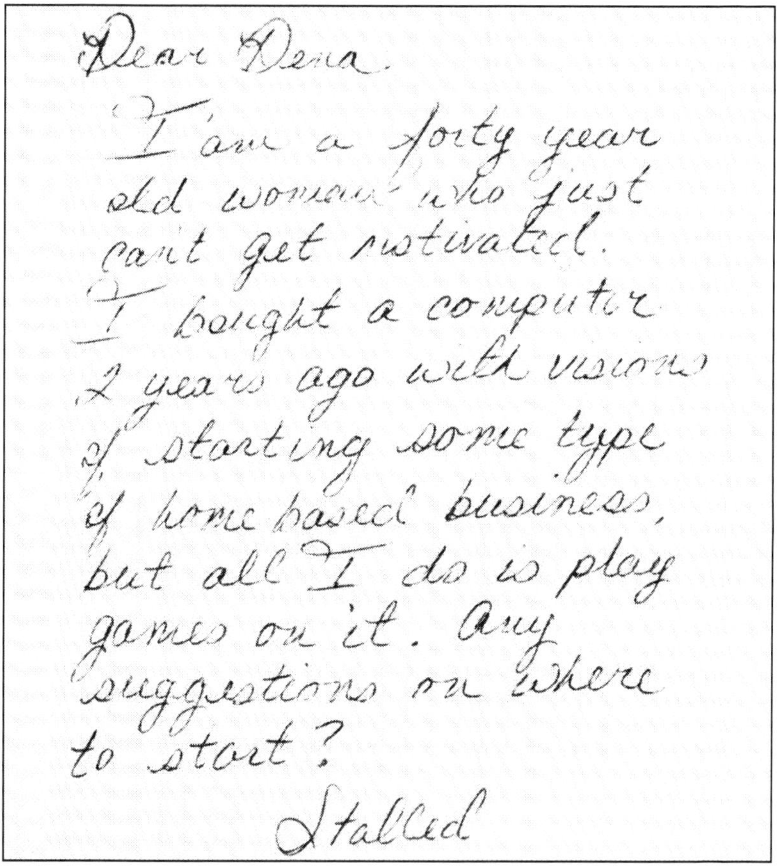
Dear Dena.
I am a forty year
old woman who just
cant get motivated.
I bought a computer
2 years ago with visions
of starting some type
of home based business,
but all I do is play
games on it. Any
suggestions on where
to start?
Stalled

Dear Dena,

I'm a forty-year-old woman who just can't get motivated. I bought a computer 2 years ago with visions of starting some type of home-based business, but still all I do is play games on it. Any suggestions on where to start? – Stalled

Dear Stalled,

I can see why you bought the computer to start a home business. You are self-reliant (underscore on "stalled" in the original but cut off here). But you're also a "people" person (medium-sized letters, right slant); you need input, interaction, and inspiration from others to help you with your weak willpower (very light t-bars) and lack of passion (very light pressure). If you don't have young children at home, I suggest you find work outside; you would be good in any of the helping fields (teaching, nursing, helping in a doctor's office, etc.).

Perhaps, you have been a housewife for years and now don't feel that you have work skills to fall back on. You show lack of confidence (low t-bars, especially in "get motivated"); you already feel a bit hopeless about it (loop in "y" in "play" beginning to turn down).

However, there is *hope. Your determination is pretty good (down-strokes on "g" and "y"), but you need strengthening of your willpower to set goals beyond the day-to-day ones. I recommend Graphotherapeutics. Before going to bed, every night for thirty nights, practice placing the t-bar higher and stronger on the stem. It can help you, on an unconscious level, find direction and confidence. Good luck!*

CHAPTER TEN

Defense Mechanisms for Handling Fears

We handle what we don't like or fear in one or all of these three ways: **"A" – fight/resist; "B" – flee/escape; "C" – give in/adjust.**

"A" – RESISTING OR FIGHTING IT

Revealed in all inflexible strokes to the right.

- Resentment: inflexible beginning stroke to the right.
- Aggression: inflexible final stroke to the right (striking out at someone?).
- Criticalness: a resentment stroke with angular "m" and "n."
- Stubbornness: wedge between sides of T-stems.
- Temper: t-bar to the right of stem.
- Irritation: dashes for dot dots on "I."
- Domineering nature: Down-slanting t-bar with feathery ending.
- Sarcasm: t-bar to right with feathery ending.
- Argumentativeness: resentment stroke with open "a" and "o."
- Defiance: buckle on "k."

Some Tidbits on Resisting or Fighting It:

- ✓ Many who resent are also very generous. They give and give but are not appreciated.
- ✓ Resentment strokes beginning below line, feeling imposed upon, unappreciated from childhood. being carried over to the present, albeit perhaps unconsciously.
- ✓ Resentment plus down-stroke: stubbornness (inverted "v").
- ✓ T-bar off to right, resentment stroke in upper zone: temper.
- ✓ Where does aggression come from? Is it from resentment? The strokes are similar.

"B" – ESCAPING OR FLEEING FROM IT

Upper Zone:

- ➢ Slant to left: withdrawal, fear of being hurt emotionally.
- ➢ T-bar to left of stem: procrastination.
- ➢ T-bar floating above stem: inclination toward daydreaming.
- ➢ Very tall t-stems: vanity.
- ➢ Very long curved word endings turning left: blaming self.
- ➢ Strokes to left: reverting to the past.
- ➢ Weak t-bars: weak will.
- ➢ Extra large loops: overactive imagination.

Middle Zone:

- ➢ Counterclockwise loop on left side of "a" & "o": deceiving self; rationalizing.

- Counterclockwise loop on right side of "a" & "o": deceiving others.
- Feathery endings to words: indecision.
- Small writing: concentration.
- Partly closed "a" and "o": evasiveness.
- Squeezed letters: suppression.
- Retraced "h": repression of feelings.

Lower Zone:

- Loop on "y" or "g" going left instead of right and ending below the line: feeling rejected.
- Long loop into next line: desire for variety.
- Small, round loop on "y" or "g" that does not reach baseline: clannishness.

Other Escapes: substance abuse (e.g., alcohol and drugs); suicide; dishonesty; fantasizing; depression; possible mental and physical illnesses.

"C" – ADJUSTING TO IT (OR "JOINING THEM")

Traits such as bluff, caution, conservatism, decisiveness, dignity, diplomacy, fluidity, extreme generosity, humor, independent thinking, intuitiveness, loyalty, narrow-mindedness, objectiveness, perfectionism, persistence, philosophical imagination, sureness, pride, reticence, selectivity, self-control, tenacity, yieldingness, thankfulness.

**Specimen #39 – example of "A"
(using resentment in coping with fears)**

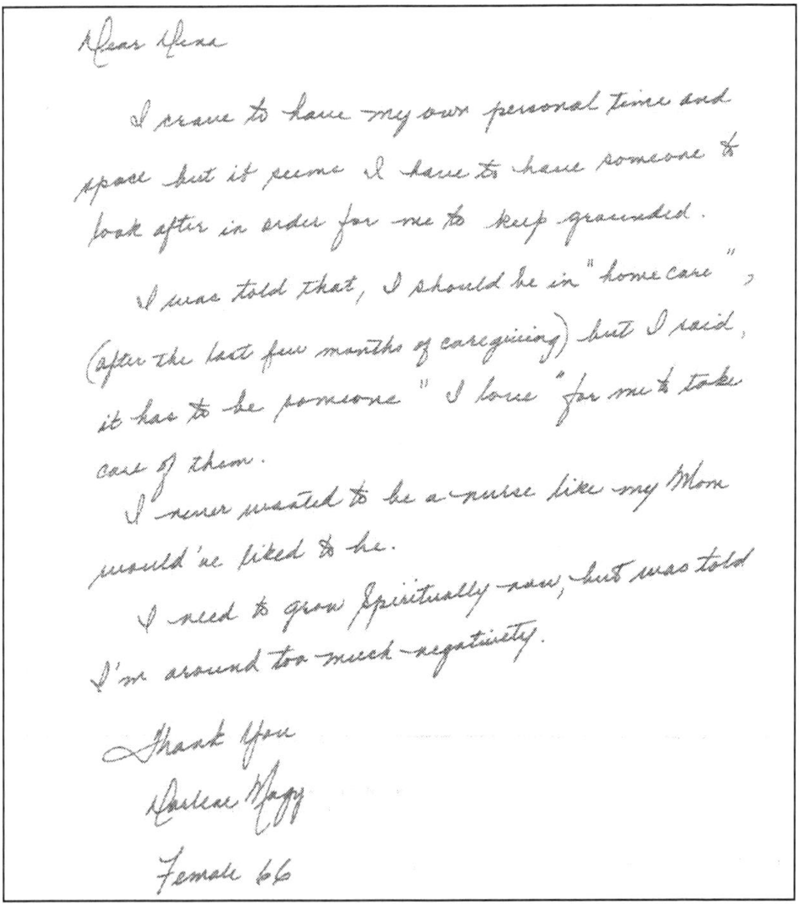
Dear Dena
I crave to have my own personal time and space but it seems I have to have someone to look after in order for me to keep grounded.
I was told that, I should be in "home care", (after the last few months of caregiving) but I said, it has to be someone "I love" for me to take care of them.
I never wanted to be a nurse like my Mom would've liked to be.
I need to grow Spiritually now, but was told I'm around too much negativity.
Thank You
Darlene Nagy
Female 66

Dear Dena,

I crave to have my own personal time and space but it seems I have to have someone to look after in order for me to keep grounded. I was told that, I should be in "home care", (after the last few months of care-giving) but I said it has to be someone "I love" for me to take care of them. I never wanted to be a nurse like my Mom would've liked to be. I need to grow spiritually now, but was told I'm around too much negativity. Thank you – Darlene Nagy, Female 66

Dear Darlene,

I wonder why a person with your obvious education and maturity (small well-spelled writing, balanced upper, lower, and middle zones), intelligence (analytical and investigative mind with angular and rounded "m" and "n"), confidence and determination (high t-bars and straight down-strokes on "y" and "g"), as well as dependability and reliability (balance and rhythm on page, spacing between letters, words, and lines)—high school teacher, psychologist, medical researcher, or some kind of administrator, perhaps, in your younger years?—I wonder why you are so emotionally up and down (wavy baseline) that you have to have someone to look after to "keep grounded." Is it because of your spiritual search (pointed "I" and pointed "I") or something else?

If I understand you correctly, the work is also to pay for food and a roof over your head. However, you have free will; you don't have to do anything. Note that the words "have to" fall suddenly at the thought. By saying instead that you choose to do it for the pay-off (room and board or whatever), work becomes lighter, easier, less unpleasant. You may even hear about and appreciate the full, interesting lives your patients have had.

But unless you change your attitude about it, I would advise you against working with "home care" patients. There are so many other kinds of work you could do. At the present time you are not suited for "nursing" anybody. A patient would sense *your resentment or "***chip on the shoulder" (a feeling of having been imposed upon and not appreciated),** *which shows itself in thirty inflexible beginning strokes—most noticeably in the words "crave," "time," "space," "someone," "love," "would've," and "spiritually," which all begin below the line—meaning the resentment, common in generous and giving people like you (long endings to words), has been carried over from childhood. Also, feelings of having been rejected or rejecting someone close (lower loop on "f" in "for" in sixth line swings left below the baseline), with some defiance (buckle on "k") and anger (temper tic "T" in "Thank"), only lessen emotional stability.*

Could the fact that you capitalized "Mom" (strong influence) with a temper tic (anger towards your mother?)—and the last hump of the "m" (curved, making a large acquisitive hook)—have something to do with your resentment? Note the "M" in Magy (your middle name) is different, showing a sense of humor (curved beginning stroke), strong resentment, strong stubbornness (wide wedge), spiritual searching (high pointed last hump), and strong determination (long, straight down-stroke with ending hook). But what is most important is the resentment stroke you drew across it. You are sabotaging yourself, getting yourself into unrewarding situations—in other words, you are your own worst enemy.

You have procrastinated (t-bar to left of stem) on fulfilling your dreams (t-bar floating above stem), vacillating between optimism (rising lines) and pessimism ("I love" drops suddenly), and between enthusiastic confidence (high, long t-bars) and a tendency to give up (concave t-bar in "time" and "it").

For your psychological and spiritual health, you need to learn compassion (for your mother? or whoever) so that you can forgive and let go of resentment; you can then go on, using freed energy to do what you love to do, want to do, instead of what you think you "have to" do, or "ought to" do.

Specimen #40 – example of "A"
(reacting to fears with resentment and sensitivity to criticism)

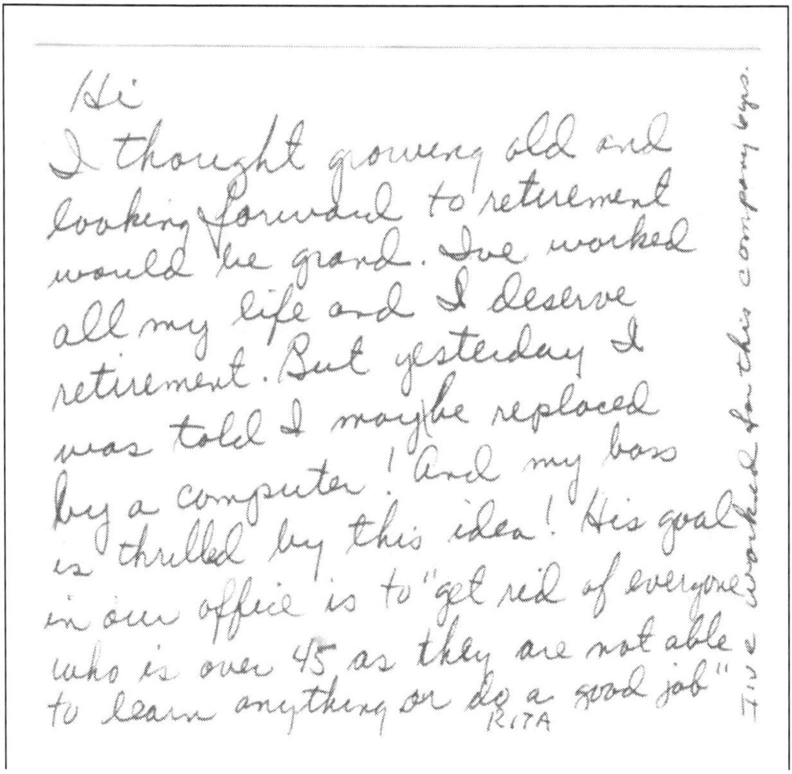

Hi
I thought growing old and
looking forward to retirement
would be grand. I've worked
all my life and I deserve
retirement. But yesterday I
was told I maybe replaced
by a computer! And my boss
is thrilled by this idea! His goal
in our office is to "get rid of everyone
who is over 45 as they are not able
to learn anything or do a good job"
RITA
I've worked for this company [illegible] yrs.

Hi,
I thought growing old and looking forward to retirement would be grand. I've worked all my life and I deserve retirement. But

yesterday I was told I may be replaced by a computer! And my boss is thrilled by this idea! His goal in our office is to "get rid of everyone who is over 45 as they are not able to learn anything or do a good job." I've worked for this company 6 yrs. – RITA

Dear Rita,

So what's your question? How to resist the coming change? How to adjust to being laid off? How to handle your fears?

You want things to stay as you're used to (down-slanting t-bars in key words "yesterday" and "computer"). Fear of change is also shown in your large right margin of the first seven lines. Naturally you resent his policy (inflexible beginning strokes in the key words "retirement," "worked," "idea," and "rid") and are rejecting him ("f" in "forward").

You're intelligent (angular and rounded "m" and "n"), friendly (rounded "m," right slant), and very generous (long word endings). Being laid off is hard to take after six years of putting out loyal and dependable good work (good rhythm, even lines.) You have a legitimate gripe. Women over 45 are not appreciated enough in the workplace (or elsewhere), and it's not fair.

However, long-standing resentment can possibly give you arthritis. You have choice. You could dissipate the resentment by suing your boss should he "let you go." By taking action, you are no longer a victim, and you might attract an even better position (executive secretary). Or you could not sue, and instead go into business for yourself (public steno or whatever) where you can be your own boss.

You need to be your own boss, because you are much too sensitive to criticism of your work (many large loops in "d"), as well as your ideas (loop in "t"), making relationships difficult (whether at work or home). The result is irritation (dashes for dots), lower confidence (weak and low t-bars in "thought," "get," and "not"), and a feeling that you don't count as a person (capital "I" smallest in the sixth line). Should you be laid off, you've got what it takes to go into business: experience, know-how, and so forth. But you would have to believe in yourself more—as well as drop the "chip on your shoulder."

Specimen #41 – example of "B"
(escaping from her fears by leaving job, and being cautious)

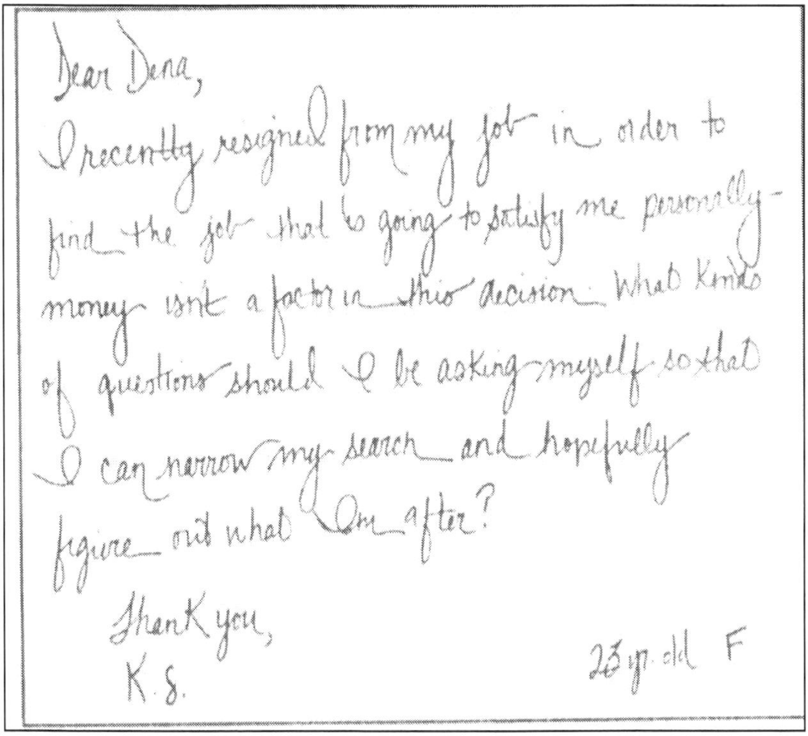
Dear Dena,
I recently resigned from my job in order to find the job that is going to satisfy me personally - money isn't a factor in this decision. What kinds of questions should I be asking myself so that I can narrow my search and hopefully figure out what I'm after?
Thank you,
K.S.
23 yr. old F

Dear Dena,

I recently resigned from my job in order to find the job that is going to satisfy me personally—money isn't a factor in this decision. What kinds of questions should I be asking myself so that I can narrow my search and hopefully figure out what I'm after? – Thank you, K.S., 23 yr old F.

Dear K.S.,

Since money is not a factor, you should be asking yourself not only what you want to get out of life, but what you want to give to life. Also, do you simply want to find an enjoyable job until you marry a man who can support you if you yourself do not have enough—or do you want a career? Do you have a passion for some particular trade or endeavor? Are you willing to study and train for it for years, whether in college or technical school? And since you do not mention going to college, do you feel unable to handle study, emotionally or intellectually? Do you want to enjoy your work and be happy? Also, you're very independent (short "d") and don't like criticism (loop on "d".) Can you work comfortably under a boss?

With your aesthetic and artistic sense (balance on page, simple capitals) and your talent for working with your hands (flat-topped "r"), you would make a good photographer, photojournalist, architect, or interior designer. However, a few things stand in the way of your achieving such goals. The most important is your lack of confidence and low self-worth (very low t-bars, especially in "recently"), not uncommon in women your age. Because of it you are much too sensitive to criticism (exaggerated loop on "d"), have a tendency to give up (concave t-bar in "that")—and in your fear, end up being much too cautious (straight word finals in the key words "find," "decision," "search," "figure," and "I").

You have a wonderful imagination working with things (large lower loop on "y") but you don't trust yourself and blame yourself when things go wrong (leftward word endings in "is," "kinds," and "that"), and get bogged down in the past (resentment from childhood in the inflexible beginning stroke to "s" in "satisfy").

You have many talents, but until you see what your belief system is doing to you, and stop rationalizing (large beginning loop in "a" in "can" and "search"), it won't do you any good to figure out what you're after. In order to achieve, you have to have a goal and determination to carry it out. You have excellent determination (strong down-strokes on "y"), but goal-setting arising from self-esteem is missing.

Graphotherapeutics can help you. Each night before going to bed, draw a number of "t's" with high and strong t-bars. In time it should give you a feeling of strength, a belief in yourself. In addition, some counseling wouldn't be a bad idea. Good luck!

**Specimen #42 (female, age 26) – example of "B"
(escaping by giving up)**

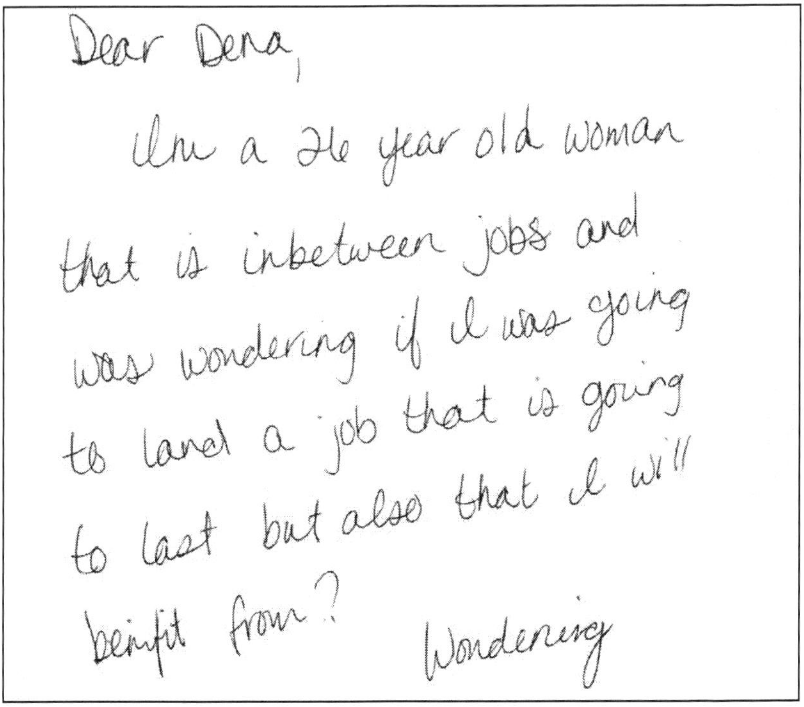
Dear Dena,
I'm a 26 year old woman
that is inbetween jobs and
was wondering if I was going
to land a job that is going
to last but also that I will
beinfit from?
Wondering

Dear Dena,

I'm a 26 year old woman that is in between jobs and was wondering if I was going to land a job that was going to last but also that I will benefit from? – Wondering

Dear Wondering,

You are intelligent (analytical and logical thinking processes), and work well with people or behind the scenes (large handwriting, right slant and upright slant) with optimism (rising lines), and an artistic sense (printed capitals) and aesthetic sense (good spacing between letters, words, and lines, balance on page).

You don't say whether you quit or were fired from the jobs. But your handwriting shows that your will is weak and you tend to give up when things get tough (low and concave t-bars in "that"). You don't complete projects or fulfill commitments (down-stroke on "g" in "going" turns left, not returning to baseline), meaning something from your past is having a negative effect on you in regards to this.

Your light pressured t-bars indicate you don't know what you really want from working. Perhaps it is just a stop-gap until you find a husband, partner, relationship? You don't say whether you are married, single, or perhaps a mother, and it would make a difference in what your priorities would be.

As it is, your goal-setting is weak. If you want results, you need to think of yourself as an "actor" in life rather than being "acted upon" (losing a job) by life. Also, jobs (especially those you lose) can greatly benefit you as a learning experience.

Specimen #43 - example of "C"
(adjusting to her fears with confidence and enthusiasm)

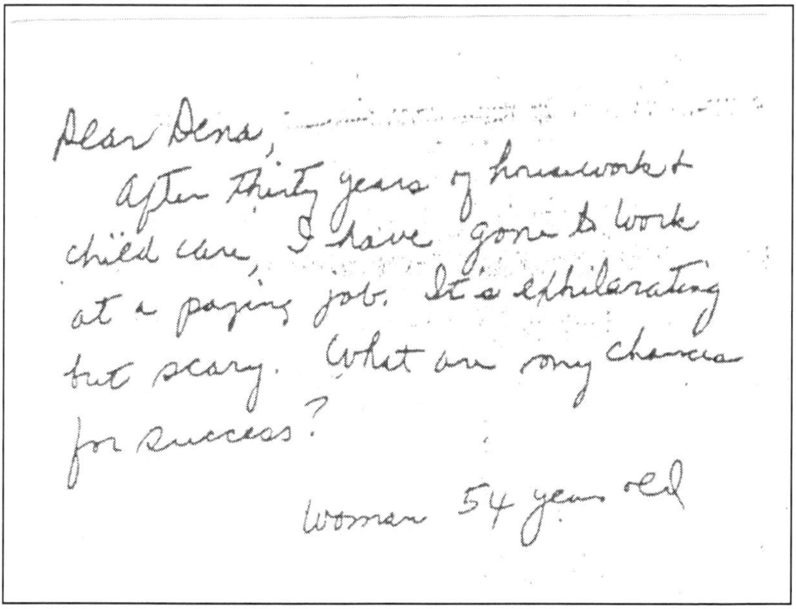
Dear Dena,
After thirty years of housework + child care, I have gone to work at a paying job. It's exhilarating but scary. What are my chances for success?
Woman 54 years old

Dear Dena,

After thirty years of housework + childcare, I have gone to work at a paying job. It's exhilarating but scary. What are my chances for success? – woman 54 years old

Dear woman 54 years old,

You'll be just great! You have good concentration (small middle-zone letters), logical thinking processes (rounded "m" and "n"), confidence in your natural abilities (good high and strong t-bars), as well as pretty good determination to get the work done (down-strokes on "g" and "y"). Furthermore, you have enthusiasm and optimism (t-bars long and slanting upwards).

It's scary, I know. Sometimes people will tell you that employers won't hire older women and you "give in" to the thought (rounded "s") and worry about it (loop in "m"). But don't worry; you'll be just great!

Specimen #44 – example of "C"
(adjusting well with optimism)

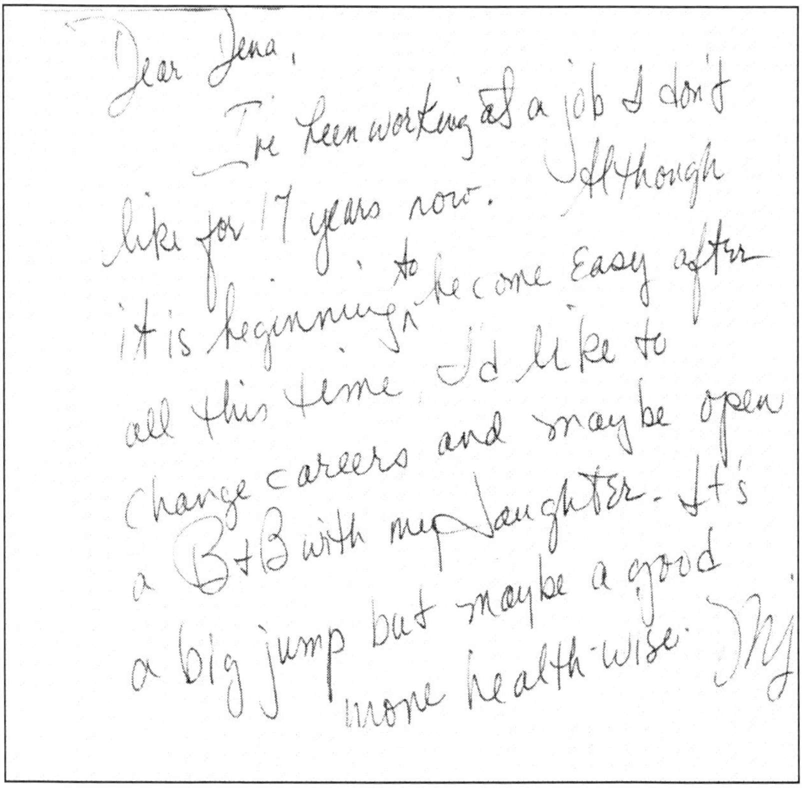
Dear Dena,
I've been working at a job I don't like for 17 years now. Although it is beginning to become Easy after all this time, I'd like to change careers and maybe open a B+B with my daughter. It's a big jump but maybe a good move health-wise. MJ

Dear Dena,

I've been working at a job I don't like for 17 years now. Although it is beginning to become easy after all this time I'd like to change careers and maybe open a B.& B. with my daughter. It's a big jump but maybe a good move health-wise. – MJ (female 59)

Dear MJ,

You have an intelligent, intuitive mind (analytical and cumulative thinking processes—angular as well as rounded "m"), with intuition (many breaks between letters). You like people (right slant large letters) and have a quick mind (fast writing), together with persistence (lasso loop in "A" in "Although"). In addition, you have fluency strokes (one letter joined to the next) showing an ability to work smoothly and efficiently; a sense of humor (curved beginning stroke in "maybe"), and general optimism (lines slanting slightly upward). All these traits are good for business, especially one dealing directly with the public. So a B & B would be the kind of business you could run successfully.

However, as you say, you hate change. The word after the large space after the word "to" is "change," and the word that comes after a large space is what you fear, causing indecision (feathery endings to words).

You don't say what kind of work you are in that you have disliked for the past seventeen years, but it has made you irritable (dashes for dots), defiant (buckle on "k"), stubborn (wedge in the "t" in the word "it" in the third line), and unwilling to take on more responsibility (inflexible beginning stroke in the second "I" that comes before the word "don't"). So perhaps a change would make you a happier person.

You have rationalized (left loop on "a" and "o") why you have stayed for seventeen years. The real reason is the fear of change and getting along with people. You know you have the ability and talent for business but sometimes lack of confidence rears its head (low t-bar in "It's"). You have communication problems (left and right loops on "a" and "o," shown especially in your note in the words "Dena," "maybe," and "thanks"). Sometimes you are completely open (no loops) and sometimes secretive (right loop on "a" and "o"), depending on how personal the subject is and whom it is you're communicating with. But it's all about trust or lack of trust.

The Bed and Breakfast business could be good for you; you like to be your own boss, where you could use your creative ideas and skills (simple large capital "I" in "I've" and capital "D"), unlike where you are now, feeling insignificant (tiny first "I") and holding onto resentment (inflexible beginning stroke). The business could also give you time to develop your interest in cultural things (Greek "e," "s" and "d") and express yourself in writing (figure 8 "g"). Good luck!

Specimen #45 – example of "C"
(adjusting with enthusiasm)

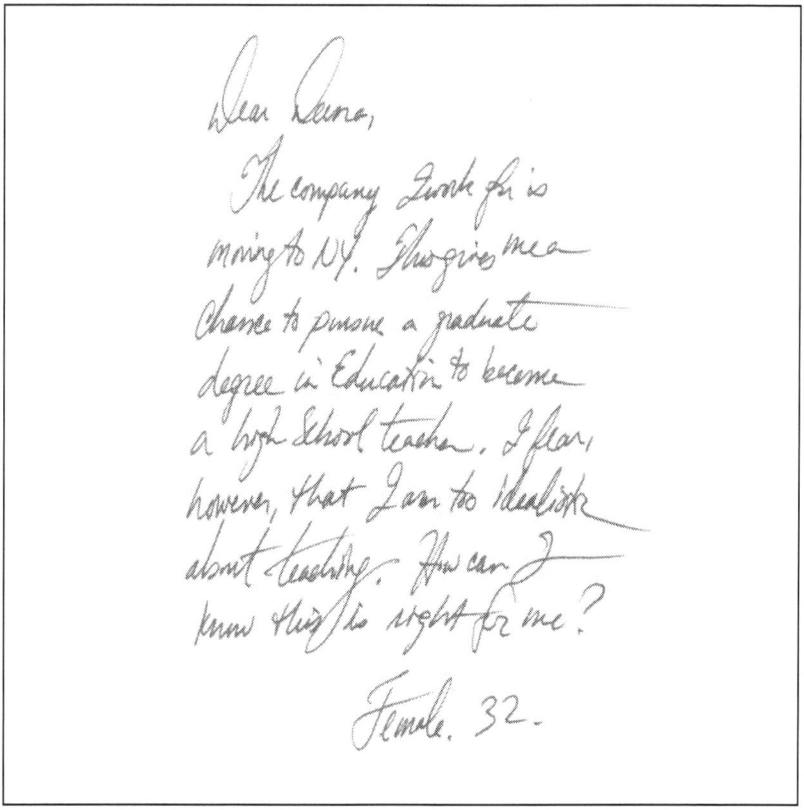
Dear Dena,
The company I work for is
moving to NY. This gives me a
chance to pursue a graduate
degree in Education to become
a high School teacher. I fear,
however, that I am too idealistic
about teaching. How can I
know this is right for me?
Female, 32.

Dear Dena,

The company I work for is moving to NY. This gives me a chance to pursue a graduate degree in Education to become a high school teacher. I fear, however, that I am too idealistic about teaching. How can I know this is right for me? – Female. 32.

Dear Idealist,

Teaching is something you care about, are enthusiastic about (very long t-bars in the key words "graduate," "teacher," and "about teaching"). You're not suited to being an elementary school teacher: you lack patience (fast writing and irritableness, revealed by dashes for dots), and you'd be bored; you like experimenting with various ideas or projects (loop on "g" invading the line below in "teaching"). But a high school teacher, yes—where your ideas and reform can be put into practice. You have what it takes: a sharp, quick analytical and logical mind (angular and rounded "m" and "n" and fast writing), efficiency, and literary talent (t-bar joining next letter, figure 8 "g").

You probably are *too idealistic (tall "h" and "l"), but then, who* isn't *at first? You will probably never live up to your own standards (very high t-stem in "teaching" with its t-bar far from the top).*

High-school teaching can be stressful, and you want to be cautious (straight final ending to "e" in "become" and "idealistic"), but I think you would regret not trying it. You're still young; if you've had enough of teaching you can return to your present work (whatever that is—computers, business, publishing?)—or write a book about high schools. Good luck in whatever you do!

CHAPTER ELEVEN

Another Short Review
Forces to Achieve: Goal Planning and Determination

1) **Emotional makeup** – slant (towards people and future, or to the past and within self).

2) **Fears** – desire for attention, indecisiveness, jealousy, suppression, repression, self-castigation, self-consciousness, self-underestimation, sensitive to criticism, stinginess, timidity, ultraconservatism, emotional withdrawal.

3) **Defenses** – Resist, Escape, or Adjust.

Resist (or fight): aggressiveness, argumentativeness, defiance, domineering nature, irritability, resentment, sarcasm, stubbornness, temper.

Escape: clannishness, concentration, daydreaming, deceptiveness, evasiveness, procrastination, secrecy, self-deceit, shallowness, superficial thinking, vanity, desire for variety.

Adjust: bluff, caution, conservatism, decisiveness, dignity, diplomacy, fluidity, extreme generosity, humor, independent thinking, intuitiveness, loyalty, narrow-mindedness, objectivity, perfectionism, persistence, philosophical imagination, positive attitude, pride, reticence, selectivity, self-control, tenacity, yieldingness.

4) **Mental processes** – size and shape (rounded or angular of middle zone "m" and "n").

Example: very small writing. (Being totally absorbed in what you're doing is actually meditation. You leave the material world and enter the inner world.)

5) **Imagination** – upper and lower loops (abstract and material)

"Our imagination is the only limit to what we can hope to have in the future."
- Charles Kettering

"Imagination is more important than knowledge. Knowledge is limited."
- Albert Einstein

6) **Communication** – looped, open or closed "a" and "o" (rationalizing, secretive, dishonest, talkative or reticent.)

Now one must take into account what the writer does or does not do with the above aspects of his personality. What traits are necessary to *achieve* in life (whether materially or spiritually)?

Forces to Achieve: Goal planning and Determination

"If you don't know where you're going, you'll probably wind up somewhere else."
- Lawrence Peter

Examine t-bars plus down-strokes on "g" and "y" (goals plus determination). If these are weak and low, practice Grapho-therapeutics. When realistic goals are set and there is determination to accomplish them, you will see the t-bar high and firm on the stem and the down-stroke on "y" and "g" straight, long, and firm. It can be achieved by continually practicing Graphotherapeutics (as demonstrated in Chapter Eight). Check your own writing for the following:

1) Height of t-bar on the stem (low, practical or visionary goals, reflecting self-esteem).
2) Height of t-stem (one's standards, pride, vanity).
3) Pressure of t-bar – will power (weak, moderate, strong).
4) Length of t-bar (enthusiasm, or lack thereof).
5) Down-stroke on "g" and "y" – determination weak, moderate, strong depending on the length, pressure, straight or curved.
6) Intensifying influences to the above: acquisitiveness, aggressiveness, decisiveness, attention to detail, directness, enthusiasm, generosity, imagination, initiative, optimism, organizational ability, persistence, definiteness, precision, pride, desire for responsibility, rhythm, good spacing, self-confidence, self-reliance, self-control, tenacity.
7) Reducing influences: caution, confusion of interests, deliberateness, inattention to detail, latent imagination, indecisiveness, perfectionism, pessimism, procrastination, self-

underestimation, lack of rhythm, irregular spacing, shallowness, yieldingness.

Now, if you are seeking work, do you have the traits necessary to get the job you want? Perhaps you need some therapy to overcome emotional problems, or more schooling, more training. Also, some of you may **experience discrimination of one sort or other,** and may have to put forth an extra effort to get ahead. It's crucial that you believe in yourself: **you must have extraordinary self-confidence and unwavering determination. But when ready, go for it – focus on your dream!**

CHAPTER TWELVE

Focus on Your Dream

"You must be who you really are; then do what you need to do, in order to have what you want."

- Margaret Young

"It is not the end of the physical body that should worry us. Rather, our concern must be to live while we're alive - to release our inner selves from the spiritual death that comes with living behind a facade designed to conform to external definitions of who and what we are."

- Elisabeth Kubler-Ross

Specimen #46

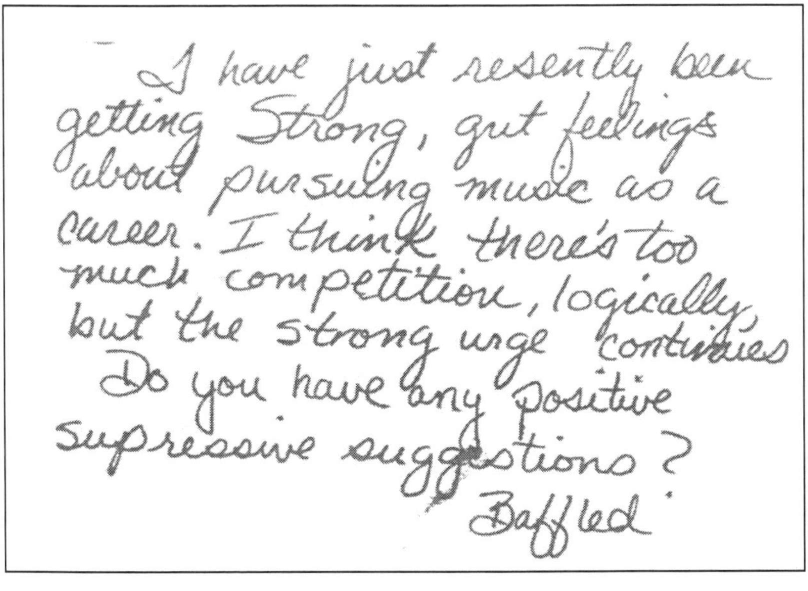

I have just resently been getting Strong, gut feelings about pursuing music as a career. I think there's too much competition, logically, but the strong urge continues Do you have any positive supressive suggestions?

Baffled

Dear Dena,

I have just recently been getting strong, gut feelings about pursuing music as a career. I think there's too much competition, logically, but the strong urge continues. Do you have any positive suppressive suggestions? – Baffled

Dear Baffled,

No. And I wouldn't give you any if I had. Anybody who has gut feelings about something should follow them, especially if he or she is young. If you do what you really enjoy doing, you'll spend so much time on it that you'll eventually become good enough to compete. You can't go wrong—only hungry sometimes.

*You have the talent—**passion** and extroverted nature for expressing yourself (large writing, right slant, heavy pressure); cultural and artistic interests (Greek "s," printed capitals, many fluency strokes); great imaginative ideas for projects (large lower loops); aesthetic sense (good rhythm and balance in writing), a mechanical aptitude for playing an instrument (flat-topped "r"), and an intuitive sense (breaks between letters). In addition, your sharp mind (angular and rounded "m" and "n") can handle the new pursuit.*

You have a strong belief in your ability to set realistic goals (straight, high, and strong t-bars), and more than adequate determination to carry them out (good, firm down-strokes on "y" and "g")—both necessary for success. However, even with your exemplary self-discipline (convex t-bars), you may also sometimes procrastinate (t-bar to left of stem), give up when you lose confidence (very low concave t-bar in "continues"), or feel self-conscious (last hump higher in "m" and "n").

But you can work on these negatives. You have what it takes. You just need to see yourself as the "I" in the fourth line (artistic and creative), rather than the first "I" (beginning with a temper tic, ending with a hook, which suggests holding onto something from the past).

Luckily, you don't have suppressive controls (crowded, retraced letters) but do possess strong intuition. Follow your heart, not your head, and your burdens (drooping lines) will lift.

Specimen #47
(writer looking for encouragement)

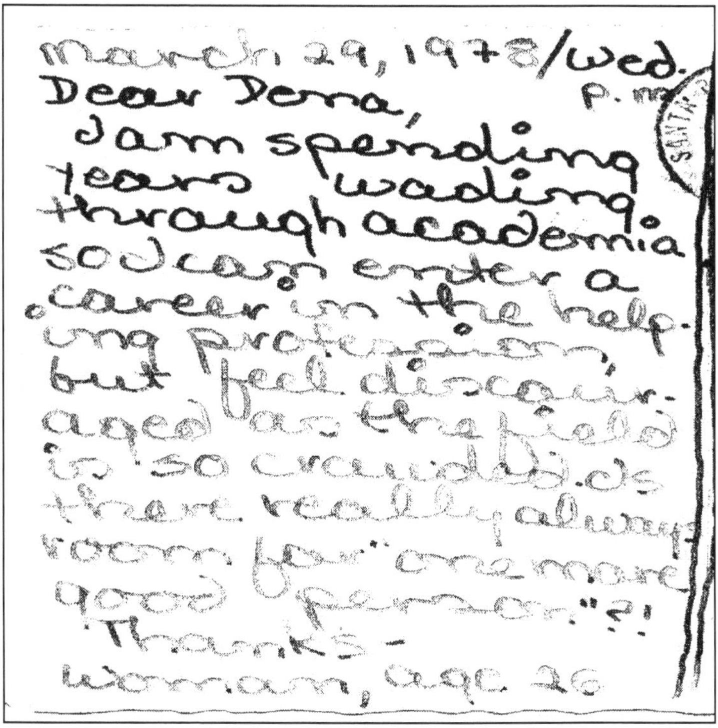
March 29, 1978/Wed. P.M.
Dear Dena,
I am spending years wading through academia so I can enter a career in the helping profession, but feel discouraged as the field is so crowded. Is there really always room for "one more good person"?!
Thanks –
Woman, age 26

Dear Dena,

I am spending years wading through academia so I can enter a career in the helping profession, but feel discouraged as the field is so crowded. Is there really always room for one more good person? – Thanks – woman, age 26.

Dear Good Person,

There is always room for one more. I can understand your impatience with academia. You don't say which particular helping field you are studying for, but what counts in any field after graduation is how good you are in the practical application of it. So hang in there even if you are not particularly cut out for scholarly pursuits (no tiny writing, no angular "m").

You're good with your hands (rounded "m") and can work objectively with people (vertical writing). You'd make a good physiotherapist, art therapist, or arts and crafts teacher. With your patience and kindness (no dashes, rounded "m" and "n", slow writing, no looped "d") and dispassionate nature (vertical slant), you could work well with disabled, retarded, or emotionally disturbed people. So if you're studying psychology, social work, or any of the other fields just mentioned, you'll be equipped degree-wise.

You feel you are unique (circles for dots), and you are. Few who desire to help others have the combination of warmth (rounded "m") and detachment (vertical writing, no word endings)—yet that is precisely the combination necessary to work in the world of suffering people. I hope you keep your beautiful childlike caring (large rounded letters, predominant middle zone) and never become disillusioned!

Specimen #48

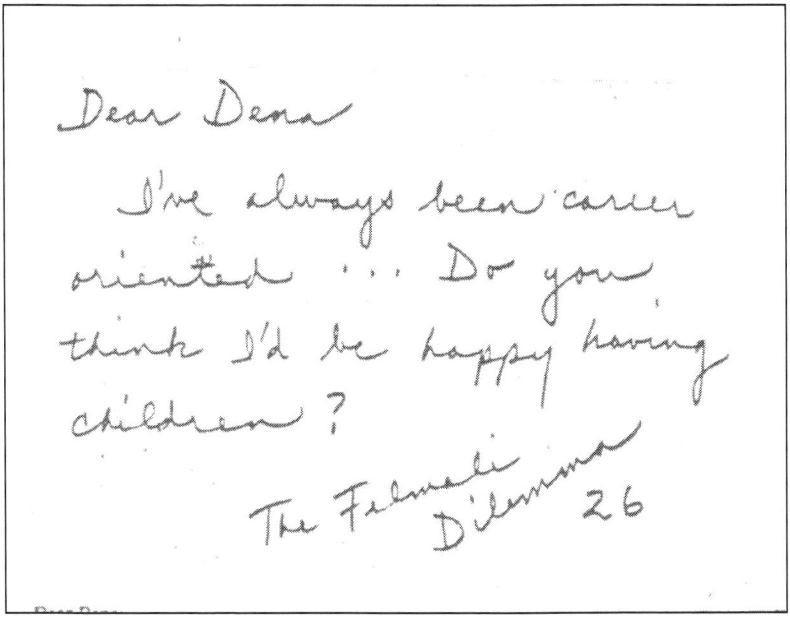
Dear Dena
I've always been career oriented ... Do you think I'd be happy having children?
The Female Dilemma 26

Dear Dena,

I've always been career oriented... Do you think I'd be happy having children? – The Female Dilemma 26

Dear Female Dilemma,

You don't say whether at present you are married, pregnant, or both (and I can't tell from the handwriting). But I can tell that you are a warm, sensitive, and caring individual (curved joining of letters, medium-sized writing, right slant, generous endings). Though you are sometimes irritable (dashes for dots), closed on some subjects (narrow "e"), and at times indecisive (feathery endings), I would say you would be about average in patience, tolerance, and discipline (traits necessary in dealing with children).

I take it you worry that career and children are not a good mix. In order to juggle work and family, you must have a sharp organized mind (angular "m" and "n," equally sized upper and lower loops), be direct and to the point (no beginning strokes), and have initiative (angular "h"). So you pass here.

I would say you could handle both career and family—if you accept the imperfections that are bound to occur in trying to be "superwoman." If you could accept your frustrations and those of the people around you without feeling guilty, you would very likely derive great satisfaction from having both career and children.

Furthermore, you are responsible (rhythm, spacing, and loop on "l"), intelligent (analytical thinking processes), and people-oriented (right slant). I think you will enjoy children. They will bring heartaches as well as joys, just as careers do. The only difference: careers you can choose; children you get "pot luck." Needless to say, I give no guarantees with my free advice.

Specimen #49

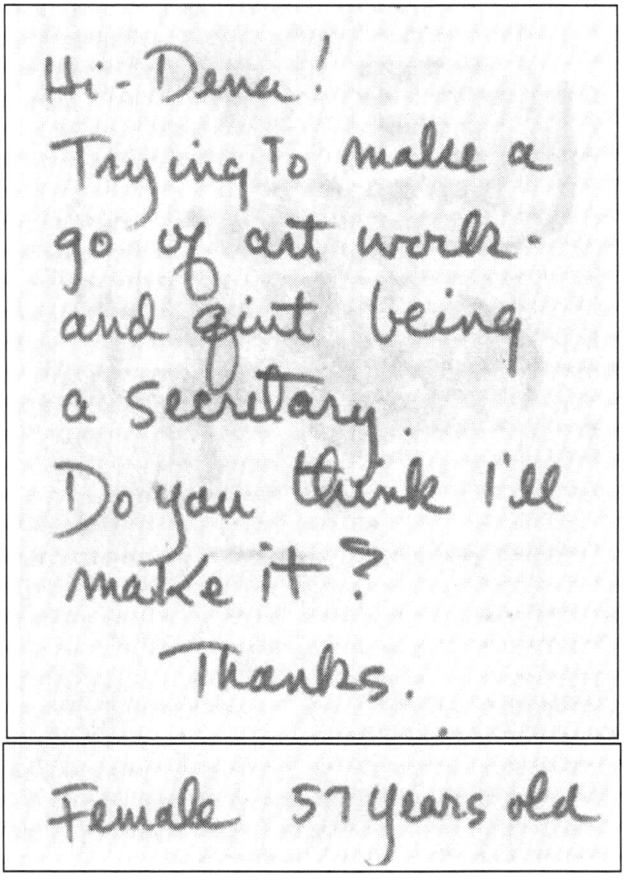
Hi - Dena!
Trying To make a go of art work - and quit being a secretary. Do you think I'll make it?
Thanks.

Female 57 years old

Dear Dena,

Trying to make a go of art work—and quit being a secretary. Do you think I'll make it? – Thanks. Female 57 years old

Dear Female 57,

Yes. You have the passion (heavy pressure) as well as the talent (simple printed capitals), intuition (breaks between letters), imagination (large loop on "f"), plus good determination (strong down-strokes on lower loops), intensified by defiance (buckle on "k"), self-control (convex t-bars), and above all confidence (long high and strong t-bars).

However, realize that you are too sensitive to criticism of your artwork and art ideas (loops in "d" and "t"), and therefore have a habit of leaving projects unfinished (incomplete lower loops in "y" and "g"). Fight this tendency and you'll be O.K. Good Luck to you!

CHAPTER THIRTEEN

Integrity and Social Traits of Employer/Employee/Partner

"There are seven things that will destroy us: Wealth without work; Pleasure without conscience; Knowledge without character; Religion without sacrifice; Politics without principle; Science without humanity; Business without ethics."
- Mahatma Gandhi

"It's not what we eat but what we digest that makes us strong; not what we gain but what we save that makes us rich; not what we read but what we remember that makes us learned; and not what we profess but what we practice that gives us integrity."
- Francis Bacon, Sr.

The dictionary defines integrity as "honesty, wholeness or integration of traits." So, is the writer trustworthy? Would he make a good employee, supervisor? Can he or she get along with coworkers? **Contributing to integrity**: sincerity, directness and frankness, broad-mindedness, generosity, self-confidence, pride, dignity, ambition, determination, loyalty, cution, self-control. **Reducing integrity:** dishonesty, weak will, lack of pride, impulsivity, prejudice, evasiveness, self-deceit, secrecy, selfishness, procrastination.

Social Traits

When choosing a business partner, you don't want someone who is resentful, domineering, dishonest, evasive, selfish, too individualistic or clannish, irritable, angry, stubborn, or shallow. So, it is crucial that you examine his or her handwriting.

On the whole, if you want someone who will be working with a lot of people, look for someone who is talkative, frank but diplomatic, optimistic, self-confident, self-reliant, sympathetic, generous, loyal, and has a sense of humor – someone, in other words, whose attention is usually outside himself. Is the writer an introvert or an extrovert? If you are looking for someone to do research for you, choose an introvert.

Honesty:

What to look for: on the whole, no loops or hooks in "a" and "o." Good rhythm and spacing; even baseline; writing that is clear and legible.

Dishonesty:

"Dishonesty is the forsaking of permanent for temporary advantages."
- Christian Bovee

What to look out for when analyzing for dishonesty:

The following traits must be consistent in the writing, not just occasional; they must be part of the writer's nature (note that the writer does not necessarily always act on his or her inherent inclination toward dishonesty):

1) Left and right loops in "a" and "o."
2) Hooks in "a" and "o" or "d," or "d" stem twisted to the right.
3) Letters or numbers that are left out, patched, or illegible.
4) Letters made in reverse direction.
5) "o" or "a" open at bottom.
6) Slow writing that is mostly and consistently illegible.
7) Signature always illegible and radically different in style from the writing specimen.
8) Lack of rhythm; very sinewy baseline.

Specimen #50
(presence of honesty, dependability and reliability)

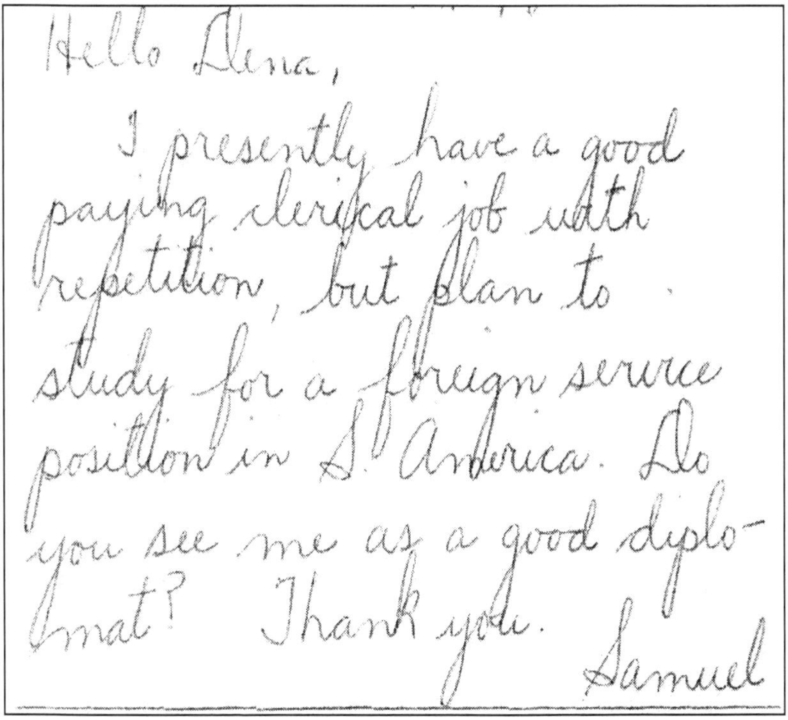
Hello Dena,
I presently have a good paying clerical job with repetition, but plan to study for a foreign service position in S. America. Do you see me as a good diplo-mat? Thank you.
Samuel

Specimen #51
(below, evaluated *possible* dishonesty)

It is important to be aware that a writer may have *tendencies* toward dishonesty but *not act* on them.

Note the following in the above sample:

1) Written amount different from number amount.
2) Zero in date, zero in amount both patched.
3) Patched "A" in "Blatt" and patched "p" in "April."
4) "t" in "ninety" inserted afterwards.
5) All "n" written as "m" except in "Dena."
6) Lack of rhythm (letters and date squeezed together, others wide apart).

Embezzling or theft:

All of the signs in the check plus weak will (light weak t-bars) and acquisitive signs (beginning loops) are only a few of the traits to look for in evaluating dishonesty or a propensity for thievery. Others are heavy pressure on paper, reversed strokes, letter retracing or omission (just to name a few), while others may actually indicate characteristics of the writer which *temper* his or her capacity for dishonesty. In sum, evaluating handwriting for traits suggesting dishonesty is a highly sophisticated and complicated endeavor, requiring much more knowledge and training than can be imparted here.

What's important is to be aware that a writer may have *tendencies* toward dishonesty and yet not *act* on them.

INTEGRITY IN OTHER AREAS

Specimen #52 (Radoslaw Ostrowsky)*

"Nearly all men can stand adversity, but if you want to test a man's character, give him power."
- Abraham Lincoln

* Radaslau Astrouski in Belorussian

Honesty (no loops, hooks in "o"); dependable, reliable (rhythm and slant), with strong ability to achieve (heavy horizontal bar, and long down-stroke on "y").

However, note also the following negative traits:

1) High upper loop, long lower (radical ideas/action, extremes in thought/practice).
2) Heavy t-bar to right of stem (very strong will-power, strong temper).
3) Short t-stem (independent mind, one who cares not what others think).
4) Heavy long final down-stroke on “y” (very strong determination used negatively).
5) Last down-stroke ends bluntly (cruelty, brutality).
6) Periods after first name initial and surname emphasize definiteness, no wavering.
7) Heavy pressure: Strong deep feelings, passion, held in, ready to explode.
8) Squeezed-together letters (suppressed feelings).
9) Down-slanting bar in second letter of surname (must have own way).
10) Drooping of last letters of surname (depression thinking of father).

Before World War II, Ostrowsky was a high school teacher, then a physics and mathematics professor. He was a Catholic who became a Communist, then an anti-Communist and devout Nazi. In 1943 the Nazis made him president of Byelorussia (“White Russia”). Working with the SS, he finally found the work he was best suited to: ordering and overseeing mass killings of innocent people. Brought to United States by the CIA, he was the highest-ranking Nazi war criminal ever to be granted American citizenship.

He and Mengele had sincere convictions, but no conscience (as generally understood.).

Specimen #53 (Dr. Josef Mengele)

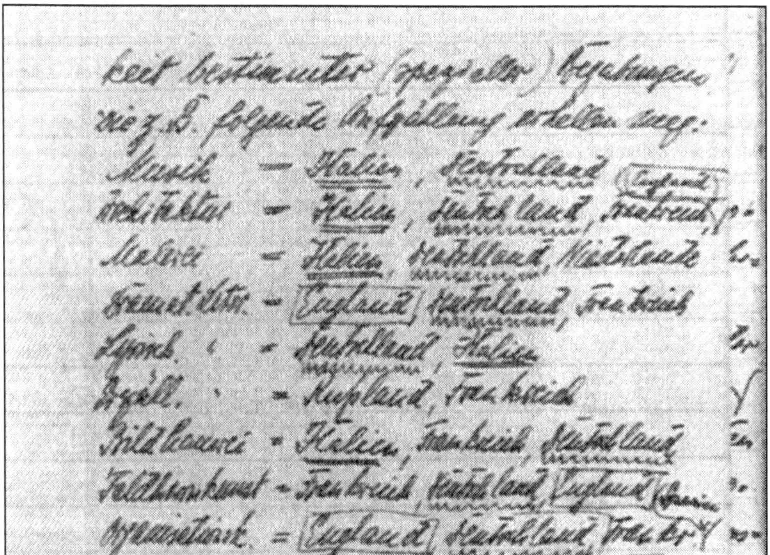

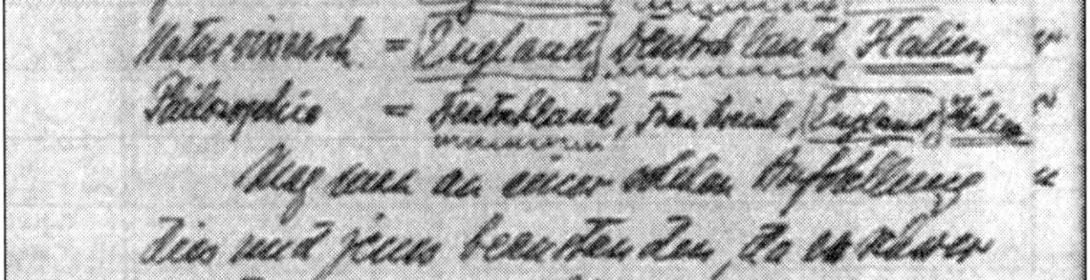

Evil is not so evident in the above specimens of Dr. Josef Mengele's handwriting, infamous Auschwitz physician who played God, pointing victims right or left and performing "medical" experiments, especially on twin children, before killing them. He came from a wealthy manufacturing family in Germany, and earned a Ph.D. in Anthropology and an M.D. from the University of Frankfurt.

The signature indicates that his father was a strong influence (surname much larger) who had an even sharper mind (comprehensive, investigative thinking processes in "n") and Josef felt depressed at the thought of him (last letters of "Mengele" fall). Josef's strong responsiveness (far right slant) of resentment, aggression (angular "M"), and temper (short stroke on capital "J") toward his father are all suppressed (squeezed and angular capital "M").

The body of the writing: he had what it took be a physician, traits necessary to achieve one's goals (good rhythm, high and strong t-bars, strong down-strokes on 'g" and "y"). Note also strong analytical and investigative thinking processes – probably high IQ.

However, he also had **negative traits**: heavy writing (strong, deep feelings) combined with squeezed-together, far-right slanted letters showing suppression of feelings which could explode impulsively under stress (t-bars to right of stem). His many inflexible beginning strokes with angular writing show resentment and a total lack of warmth. A hyper-critical nature is also evident, a trait which could account for his ardent Nazi ideology – which I suppose, for him, was *his* conscience (what nearly anyone else would think is evil he thought was good).

I often wonder: how could he, as a *physician* who came from an educated, well-to-do family, do what he did? I believe it was his apparent lack of conscience – morality as we understand it – and this is not discernible in his handwriting, at least to me.

We like to vote for or hire a person who has confidence, high self-esteem, and the ability to achieve goals – but beware, if the person's notions of good and evil differ radically from those of society at large.

In the next chapter we will study graphological signs to look for or look *out* for in choosing personnel or an employer.

CHAPTER FOURTEEN

Personnel (and Employer) Selection

"The closest to perfection a person ever come to perfection is when he fills out a job application form."
- Stanley J. Randall

"Enthusiasm is the greatest asset in the world. It beats money, power and influence."
- Henry Chester

Choosing a Repairman

Graphoanalysis is great for choosing employees. My husband and I owned an electronics store and needed a repairer of stereos, someone experienced mechanically or someone with manual dexterity we could train who would stay with us for a long time. We put an ad in the paper, and I screened the applicants. When I found a guy (no females applied) that had a flat-topped "r," I handed him a stereo to repair. He was especially good at it, but his handwriting indicated he had psychological problems; he was emotionally unstable. I didn't want to hire him, but my husband (who didn't believe in handwriting analysis) felt that we should; the guy was a genius when it came to fixing things. So I gave in.

He was great for a few weeks. Then one day he simply didn't show up. He had disappeared. Perhaps he had been on drugs or in a depression.

Another applicant's handwriting indicated a very reliable, very intelligent, sociable and responsible person. In addition, he was even good with his hands – yet I turned him down. I told him that I felt he would not be happy fixing stereos; he could easily obtain something better. His handwriting showed he liked to work directly with people; he was college material and very intelligent. He then revealed that he was studying psychology at the local university and was looking only for summer work for extra money. I wished him all the best.

Eventually, our own son-in-law fitted the bill better than all of them, and has been with us for many years, doing excellent work.

Tips for Employers

If you're looking for someone to work outdoors and alone or to do research, you'd pick an introvert who is into his own mind. However, some people *appear* to be extroverts or introverts but are not.

For example, I chose to be a laboratory technologist not just because I have an analytical mind, but because I knew I'd not be working directly with people but with machines and mostly alone; I was uncomfortable around people; I didn't know how to make small talk. I felt safe in the windowless basement with my microscope and machines. However, part of my job was to go to the wards and take blood from patients for testing. It wasn't long before I found that I loved it; I loved talking with patients as I stuck the needle in them. My handwriting is not tiny but small (good for research) and I would seem to people to be an introvert, lost in my own thoughts, being self-absorbed, not noticing what's around me — but I'm not completely. The slant is definitely to the right, and I like being with people, *but not all the time.*

On the other hand, a true introvert can appear like an extrovert, very outgoing and talkative, but it's only a show — a cover for his introverted, *self-absorbed* nature of anticipating negative reactions from outside himself. In contrast, the extrovert is immediately aware of people and things outside himself; he is not self-absorbed. Look at the handwriting for a truer picture.

Tips For Seeking Work

I've been employee as well as employer, and can see things from both perspectives. First, as a young seeker of work, I understood some things instinctively. For example: you do not show qualifications that would not help in the work being sought. If you really want the job, you show only what is required for it, or the employer will feel, rightly so, that you are overqualified and should seek a better job. In hard times you could wait a long time.

For example: in 1947 I had just completed training as a medical technologist in Canada (where I was born). Not finding work and needing whatever job I could get to pay the rent, I applied for a filing job in a hospital, omitting to mention, of course, that I was in fact a *licensed* laboratory technologist. I merely said I thought I could do the filing because I was careful and dependable. Perhaps the woman responsible for hiring instinctively sensed those traits in my handwriting (good rhythm, even baseline, slight right slant, dot over "i", t-bar placed high on stem showing

```
confidence, with good down-strokes on "g" and "y"
showing determination to achieve my goal.)
```

A Question of Discrimination: The next "Dear Dena" asks if she should "give in" to being laid off after twenty-four years of service at the university, or continue to fight her dismissal.

Specimen #54 "M"
(employer/employee)

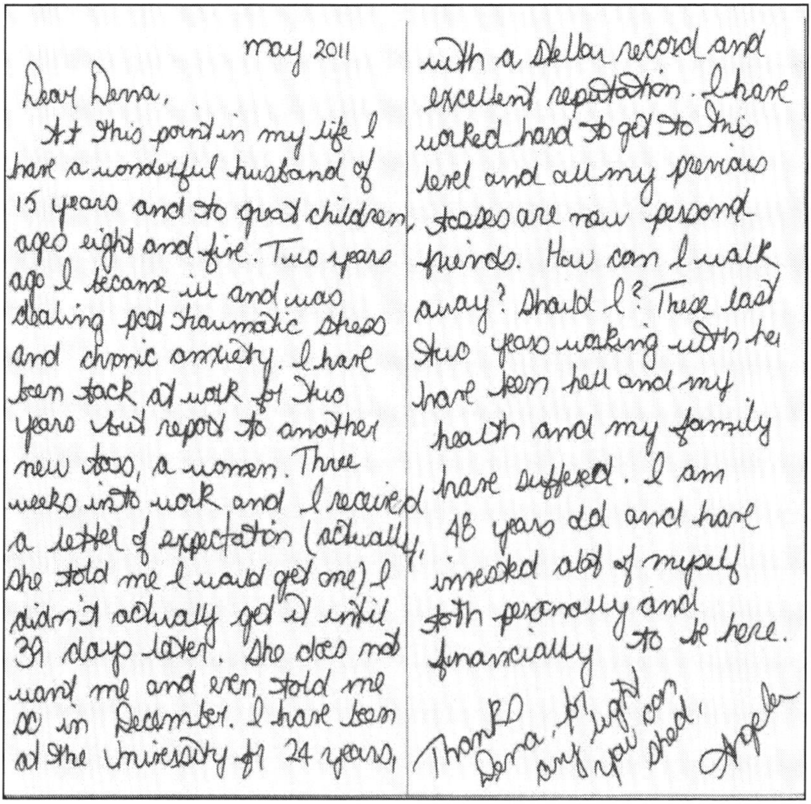
may 2011

Dear Dena,

At this point in my life I have a wonderful husband of 15 years and two great children ages eight and five. Two years ago I became ill and was dealing post traumatic stress and chronic anxiety. I have been back at work for two years but report to another new boss, a women. Three weeks into work and I received a letter of expectation (actually, she told me I would get one) I didn't actually get it until 39 days later. She does not want me and even told me so in December. I have been at the University for 24 years, with a stellar record and excellent reputation. I have worked hard to get to this level and all my previous bosses are now personal friends. How can I walk away? Should I? These last two years working with her have been hell and my health and my family have suffered. I am 48 years old and have invested alot of myself both personally and financially to be here.

Thanks Dena, for light any you can shed.

Angela

Dear Dena,

At this point in my life I have a wonderful husband of fifteen years and two great children ages eight and five. Two years ago I became ill and was dealing post-traumatic stress and chronic anxiety. I have been back at work for two years but report to another new boss, a woman. Three weeks into work and I received a letter of expectation (actually she told me I would get one) I didn't actually get it until 39 days later. She does not want me and even told me so in December. I have been at the university for 24 years with a stellar record and excellent reputation. I have worked hard to get to this level and all my previous bosses are now personal friends. How can I walk away? Should I? These last two years working with her have been hell and my health and my family have suffered. I am 48 years old and have invested a lot of myself both personally and financially to be here. Thanks Dena, for any light you can shed. – Angela [female 48]

Dear Angela,

You don't say what your work actually is, but you do it well—methodically (slow rounded letters) yet efficiently (t-bar joining next letter). You like working with people (large letters), but try not to show your conflicting emotions (variable slant).

Your question: should you walk away? Yes, but with the help of your physician who treated you for chronic anxiety and stress, or someone else who is qualified. There is much conflict in your writing. You ordinarily like people and are friendly (large letters, rounded "m" and "n," some right slant) but at the same time are fearful of being close to people (extremely narrow spacing between some letters as well as wider spacing in the same word, e.g., the word "old"); you desire to be with people and also away from people (larger than normal spacing between words as well as normal spacing); you blame yourself for your situation (many "t" endings turn left), and at the same time you are very defiant (very large buckle on "k") about it, and resentful about it (inflexible beginning strokes in "can" and "away").

You're very open-minded (wide "e") toward people, yet you are rejecting someone close (lower loop on "f" swings left before the baseline, especially in "family").

Furthermore, you don't like change (traditional capital "D"), and cling to security (no left margin). At the same time, you're non-traditional (unusual "b"), independent (short "d" stem), and ambitious for advancement at work (small beginning hooks).

Your communication with others is confusing. Trying to protect yourself from hurt, you can be evasive (hook in "a" and "o"), or tightly closed-mouthed (retraced on top), giving others the feeling you haven't told the whole story. As a result, people can find you hard to really know, especially when you rationalize at times (large left loop on "a" in "later")—meaning, in some area you are (unconsciously) not completely honest with yourself.

Finally, I think your strong persistence (large lasso loops in "expectation," "reputation," and especially "Angela") in staying at work would be better used to attend now to your health and well-being. First things first. Take care.

Handling Prejudice
(Whether Race, Religion, Color, Gender, Sexual Orientation, Age, Weight, or Disability)

In the real world you may come across prejudice. There are many ways of handling this, depending on one's personality, beliefs, physical/

mental stamina, and pocketbook.

I was hired as file clerk even though on the application I put "Jewish" under "nationality" (as was *expected* and not "Canadian" as you would think). I was told that I was picked over a stack of applicants, and that if I wanted the job, I had to be a "secret" Jew as none were allowed to work in the hospital, and I was being hired to irritate someone she disliked. This meant I was not to be called by name, and not ever let on that I was Jewish, which didn't mean much as I worked in a windowless basement, alone with the records.

But at times I had to bring up records or X-rays to different departments, and one day I happened to be where there was unhappy commotion between doctors and office heads. Medical reports to be completed were piling up because the typist was ill and not coming back. I turned to them and said simply: "I can type." **This is called initiative (convex "t" ending)**. My boss was surprised but let me take it while she got someone else to do the filing. I had already taught myself to type years before. All I had to do was transcribe what I heard on the "dictaphone" (as it was called in those days) onto the typewriter. I took the medical dictionary home and studied it carefully. I was already a good speller, but I needed to be more familiar with the terminology **[I had a realistic goal (t-bar high on the stem), with determination (strong down-strokes on "y" and "g") to achieve the goal (making a living)]**.

In time I was given a raise (I would correct the doctor's bad grammar and spelling if given in writing) and became operation room secretary, taking dictation from all the surgeons using a combination of longhand and Gregg (which I had learned years before). Finally I became personal secretary to the registrar of the hospital where I typed the complete history of a patient's hospitalization, with another raise. **I was now making much more as a secretary than I ever could as a technologist. But I hated sitting at a desk; I missed doing what I had been trained to do:** bacteriology, chemistry, hematology, histology.

But give up what I had worked so hard to obtain? Fate stepped in. To make a long story short, when one of the surgeons made an ugly anti-semitic remark to me, I told him I was Jewish and he proceeded to get me fired. (There were no laws against all of this at the time)

I was called into the office of the hospital superintendent, Mr. McPherson, who informed me that Dr. Duffy was trying to get me fired. He said he understood it was because Duffy had discovered I was Jewish. How did I get into the hospital in the first place, he wanted to know. Who hired me? I told him about Miss St. John. After a few moments of silence, he tapped his pipe on a dish, then rose from behind his desk. "Well," he said, "it's up to you. If you can stand it, I'll back you. Or you can leave, and not suffer being where you're not welcome. It's all in the way one looks at it."

We were both silent for a moment. "Unfortunately," he said, finally, "in my job I have to deal with a majority of anti-Semites."

Well, I was stubborn and wasn't about to let Dr. Duffy win. "I'll leave," I told McPherson, "when *I* choose. I won't let him think he can intimidate me."

"O.K." he said, "but it won't be easy."

And it wasn't. He made my life miserable complaining about me and my work to everyone. But I was determined not to give him the satisfaction by quitting.

I was now in a position some employees find themselves in today: should I stay on principle or leave and go find a job where I was at least wanted? Should I leave the good work and pay for

possibly no job or one I might not like and with much less pay? For quite some time I stuck it out – on principle. I didn't want to give them the satisfaction of forcing me out through bullying and harassment.

But then I remembered I was having headaches sitting at a desk even *before* all this had happened. **I decided I would leave, not because of *them,* but for me.** So maybe I should thank the anti-Semitic surgeon. **He helped me get back on track, back to what I really wanted to do.** I applied to the Jewish General Hospital and went back to the work I loved at much less pay, and the headaches disappeared.

This was *my* way of handling the situation. Each person meeting prejudice must make his or her own decision, according to the world s/he's living in at the time, and his or her own emotional makeup and beliefs. I don't think there is really one right or wrong way, as the world keeps changing, with new laws being enacted and old prejudices slowly fading. Also, sometimes what seems like a bad situation turns out to be for the good, after all.

Personnel Selection

How To Choose a Secretary

In 1975 a businessman hired me to analyze a few handwriting samples for the position of personal secretary. He handed me a number of applications. I analyzed each for intelligence, dependability, initiative, and good character, and sent in my report, so that he could choose for himself who best suited him. He thanked me and paid me.

Sometime later, I was curious to know if he hired the one I thought was most mature and dependable. "No," he answered. "I hired the young and pretty one." (Today he'd be sued.)

Israelis See Handwriting as True Personality Test

By DAN FISHER, *Times Staff Writer*

JERUSALEM—A young Israeli computer technician and his wife went apartment-hunting recently

value as a mirror of personality is much more controversial. And in the United States, graphologists

ABOVE: Europe and Israel are open to graphology, using it mostly in personnel selection.

When Integrity Is Especially Important: How to Choose a Bookkeeper or Cashier (or: How Not To Be Embezzled From)

Dishonesty is not absolutely discernible from handwriting. Various combinations of traits showing different shades of dishonesty are not cut-and-dried. The graphoanalyst must evaluate carefully. One can be dishonest with oneself, as well as with others, and on an unconscious level. One could be evasive, manipulative, secretive, or even just trying to protect oneself or someone else. Many factors are involved in whether or not a person will deliberately steal, for example.

However, there are some signs to watch out for. Look for acquisitive hooks (large beginning hooks) together with weak concave t-bars low on the stem, as well as left and right loops in "a" and "o," hooks in "a" and "o," irregular slant, rhythm, and baseline. Also, if you see a letter or word that has been "corrected," or so illegible it's a scrawl, or you see different slants and pressures in only a few lines, **reject the applicant**.

My husband chose the pretty bookkeeper (before I had studied graphology). Not only did we nearly go bankrupt, it was a recipe for divorce. So learn your lessons well – and apply them.

And Don't Make a Judgment From Only a Signature!

Look at the body of the handwriting below and then that of the signature. How different! One's signature is how one sees oneself or *wishes* to be seen by the world, and can also be how one feels about one's father (surname) – whereas the body of the writing indicates one's real personality and character.

Specimen #55
(signature doesn't match the body of the writing)

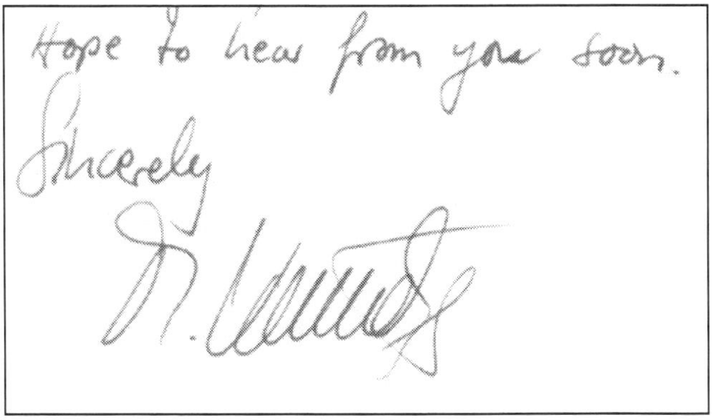

Looks Can Be Deceiving – Trust Graphology

To help raise money for a good cause, I was to entertain a large gathering of people at a hilltop mansion with my "quickie" analyses. To make it more fun, I dressed as a gypsy and set myself up with a little table and two chairs at a strategic spot - and one by one they came. All were amazed at how accurate I was. There was a lull, so I went for a drink, sat back in my chair, and relaxed. A strikingly beautiful woman in a stunning form-fitting gown was striding confidently toward me. "A movie star," I was thinking, "egotistical, vain, cool, selfish. I can just picture those traits in her handwriting."

She sat down and wrote - and what a surprise! I told her that she had a brilliant mind, was definitely Ph.D. material, would have a profession of some sort partially working with people, at other times researching in one of the helping fields. She smiled and said she was an M.D. radiologist in a hospital.

CHAPTER FIFTEEN

Employer/Employee/Coworker/Client Conflicts

Specimen #56
(employer/employee problem)

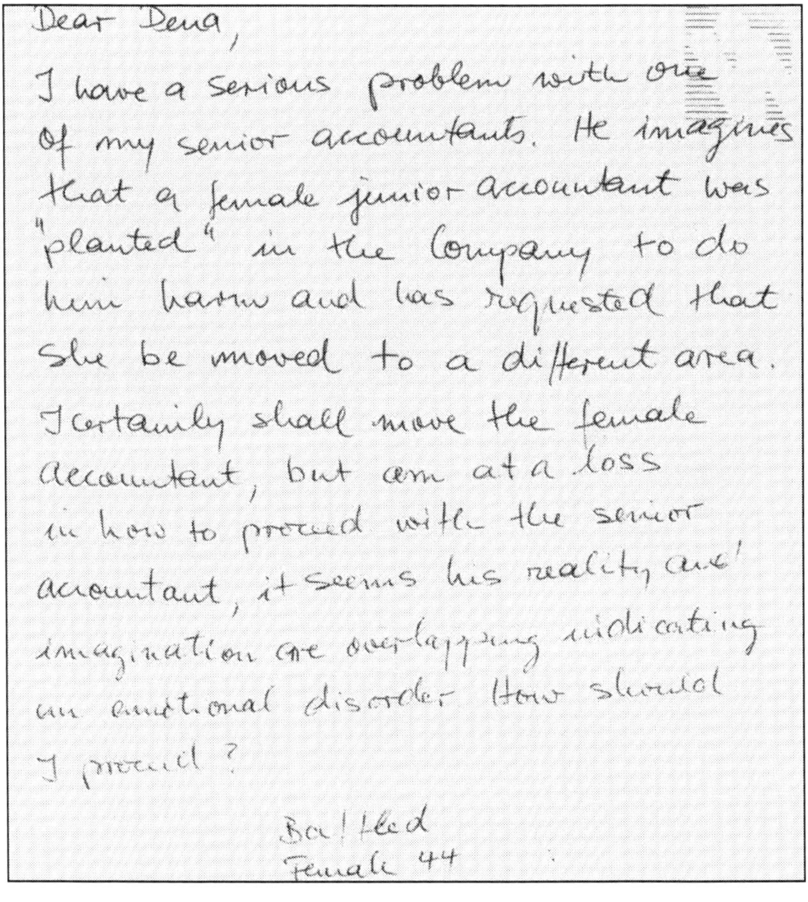

Dear Dena,

I have a serious problem with one of my senior accountants. He imagines that a female junior accountant was "planted" in the Company to do him harm and has requested that she be moved to a different area. I certainly shall move the female accountant, but am at a loss in how to proceed with the senior accountant, it seems his reality and imagination are overlapping indicating an emotional disorder How should I proceed?

Baffled
Female 44

Dear Dena,

I have a serious problem with one of my senior accountants. He imagines that a female junior accountant was "planted" in the company to do him harm and has requested that she be moved to a different area. I certainly shall move the female accountant, but am at a loss in how to proceed with the senior accountant, it seems his reality and imagination are overlapping indicating an emotional disorder. How should I proceed? – Baffled Female 44

Dear Baffled,

If I had the handwriting of your senior accountant I could better advise you. You are very bright, sharply analytical person (sharp "m" & "n"), and you work well and efficiently (many fluency strokes of one letter joining another or the crossing of a t-bar.). If he is a slow plodding thinker (rounded "m"), you would have to be patient with him. Your capital "I" indicates you were educated in Europe, and your work habits are probably different from Americans. How are his? You are not overly sensitive to criticism. However, if he is, (big loops on "d"), you would have to handle him gently.

You can be aggressive at times (final inflexible stroke on "q" in "requested"), a bit secretive (small right loop on "o" and "a") and evasive (hook in some "a" and "o"). This together with the tendency sometimes to be critical (beginning stroke on "w" in "with", together with sharp "m") –could give you trouble with those under you, unless you take care to be sensitive to those with lower self esteem and intelligence.

If he is equal to you or better, and is argumentative and defensive, you would keep your cool; you don't like arguments (retraced "d" &"t" stem). You're quite intuitive (breaks between letters), have a feeling for people (slight right slant, large letters), and are creative (flat topped "r").

Just pick a time when you are less irritable (dashes for "imagination"). On the whole you have a good sense of self (realistic high t-bar in "imagination" and good down-strokes on "g" and "y"). However, sometimes you lack confidence and set your goals too low (low t-bar in "at" and "it")—for a person of your ability and intelligence. Also in some area of your life (intimate relationships?) you tend to rationalize (large left loop on "a" and "o").

Incidentally, what do you do for hobbies after work? You have interest and talent for cultural things, art, music, literature.

As for your employee, if he's still acting paranoid after you've moved the female employee, and seems a danger to you and your firm, I would get an attorney to guide you with the first steps in handling the situation.

To help me in my graphology research, I asked "Dear Dena" writers for honest responses to my answers, with the following note:

"It may contain your feelings on reading it, where you think it was inaccurate or false, where I was "right on," what I missed, what you think of my idea or style, or anything else you may think of. Enclosed is a self-addressed stamped envelope."

Among the many replies, one of the more interesting was from "Baffled Female 44":

Dear Dena,

I appreciate your answer and must compliment you! I was educated through High School in Europe, but went to college in the U.S. It's true I am a little sensitive to criticism and speak my mind without regard to rank and class but I forget or ignore the strokes necessary for people in lower positions under extreme pressure. I do have problems occasionally with people of lower intellect, but only if coupled with arrogance and/or defiance.

The only problem with your analysis I have is the t-bar. I do not have low self-esteem; the low bar comes from a fad during my childhood of looping my t's like the Americans, making curly "a," "s," and "g." I bet if the writing was surveyed region or time-wise (southern Germany, early to mid 50's), a pattern would emerge. I am an extremely versatile person, with artistic (painting, writing, poetry) and psychic abilities.

Specimen #57

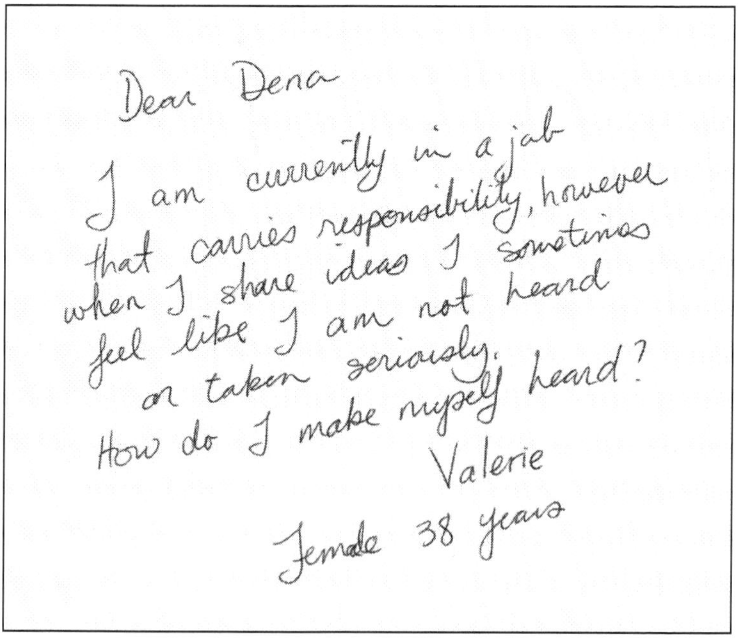
Dear Dena
I am currently in a job
that carries responsibility, however
when I share ideas I sometimes
feel like I am not heard
or taken seriously.
How do I make myself heard?
Valerie
female 38 years

Dear Dena,

I am currently in a job that carries responsibility, however when I share ideas I sometimes feel like I am not heard or taken seriously. How can I make myself heard? – Valerie, Female 38 years

Dear Valerie,

With your basic optimism (rising lines) and your sharp analytical mind (angular "m" and "n"), you work directly and to the point (no beginning strokes), efficiently and smoothly (fluency strokes in "f") in work you are familiar and comfortable with.

You want to get ahead (light hook on capital "I") but are not keen on taking on a lot of responsibilities, or else you would have made a loop on the capital "I."

Though you are full of ideas for projects (large loop on "y" in "responsibility"), you procrastinate (t-bar to the left of stem in "currently") or do not complete them (unfinished loop in "seriously"). Could it be you are not in your usual field and are uncomfortable?

Artistic and creative abilities are evident (simple printed capitals). You have manual dexterity for painting or design (flat-topped "r"). You could also do well in one of the helping fields, working with people (moderately sized writing and medium right slant). However, you are a little too sensitive to criticism of your ideas (loop in "t"). As a result, you can at times be moody (uneven baseline and irregular margins) with a lack of belief in yourself (very low and weak t-bar in the key word "not").

I think your co-workers and employer sense your wavering of confidence (t-bar sometimes high on stem and sometimes low and weak), making them wary of trusting your ideas. Rather than feeling defiant (buckle on "k") or depressed (drooping letters in key word "heard"), try not to care about being not heard. If confidence is not always felt, put on an act, and soon it will be real.

You can also practice graphotherapeutics. Simply take the word "not," with its low and weak t-bar on a looped t-stem. and when you write make a "t" without a loop and with a t-bar high and strong on the stem. Do this thirty times a night for thirty nights. At first it will feel strange, but soon you will make yourself heard as you project confidence in yourself with no oversensitivity to criticism. Good luck!

Specimen #58

"In looking for people to hire, look for three qualities: integrity, intelligence, and energy. And if they don't have the first, the other two will kill you. "
- Warren Buffet

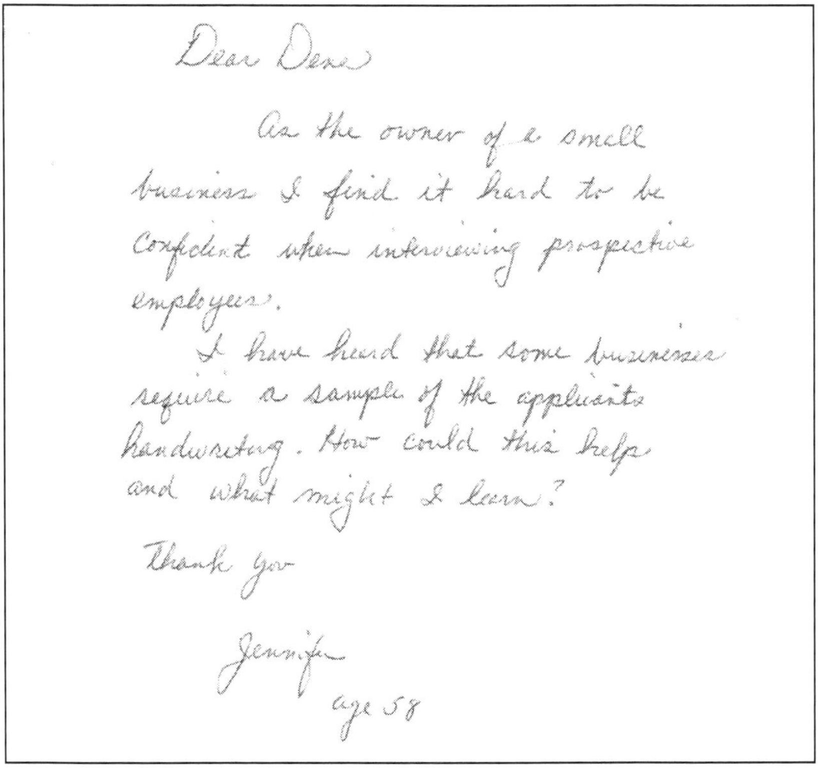

Dear Dena

As the owner of a small business I find it hard to be confident when interviewing prospective employees.

I have heard that some businesses require a sample of the applicants handwriting. How could this help and what might I learn?

Thank you

Jennifer
age 58

Dear Dena,

As the owner of a small business I find it hard to be confident when interviewing prospective employees. I have heard that some businesses requiere a sample of the applicant's handwriting. How could this help and what might I learn? – Thank you. Jennifer, age 58

Dear Jennifer,

How can graphoanalysis help in choosing an employee? Very good question. However, I could be of more help had you told me what kind of business you have. I could then tell you the traits necessary for the particular work it requires. Without it, I can only generalize.

1) Does the work entail manual dexterity? Look for a flat-topped "r."

2) Will the employee work at the cash register? You don't want an embezzler. Look for loops and hooks in oval letters; acquisitive and final hooks to words; letters, words, or numbers that are missing, patched, or crossed out, just to name a few clues. Other kinds of dishonesty are many, difficult to ascertain with certainty, and are usually combinations of traits.

3) Is the work predominantly mental? Look for smaller writing with sharp angular "m" and "n" for analytical work, deep angular strokes for the investigative type, and rounded "m" and "n" for working slowly, carefully, or caring for people. If it's to do research, look for clear, distinct, yet tiny writing.

4) Is it painstaking work, with attention to detail? You want someone who dots his "i" above the letter—no dashes. The writing should not be fast and sloppy.

5) Is he or she supersensitive? You'll have trouble getting along if the employee is too sensitive to criticism (large loop on "d"), but the employee may nonetheless do good work.

6) Does the work involve dealing with people closely, intimately? Look for writing not too large, not too small, at a moderately right slant, with good rhythm, spacing, and pressure, with finals showing generosity—a giving of self and time.

7) Is it sales work? You'll want an extrovert with ambition (acquisitive hooks), medium to large writing, right slant, strong and high t-bars, straight down-strokes on "g" and "y", showing confidence and determination, as well as the "lasso" stroke showing persistence. The writing could be fast, a bit sloppy, with perhaps some aggressive strokes (inflexible ending strokes).

8) Is it a teaching position? The writing would be similar to one working with people. If it is with children, especially children with handicaps of some sort, patience is a must; slow and careful writing is best, with right slant, no dashes for dots, with no inflexible beginning strokes (resentment).

9) Personality and character: you want someone you can get along with. You don't want someone who only wants to do it his or her way (down-slanting t-bars). However, you do want initiative (curved ending on "t"), intelligence (various thinking processes), and confidence (t-bars high on the stem). For compatibility you want a sense of humor (curved beginning stroke on "m"), someone not on drugs (tremor in writing), one who is dependable and reliable, no matter the kind of work to be done. The writing should show rhythm, good spacing, and an even baseline, with no procrastination (t-bar to left of stem) and no temper (t-bar to right of stem), temper tic (short straight beginning stroke), or resentment (inflexible beginning stroke to a letter or word), and certainly no strong aggression (inflexible ending strokes to the right)—or dishonesty.

I could go on and on. I have done personnel selection for businesses, and have used it in my and husband's electronics business. I hope I have convinced you that graphology is a great help in this—despite your doubts and pessimism regarding it ("help" drops, as well as the sentence "what might I learn?").

You say it's hard for you to be confident in interviewing employees. Why? With your good analytical mind (angular "m" and "n"), caring disposition (medium-sized writing, right slant), generosity (long endings to some words), dependability and reliability (rhythm, spacing on page and between letters, words, and lines), and efficiency in work (t-bar joining next letter)—still, at times, you lack confidence (very low t-bars in "what," "might," and the tiny "I" in the last line). Why do you underestimate yourself?

You have great imagination for projects (lower loops), as well as an aesthetic sense (placement on page), but postpone those dreams (t-bar floating above and to the left of stem in "Thank"). You are suited to be in one of the helping fields (teaching, nursing, psychology, health, or spiritually-oriented work.)

Whatever your business, after you've interviewed an applicant, study his or her cursive writing. If s/he only prints, get that as well. Have him or her write on unlined paper. Later study and compare the writing with what I have given you to screen out obvious rejects. Then just use your intuition (breaks between letters). Good luck!

By now you have looked at your own handwriting, those of your employees or your employer. Are you in the right workplace, at least for now? Do you have goals for the future? Are you confident you can achieve your dreams?

Most importantly, are you now aware of how you can change your shortcomings to more positive traits – simply by changing some strokes in the handwriting?

Do you now wish to test yourself on graphology? In the next chapter you can practice with the “Quickies.”

CHAPTER SIXTEEN

Teaching Graphology Using "Quickies"

Quickie # 1

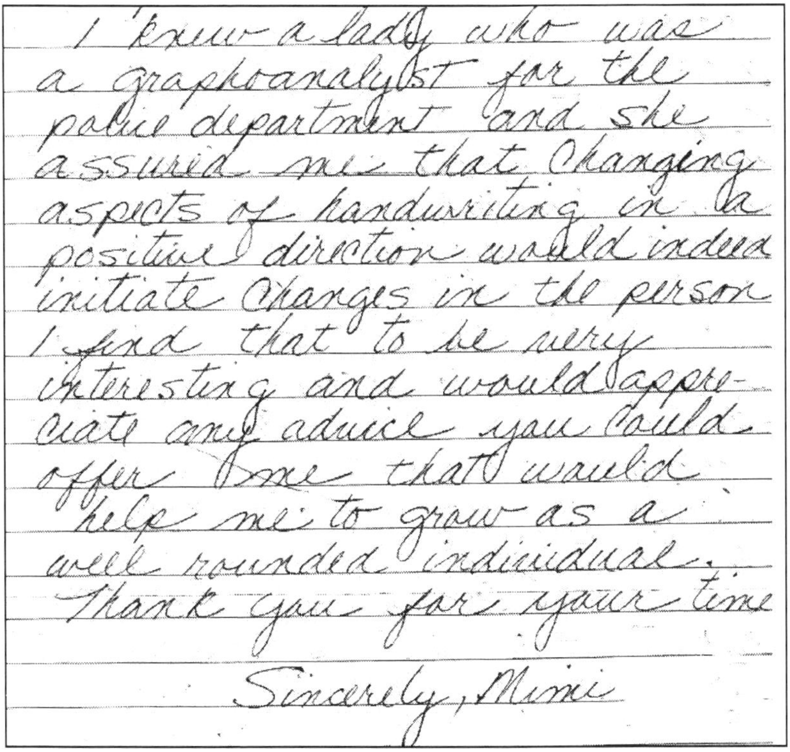
I knew a lady who was
a graphoanalyst for the
police department and she
assured me that changing
aspects of handwriting in a
positive direction would indeed
initiate changes in the person
I find that to be very
interesting and would appreciate any advice you could
offer me that would
help me to grow as a
well rounded individual.
Thank you for your time
Sincerely, Mimi

Quickie #1 (female, no age, Mimi)

Extroverted, loves people (very large writing, right slant).

Very generous (very long endings to words).
Dependable, reliable (non-varying slant, size of middle zone letters).
Attention to detail, loyal (dot right above "I").
Honest (no loops or hooks in "a" or "o").
Sets realistic goals (t-bars firm and high on stem).
Strong determination to achieve goals (straight , long down-strokes on "g" and "y").
Artistic and creative (printed capitals especially capital "I").
Cultural interests (Greek "s").
Intuitive (breaks between letters).
Takes pride in her work (height of "t" in "handwriting").
Organized, neat (good rhythm, equal upper and lower loops on "f").
Defies convention (large buckle on "k").
Dislikes arguments (no loop in "d" or "t").
Needs own space (very wide spacing in words "offer me that").
Some resentment (inflexible beginning stroke in "y" in "your").
Repressed feelings (retraced "h" in "that" and "help").
Self-conscious about something (second "l" in "will" higher).
Too many irons in the fire (lower loops dangling into line below).
Desire to have or achieve (end stroke on "m" and "n").
Mostly open-minded, but closed in some area (narrow "e" in "knew").

Quickie # 2 (female, no age, Marilyn)

5 April 88

Dear Handwriting Analysist,

What interesting things can you tell me about my personality from my handwriting? I am considering some vocational changes or alterations so a little unbiased input would prove helpful.

Am also curious as to what type of research you're doing with handwriting or is this a gimmick to locate penpals? Usually the "personals" column is devoted to a singles search and not handwriting research.

I do believe our handwriting reveals the working of our mind. It would be difficult to fool a sincere and well trained graphoanalysist when it comes to personality traits.

Hope this is enough of a sample of my writing for you to work with in your project and I'm looking forward to your analysis.

Sincerely,

Quickie # 2 (female, no age, Marilyn)

Sharp analytical mind (all angular "m" and "n").
Direct, to the point (no beginning strokes).
Objective, cool-headed, but can appear aloof (predominantly upright slant).
Dependable, reliable (uniform slant, spacing of letters, words, lines).
Organized (upper and lower loops of "f" are equal).
Strong attention to detail (every dot is above the "i").
Frank (some open "a" and "o") and honest (no loops or hooks in them).
Likes people (medium-sized writing, right slant).
Kind (curved joining of letters).
Open-minded (open "e").
Can be generous when called for (endings on words "changes, curious, analysis").
Cautious when necessary (ending on the word "gimmick").
Very loyal (every dot is directly above the letter "i").
Intuitive (breaks between letters).
Healthy confidence, strong determination (high t-bars, good down-strokes on "g" and "y").
Strong manual dexterity (rounded "r").
Writing ability (figure eight "g").
Artistic and creative, esthetic sense (printed capitals, rhythm, spacing on page).
Good at implementing given ideas (lower loop on "f").

Needs own space (spacing between words much wider than normal).

Summary:

1. **An achiever, good healthy balance in all areas of life.**
2. **Not a *big* risk taker; but also has few or no real fears**
3. **A little conflict with traditional/non-traditional roles or occupations**
4. **Vocational: Would make a good Certified Public Accountant, architect, musician, linguist, manager of an art gallery or small museum, anthropologist, pathologist, research writer or researcher in psychology, sociology or history.**

Quickie # 3 (male, no age, Jose Bogea)

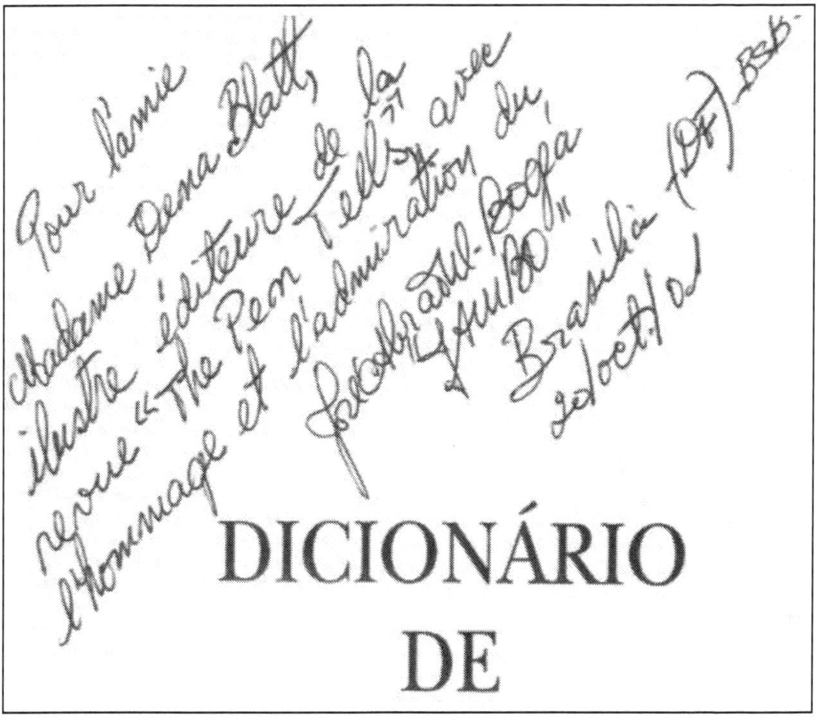

Quickie #3 (male, no age, Jose Bogea)

Strong feelings (heavy pressure writing).
Keen manual dexterity (rounded "r").
Sharp analytical and investigative thinking processes.
Artistic and creative abilities (heavy pressure, printed capitals, rounded "r").
Very open-minded (very wide "e") Some irritation (dashes for dots).

Self-conscious about something (second "l" in "tells" higher).
Sensitive to criticism of his ideas and his work (loop on "t" and "d").
Strong will (heavy t-bar in "Blatt" and "admiration").
Confidence and belief in self ("t-bar" high on stem).
Rarely thinks of giving up (*slightly* concave t-bar in "editure" and "et").
Uses self-control (slightly convex t-bar in "ilustre" and "oct").
Persistence (lasso tie in "T" in "The" and "Tells").

Have you learned some graphology thus far? Would you like to test yourself? Check your knowledge with the Q & A in the following chapter.

CHAPTER SEVENTEEN

Test Yourself with Q & A's on "Dear Dena's"

Q & A #1

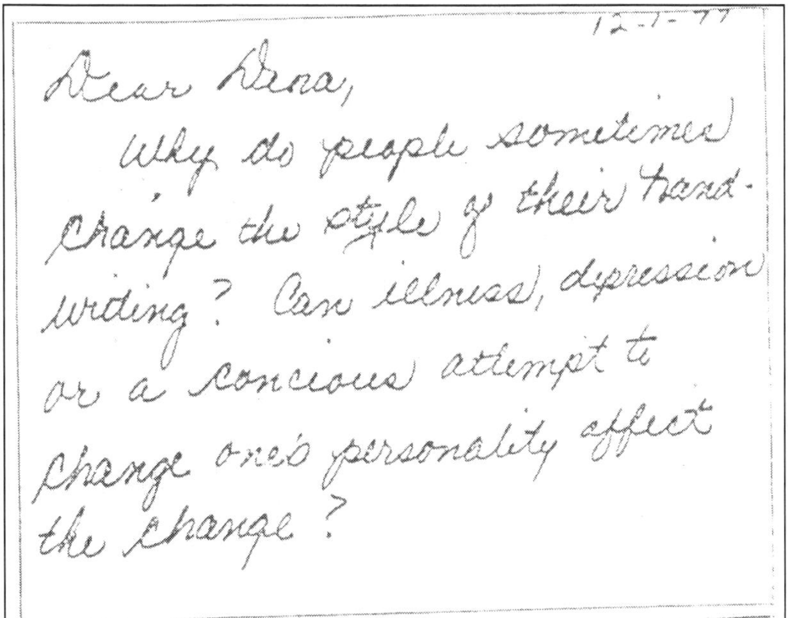

12-7-77

Dear Dena,

Why do people sometimes change the style of their hand-writing? Can illness, depression or a concious attempt to change one's personality affect the change?

1) Identify at least ten traits in the above handwriting.
2) What work would the letter writer be best suited to?

Q & A #2

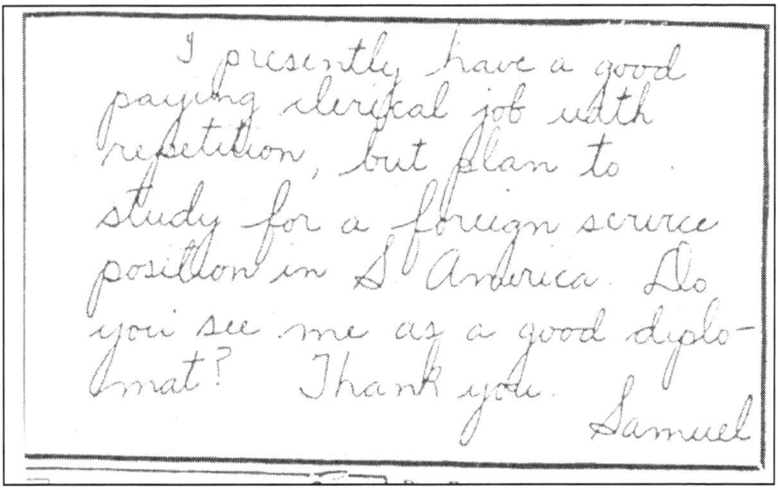
I presently have a good
paying clerical job with
repetition, but plan to
study for a foreign service
position in S. America. Do
you see me as a good diplo-
mat? Thank you.
Samuel

1) If your answer is yes, why? If no, why not? What does Samuel fear?

Q & A # 3

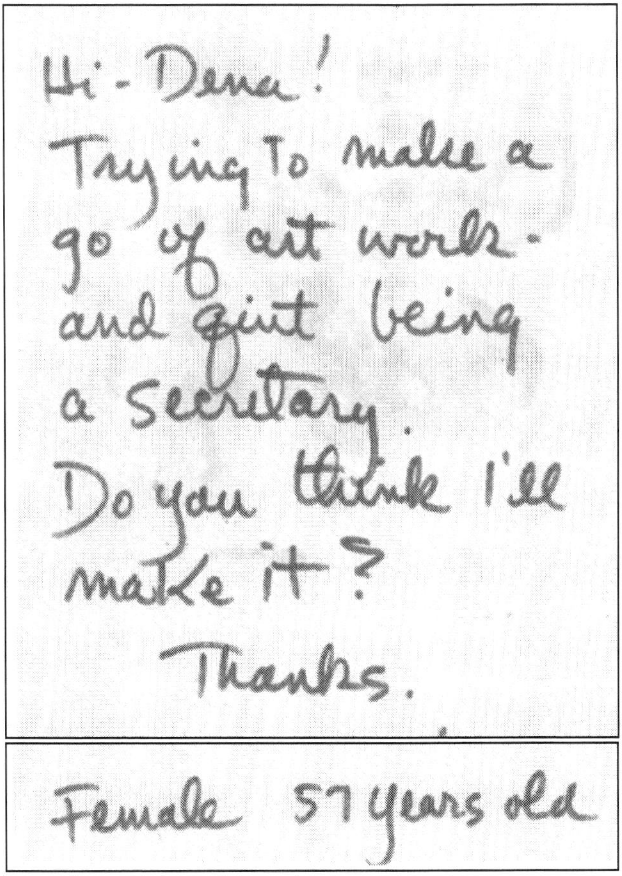

Hi - Dena!
Trying To make a
go of art work -
and quit being
a secretary.
Do you think I'll
make it?
Thanks.

Female 57 years old

1) Do you think she'll make it? If yes, why?

Q & A #4 (female 34 yrs.)

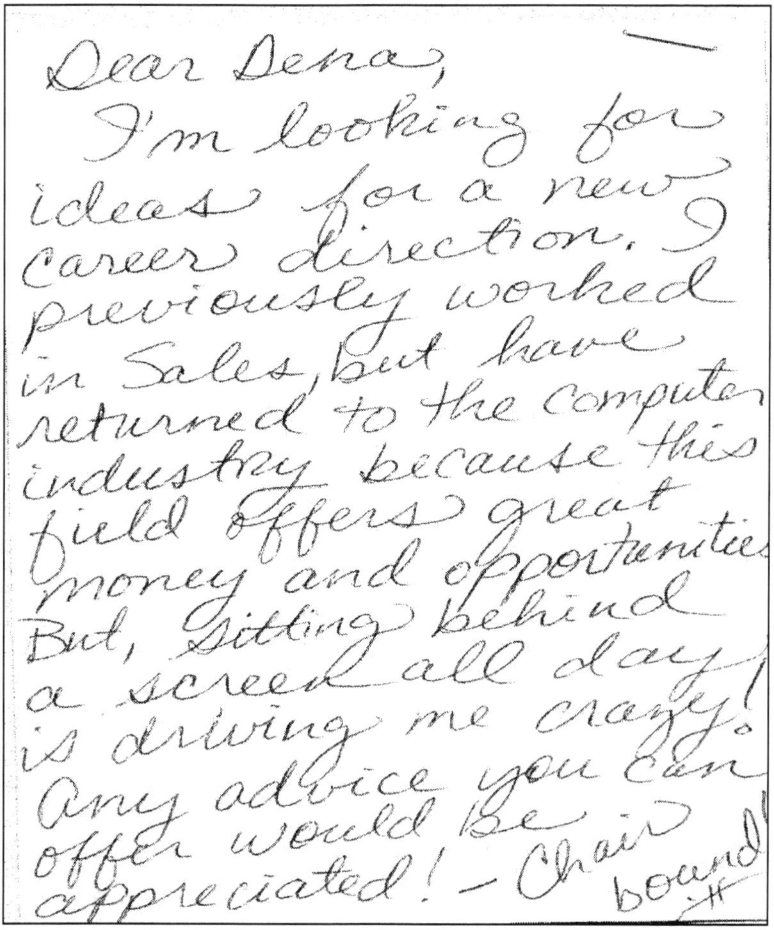
Dear Dena,
I'm looking for ideas for a new career direction. I previously worked in Sales, but have returned to the computer industry because this field offers great money and opportunities. But, sitting behind a screen all day is driving me crazy! Any advice you can offer would be appreciated! – Chair bound :)

1) Is computer work, sales, or teaching best suited to her? Why?
2) Do you think she will make a change or "hold on" to what she has? Why?

Q & A # 5

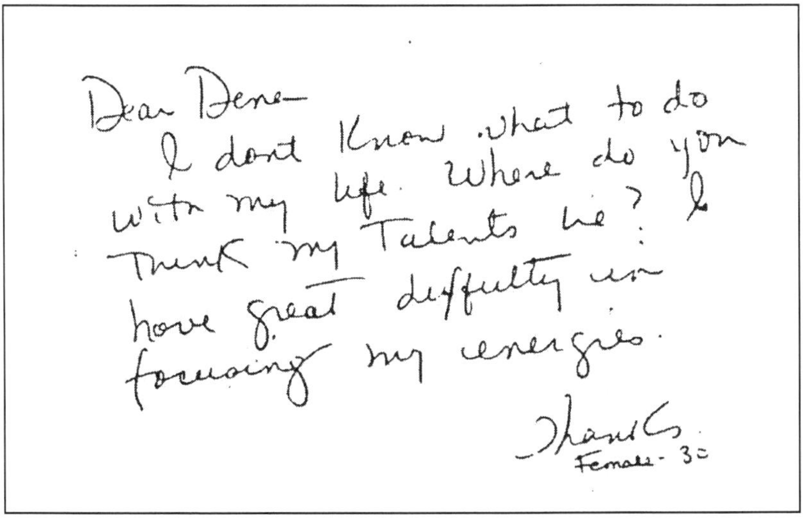
Dear Dena—
I dont Know what to do
with my life. Where do you
Think my Talents lie? I
have great difficulty in
focusing my energies.
Thanks
Female - 30

1) What talents and positive traits are revealed in the handwriting?
2) Why does she have difficulty focusing?

Q & A # 6

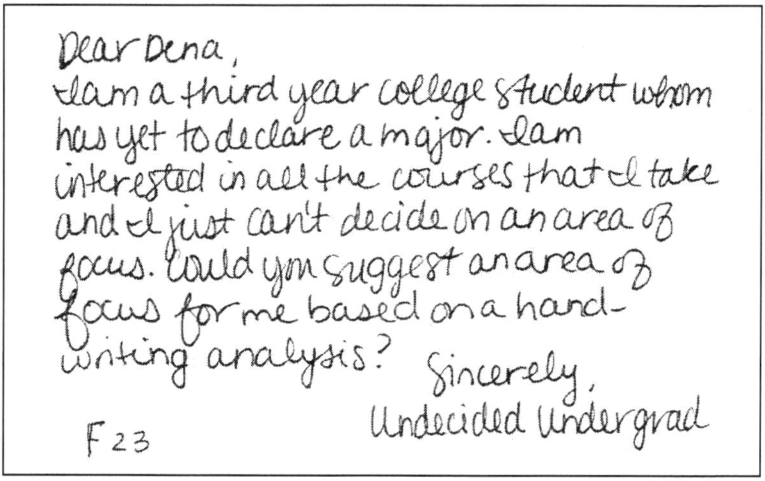
Dear Dena,
I am a third year college student whom has yet to declare a major. I am interested in all the courses that I take and I just can't decide on an area of focus. Could you suggest an area of focus for me based on a hand-writing analysis?

Sincerely,
Undecided Undergrad

F23

1) Do you believe she is really interested in all the courses?
2) If your answer is negative, where in the handwriting is the clue?
3) What kind of work is she best suited to, and why?
4) What does the heavy writing indicate?
5) Her writing is predominantly middle zone. What does that mean?
6) What does her t-bar in "can't" tell you?

Q & A # 7

Dena,

I have a B.A. in Child Development. Although I find it useful in bringing up my own child, I realize I do not want to work in this area. Would it be possible to suggest other possible career choices based on a handwriting analysis?

23 year old mother

1) What career choices would you suggest for her?

Q & A # 8

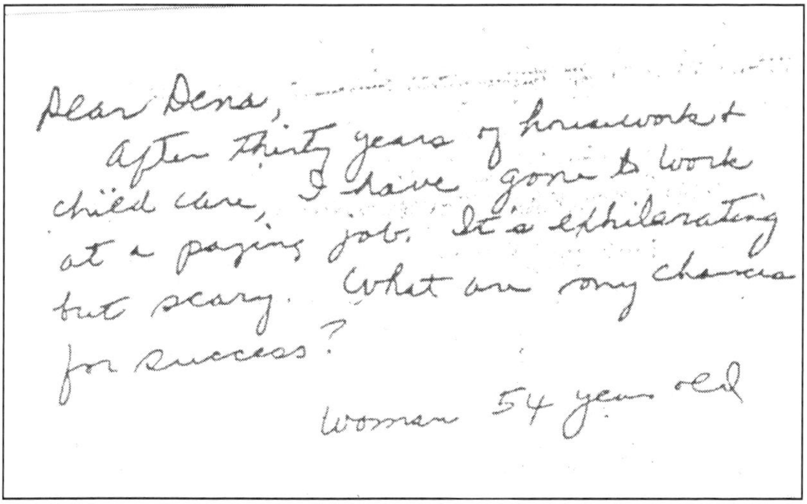

Dear Dena,
After thirty years of housework & child care, I have gone to work at a paying job. It's exhilarating but scary. What are my chances for success?

Woman 54 years old

1) What traits indicate that she should not worry?

Q & A # 9

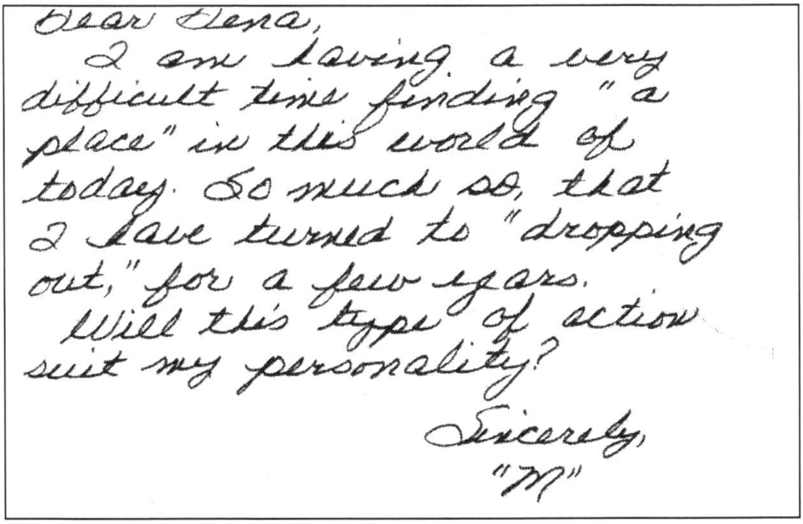
Dear Dena,
I am having a very difficult time finding "a place" in this world of today. So much so, that I have turned to "dropping out," for a few years.
Will this type of action suit my personality?
Sincerely,
"M"

1) If yes (to her question), what are your reasons for believing so?
2) What do the wide spaces between words and retraced "h" suggest?

Q & A #10

Dear Dena:
Help! I'm a recent grad, and ~~altoo~~ although
I struggled really hard to get through
school as a mom and wife - Commuting
long distances to finish my education
I'm finding it difficult to muster
up the confidence to get out there
and do it! I've gotten a good job,
but not in the field of my study.
I've taken little steps like obtaining
a business license so I can get
going in the right direction, but
finding it hard to comit the time
needed to get a business going $
work 40-hours without neglecting
my family. It wasn't easy to
justify less time with the family
to finish school, and finding
it even harder now. I'm disatisfied
with the pace. Am I expecting too
much, am I stalling or just afraid?
- Esteing

1) What does the large right border tell you, and what does she fear?

2) In what key words does she show depression?
3) What other traits are holding her back?
4) Is she optimistic, pessimistic, or both? Is she moody?
5) Is business good for her?

Q & A # 11

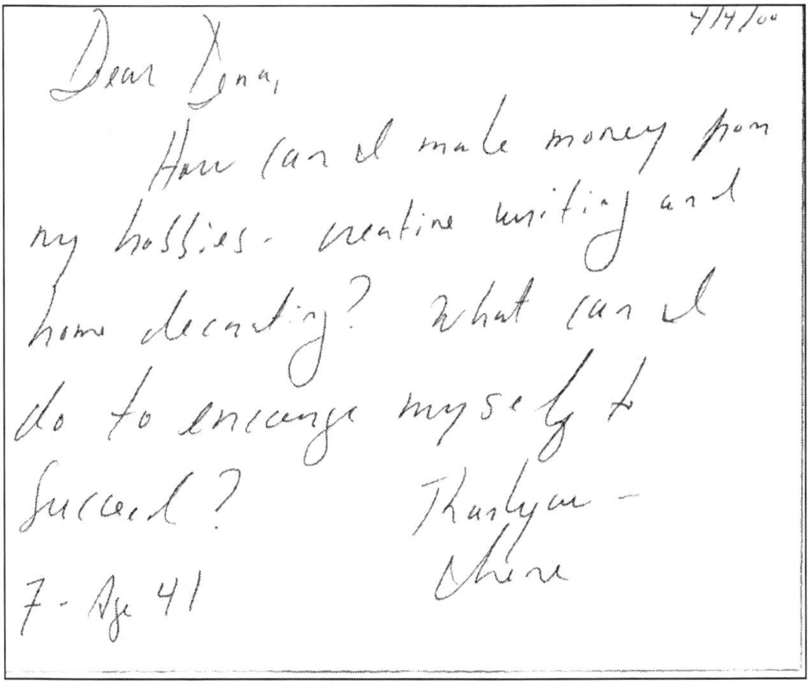
4/14/00

Dear Dena,

How can I make money from my hobbies - creative writing and home decorating? What can I do to encourage myself to succeed?

Thank you -
[illegible]

7 - Age 41

1) Name at least five outstanding traits – four very positive and one very negative. What does she unconsciously fear?

Q & A # 12

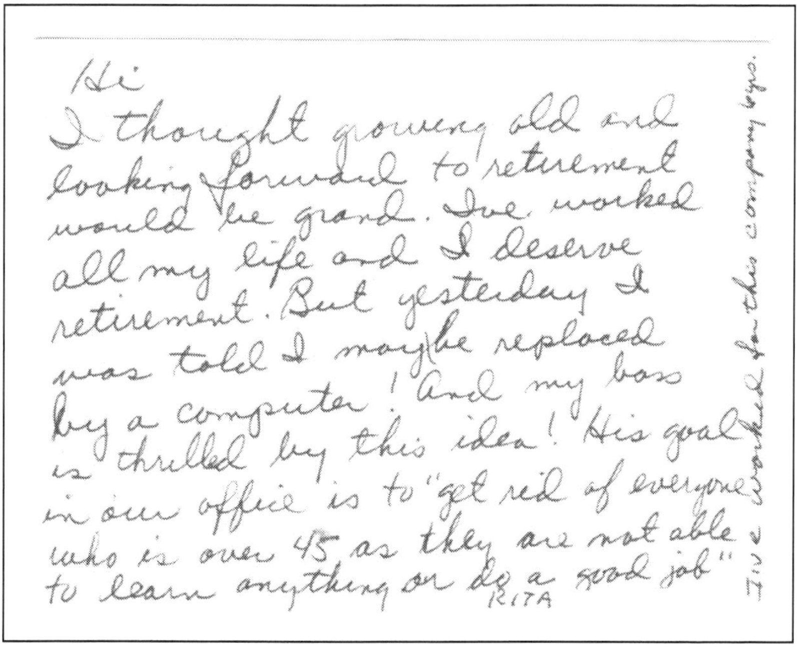
Hi
I thought growing old and
looking forward to retirement
would be grand. Ive worked
all my life and I deserve
retirement. But yesterday I
was told I maybe replaced
by a computer! And my boss
is thrilled by this idea! His goal
in our office is to "get rid of everyone
who is over 45 as they are not able
to learn anything or do a good job"
RITA

I've worked for this company 6 yrs.

1) What two traits could make it difficult for her to work under a boss?
2) What is the meaning of the patched capital "I in 4th line?

Q & A # 13

October 28, 1977

Dear Dena:

I've read your column copies over and over, and I'm learning more each day. You're a delightful writer and obviously a master in your field. Is "Dear Dena" included every week in The Journal? If so, I'll be certain to subscribe a.s.a.p. if subscription is wide open to the public.

1) What kind of work do you think the writer is suited to?

ANSWERS TO "DEAR DENA" QUESTIONS

Q & A # 1

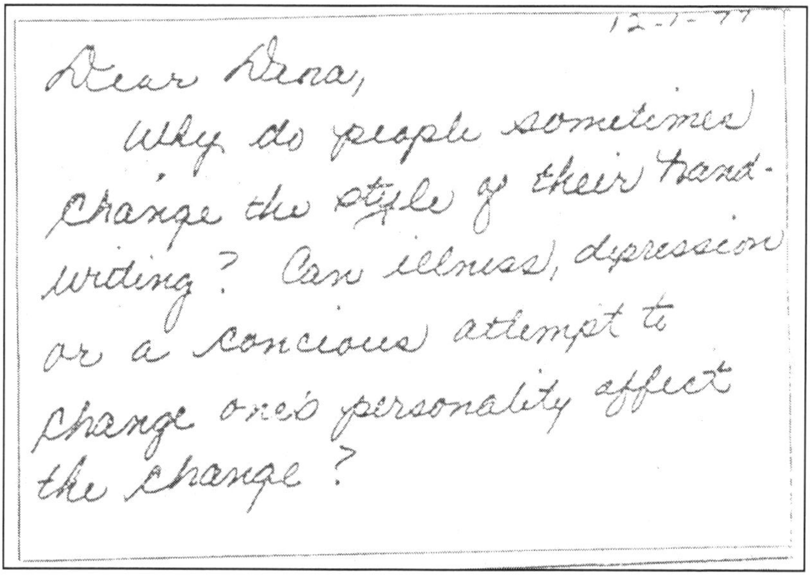

12-7-77

Dear Dena,
Why do people sometimes
change the style of their handwriting? Can illness, depression
or a concious attempt to
change one's personality affect
the change?

Questions:

1. Identify at least ten traits in the handwriting.

2. What work would the letter writer be best suited for?

Answers to #1:

1) Likes to work with and help people –medium writing, right slant
2) Good mind – rounded and angular, good spacing, rhythm, balance on page.

3) Resentment stroke on “change”, “conscious” and “writing”
4) Repression in retraced “M” and “h” in “hand”
5) Holding onto resentment- tiny hook on resentment stroke
6) Resentment from childhood – stroke begins below the line.
7) Wanting attention or love “upward ending on “sometimes” “illness”
8) Procrastination (t-bar to left of stem in “writing” “personality”
9) Generosity –generous endings to words.
10) Feeling of hopelessness about something –downturned ending on “y” in “why”
11) Traditional values - traditional capital “D”
12) Diplomacy – tapering words “change”
13) Independent minded –very short “t” in “the”, “d” in “do”
14) Narrow-minded on some subjects- very narrow “e” loop
15) At times frank and hones –open “o”
16) Reticent at other times – retraced “a” in “change”
17) Realistic goals (t-bar placed to fulfill reasonable standards)
18) Only sometimes lacks confidence (lower t-bar on last “the”)
19) Rare weak will –very weak t-bar in “sometimes”
20) Battling depression – drooping ending to “sometimes,” “illness,” “conscious”
21) Good determination and can work alone – down-stroke on “g” and “y”
22) Sabotages self – crossing of down-stroke on “y” in “style”
23) Stubborn at times – wedge in “t” in “attempt”, “affect”

24) Decisive – firm endings to words
25) Narrow philosophical or religious beliefs --narrow upper loops.

Answer to #2:

Teaching, nursing, secretarial.

Q & A # 2

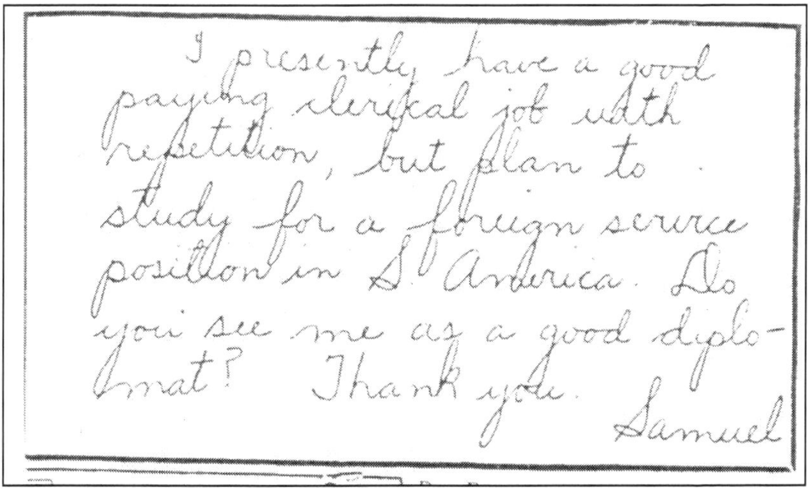
I presently have a good paying clerical job with repetition, but plan to study for a foreign service position in S. America. Do you see me as a good diplo-mat? Thank you. Samuel

Questions:

1. **If your answer is yes, why? If no, why not?**
2. **What does Samuel fear?**

Answers:

1) No. He is completely honest, too honest – no secrecy loops, no diplomacy (no tapering) and he can be defiant regarding philosophical or political issues (buckle on “k”

in upper zone). He is too traditional (traditional capitals) and doesn't have enough belief in himself (tiny "I" compared to other capitals). He also fears the study required (word after large space after "to" is "study"). He is more suited to clerical work (slow, careful).

2) He fears what is after the space after the word "to," which is "study."

Q & A # 3

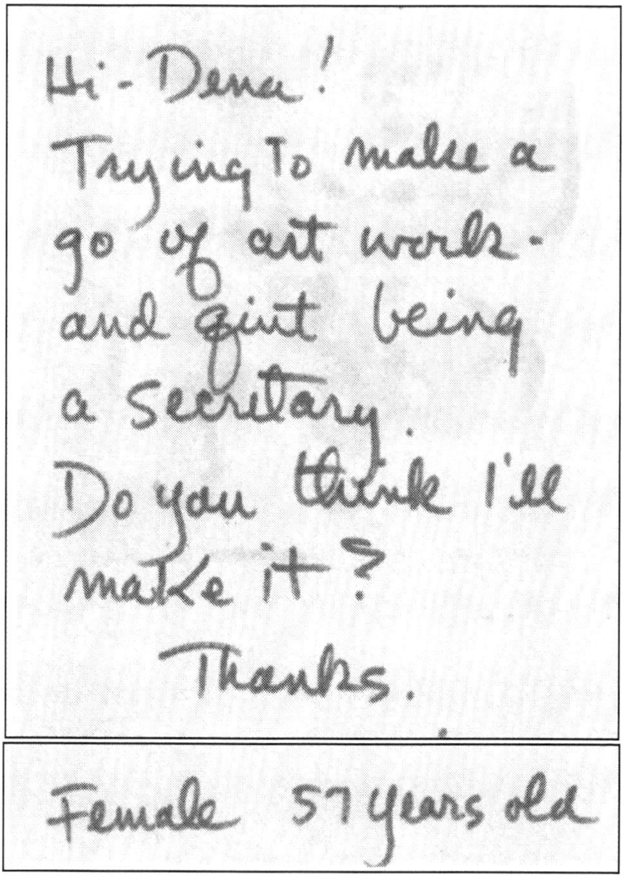
Hi - Dena!
Trying To make a
go of art work -
and quit being
a secretary.
Do you think I'll
make it?
Thanks.

Female 57 years old

Question:

1. **Do you think she'll make it? If yes, why?**

Answer:

1) Yes. Because she has artistic talent (printed capitals), aesthetic sense (balance on page) and intuition (breaks between letters) she sees herself as an artist "stick "I"), has passion (heavy writing), objectivity (upright slant), confidence (high and strong t-bars), determination (strong down-strokes on "y"), ability to work alone (no loop on "y"), sharp analytical and investigative mind (angular "m" and "n")defiance towards obstacles (buckle on "k" and huge "k" in "make", and though sometimes feeling "down" (slight drooping of words and lines) and sometimes sensitive to criticism (loop on "t"), is bound to have her way (some down-slanting "t-bars").

Q & A # 4

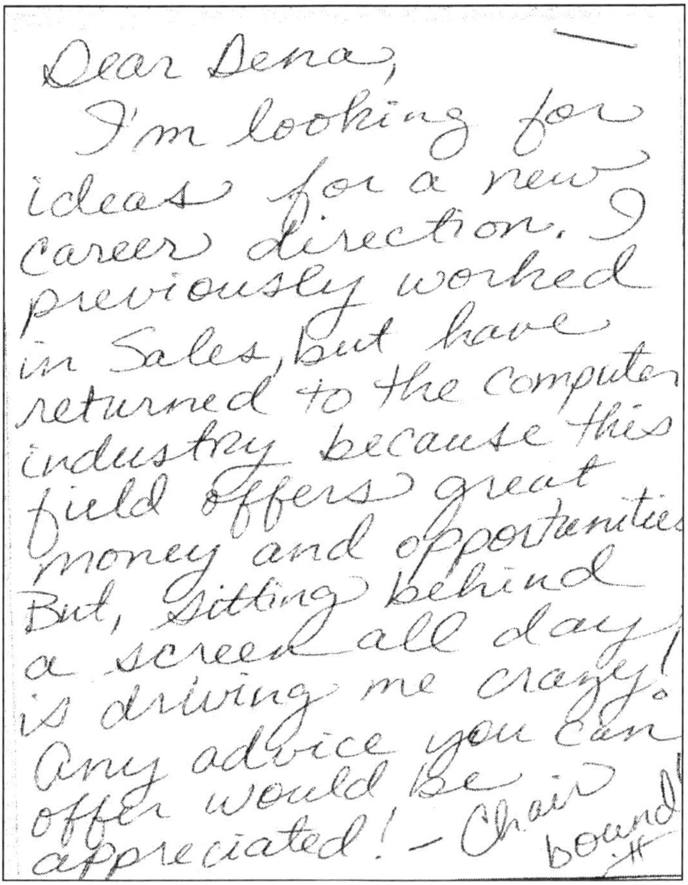
Dear Dena,
I'm looking for
ideas for a new
career direction. I
previously worked
in Sales, but have
returned to the computer
industry because this
field offers great
money and opportunities
But, sitting behind
a screen all day
is driving me crazy!
Any advice you can
offer would be
appreciated! – Chair
bound

Questions:

1. **Is computer work, sales, or teaching best suited to her? Why?**

2. Do you think she will make a change or hold on to what she has? Why?

Answers:

1) Sales or teaching is best suited to her because she likes people (medium to large size, right slant), she can move around, and have various experiences (lower loop dangles into line below). She needs to express her emotions and feelings to people, not primarily machines (large letters, right slant).

2) She will most likely hold onto what she has (ending hooks in key words "offers," "sitting" and "chair") because she lacks ambition (no beginning hooks) and willpower (very weak and low t-bar in "but" and "sitting") and is indecisive (feathery endings to some words).

Q & A # 5

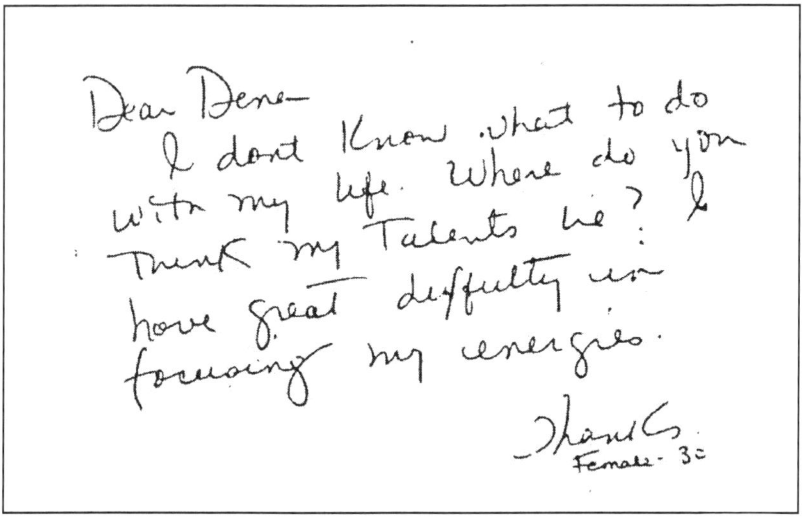
Dear Dene—
I dont Know what to do with my life. Where do you Think my Talents lie? I have great diffulty in focusing my energies.
[illegible]
Female - 3[illegible]

Questions:

1. **What talents and positive traits are revealed in the handwriting?**
2. **Why does she have difficulty focusing?**

Answers:

1) Artistic, creative (printed capitals), writing and speaking ability (figure 8 "g" and fluency strokes), ability to concentrate on long-range study (small middle zone), enthusiasm and self control (long convex t-bars), optimism (rising lines), good determination (firm down-strokes on "y"), works well with people (moderate right slant).

2) She has difficulty focusing because she could be successful in *any* field she chooses. She could go for a Ph.D. in psychology, medicine, run a magazine or newspaper, or be a writer – in the helping and cultural fields.

Q & A # 6

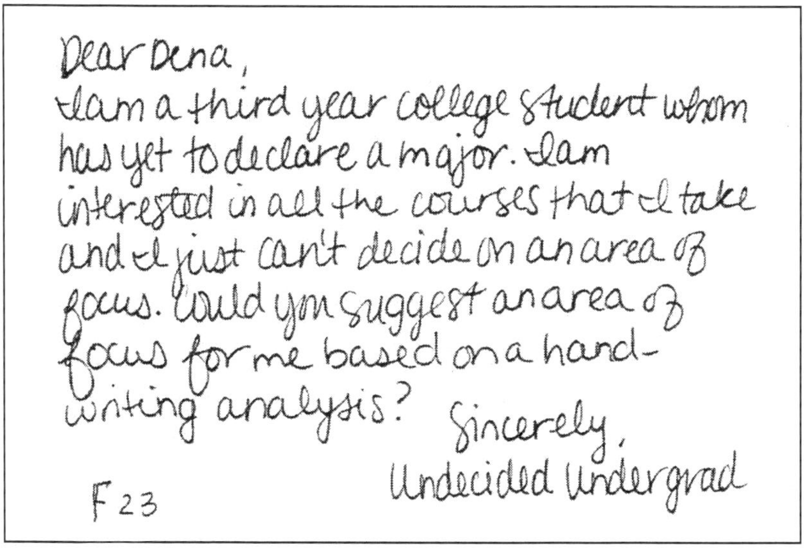
Dear Dena,
I am a third year college student whom has yet to declare a major. I am interested in all the courses that I take and I just can't decide on an area of focus. Could you suggest an area of focus for me based on a hand-writing analysis?
Sincerely,
Undecided Undergrad
F 23

Questions:

1. **Do you believe she is really interested in all the courses?**
2. **If your answer is "negative" where in the handwriting is the clue?**
3. **What kind of work is she best suited to, and why?**
4. **What does the heavy writing indicate?**

5. **Her writing is predominantly middle zone. What does that mean?**
6. **What does her t-bar in "can't" tell you?**

Answers:

1) No.

2) The word following the large space after "am" is what she fears or dislikes so I don't think she's really interested in all of them. There was long hesitation before "interested."

3) Creative writing, art work, working with children (heavy pressure, printed capitals)

4) Passionate, strong feelings, good for art.

5) Concerned with day-to-day goals only.

6) She lacks self-confidence, and has few expectations for self (short t-stem, low t-bar).

Q & A # 7

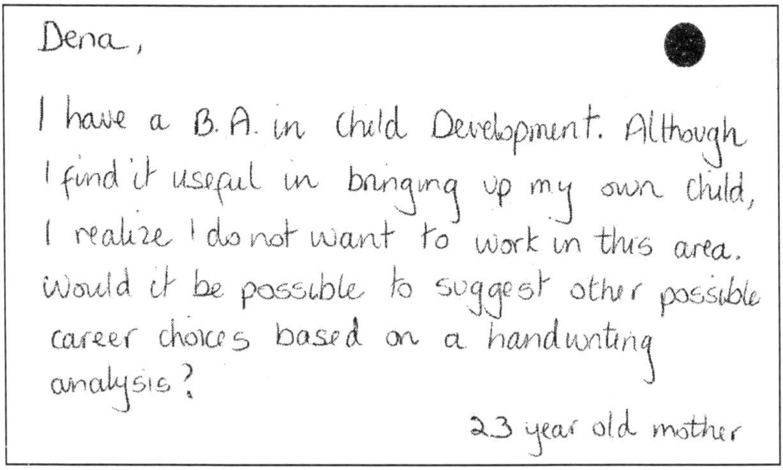
Dena,

I have a B.A. in Child Development. Although I find it useful in bringing up my own child, I realize I do not want to work in this area. Would it be possible to suggest other possible career choices based on a handwriting analysis?

23 year old mother

Question:

1. **What career choices would you suggest for her?**

Answer:

1) Art therapy; photography; arts and crafts for children; interior design.

Q & A # 8

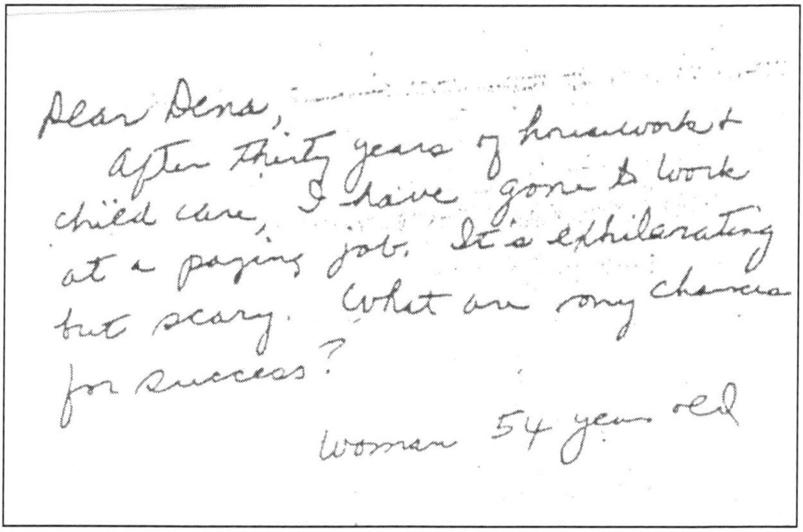

Dear Dena,
After thirty years of housework & child care, I have gone to work at a paying job. It's exhilarating but scary. What are my chances for success?

Woman 54 years old

Question:

1. **What traits indicate that she should not worry?**

Answer:

1) She has good confidence, realistic goals (strong t-bars high on stem), good determination (good down-strokes on "y"), enthusiasm (long t-bars), ability to concentrate (small middle zone letters), optimism (rising t-bars), emotional maturity (rhythm, balance on page, space between letters, words, lines, no beginning strokes, moderate right slant). Only one drawback: she is a little too sensitive to criticism (large loop on "d"), especially about her age.

Q & A # 9

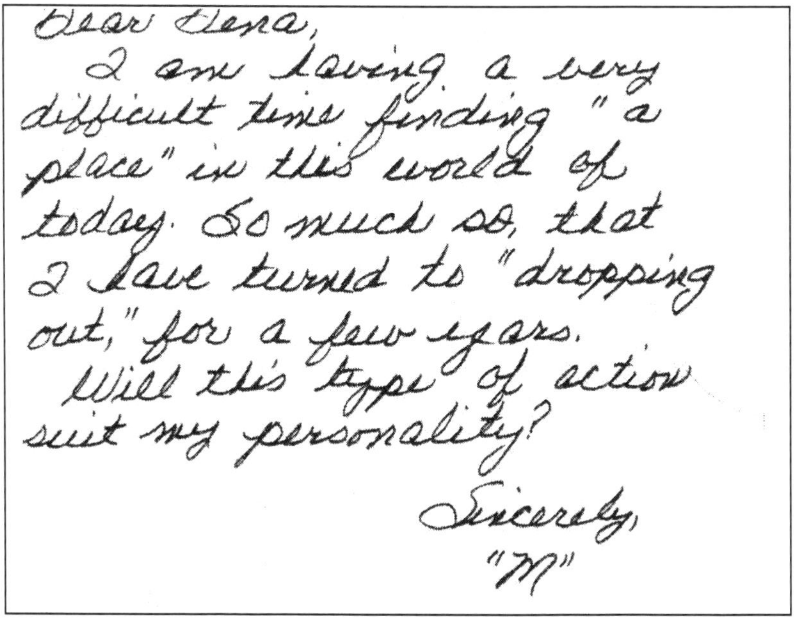
Dear Dena,
I am having a very difficult time finding "a place" in this world of today. So much so, that I have turned to "dropping out," for a few years.
Will this type of action suit my personality?
Sincerely,
"M"

Questions:

1. **Is "dropping out" good for him? If yes, what are your reasons?**
2. **What do the wide spaces between words as well as retraced "h" suggest?**

Answers:

1) Yes. We don't know if the writer is male or female and his/her age, and we don't know exactly what "dropping out" really entails, but I would say yes, for awhile. The writer is not a fighter and is not competitive (no angular letter joining). He or she is searching philosophically (pointed upper loops), is rather rigid or inhibited (slow

retraced strokes), deep strong feelings (heavy pressure), resentful (beginning stroke on "will"), not wishing to take on a lot of responsibility (no loop on capital "I"), is very different somehow in beliefs and actions (reversed loop in "y" in "years"), and very self-conscious about something (last hum on "m" and "n" higher).

2) S/he also wants or needs more personal space (wide space between words), and there is repression of strong feelings (retraced "h"), which he/she feels a need to express (all right slant). If the time is spent on learning about him/her self or spirituality, I would say yes.

Q & A # 10

Dear Dena:

Help! I'm a recent grad, and ~~althoo~~ although
I struggled really hard to get through
school as a mom and wife - commuting
long distances to finish my education
I'm finding it difficult to muster
up the confidence to get out there
and do it! I've gotten a good job,
but not in the field of my study.
I've taken little steps like ~~to~~ obtaining
a business license so I can get
going in the right direction, but
finding it hard to commit the time
needed to get a business going &
work 40-hours without neglecting
my family. It wasn't easy to
justify less time with the family
to finish school, and finding
it even harder now. I'm dissatisfied
with the pace. Am I expecting too
much, am I stalling or just afraid?

- Estring

Questions:

1. **What does the large right border tell you, and what does she fear?**

2. In what key words does she show depression?
3. What other traits are holding her back?
4. Is she optimistic, pessimistic or both? Is she moody?
5. Is business good for her?

Answers:

1) The first thing I notice is of course, the large right border that begins and ends in normal width, with a deep curve in between. The left border also wavers but not as much. The right border is, on the whole, abnormally wide—meaning a fear of people and the future. She fears she can't justify the time away from family (word after space after "to") and she fears "finding it even harder."

2) She shows depression in drooping key words "education," "family," "license," "time needed," "stalling," "direction."

3) Other traits holding her back are procrastination (t-bar to left of stem), weak will (light t-bar in "neglecting", lack of confidence (low t-bar in "distances", "but", "not" desire to give up (concave t-bar in "commuting", "without", "expecting" and "dissatisfied").

4) She begins optimistically but becomes pessimistic (convex lines).

5) Business **is good for her** because she needs to work for herself; she is much too sensitive to criticism (large loop on "d" in "good") to work under someone, she has a good mind (analytical–angular strokes), intuitive (breaks between letters); she works efficiently (fluency strokes

of joining one letter to the next); she is determined (good down-strokes on "y" and "g") and stubborn (wedge in "t" in "but"). But it is **not good** for her because she has weak will for setting goals, is too fearful, is under a lot of stress and is very irritable (dashes for dots), feels like giving up, and worst of all, lacks confidence (low and weak t-bars). Is she expecting too much, is she stalling, or just afraid? I would say all three. And for good reason; business demands a lot and to be successful one does sacrifice family somewhat. It's a choice.

Q & A # 11

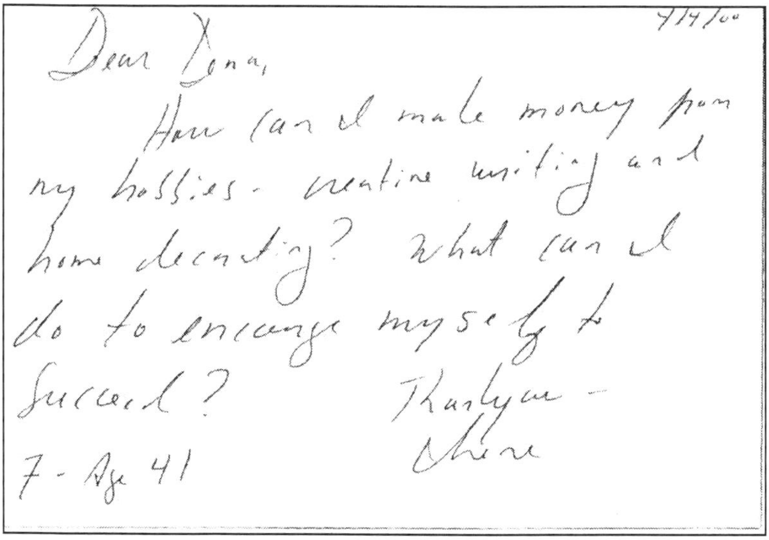

7/14/00

Dear Dena,

How can I make money from my hobbies - creative writing and home decorating? What can I do to encourage myself to succeed?

Thank you -
Cherie

7 - Age 41

Questions:

1. **Name at least five outstanding traits—four very positive and one very negative.**

2. **What does she unconsciously fear?**

Answers:

1) **Positive outstanding traits:** strong intuition (breaks between letters, great imagination (large lower loops), cultural interests (Greek "s"), artistic and creative (printed capitals), aesthetic sense (good spacing between letters, words, lines, and page) writing talent (figure 8 "g" and fluency strokes), diplomacy (tapering words), open and honest frankness (open and clean "o" and "a") good determination (long down-strokes on "g"), ability to work alone (down-stroke on "y" with no loop), ability to concentrate (small to tiny middle zone), analytical and logical thinking processes (rounded and angular "m" and "n"), and sense of humor (beginning stroke on "m" and "w"). Her one very negative trait: very little confidence and very little self-esteem.

   Negative outstanding traits: Very little belief in herself (extremely low t-bars) – resulting in weak will (light t-bars), pessimism (drooping last letters of key words "myself" and "succeed"), and the tendency to give up (concave t-bar in "to").

2) What she fears is success itself (the word following the large space after "to" is what she fears – and it is "succeed").

Q & A # 12

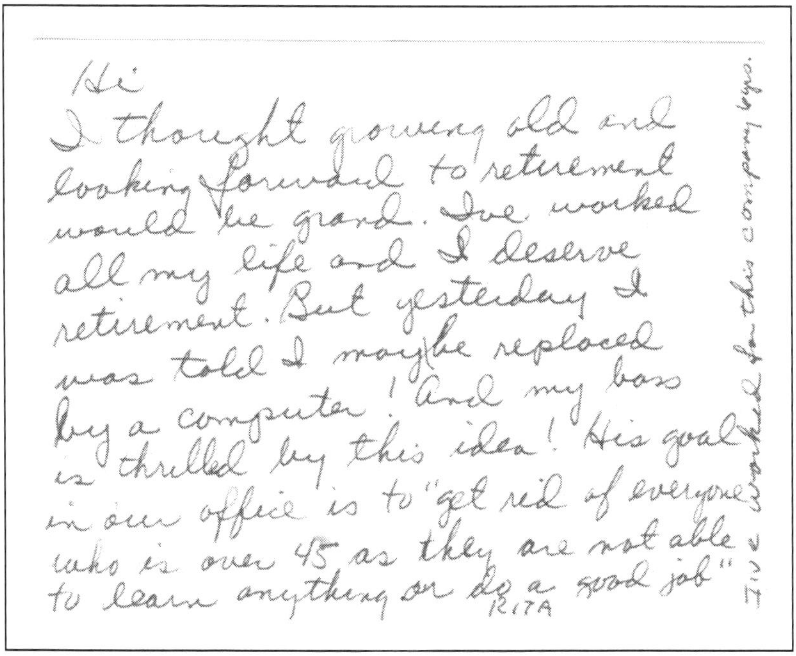
Hi
I thought growing old and
looking forward to retirement
would be grand. I've worked
all my life and I deserve
retirement. But yesterday I
was told I may be replaced
by a computer! And my boss
is thrilled by this idea! His goal
in our office is to "get rid of everyone
who is over 45 as they are not able
to learn anything or do a good job"
RITA
I've worked for this company 6 yrs.

Questions:

1. **What two traits could make it difficult for her to work under a boss?**
2. **What is the meaning of the patched capital "I in 4th line?**

Answers:

1) The strong sensitivity to criticism (large loop on "d" and "t") and a desire to do things her way (some down-turned t-bars).

2) She enlarged the loop on capital "I." On an unconscious level she was trying to bolster her feeling of low self-worth indicated in the original tiny capital "I."

Q & A # 13

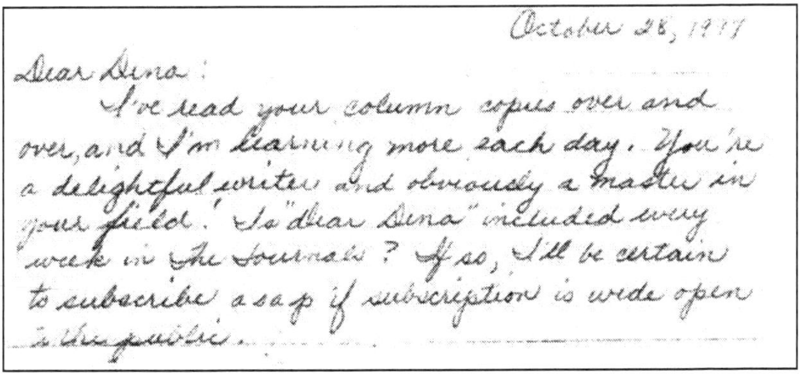
October 28, 1997

Dear Dina:

I've read your column copies over and over, and I'm learning more each day. You're a delightful writer and obviously a master in your field. Is "dear Dina" included every week in The Journal? If so, I'll be certain to subscribe a.s.a.p. if subscription is wide open to the public.

Question:

1. **What kind of work do you think the writer is suited to?**

Answer:

1) Any of the helping fields: teaching, nursing, social work, massage therapist, various therapies for the body and mind.

CHAPTER EIGHTEEN

Careers of Well-known Personalities – and Their Handwriting

Knowing the careers of famous and infamous people, it's interesting to see if their handwriting matches their peronalities and their choice of work. Generally speaking, those wishing to be in the spotlight, like entertainers, have large and heavy handwriting. More modest persons and thinkers have a predominantly small script. Before voting for our politicians, wouldn't it be great if we had not only their signatures, but a significant sample of their ordinary handwriting, as well? I prefer not to analyze a signature without at least a modest handwriting specimen in addition to it, as analysis of the signature alone can yield an erroneous interpretation of the writer's personality and character. However, I have done so in instances in which such additional specimens were simply unavailable to me and the writers were prominent or interesting in some way. Below are some signatures which match their specimens, and others which differ radically:

Specimen "A" (Joan Baez) & Specimen "B" (Thomas Edison)

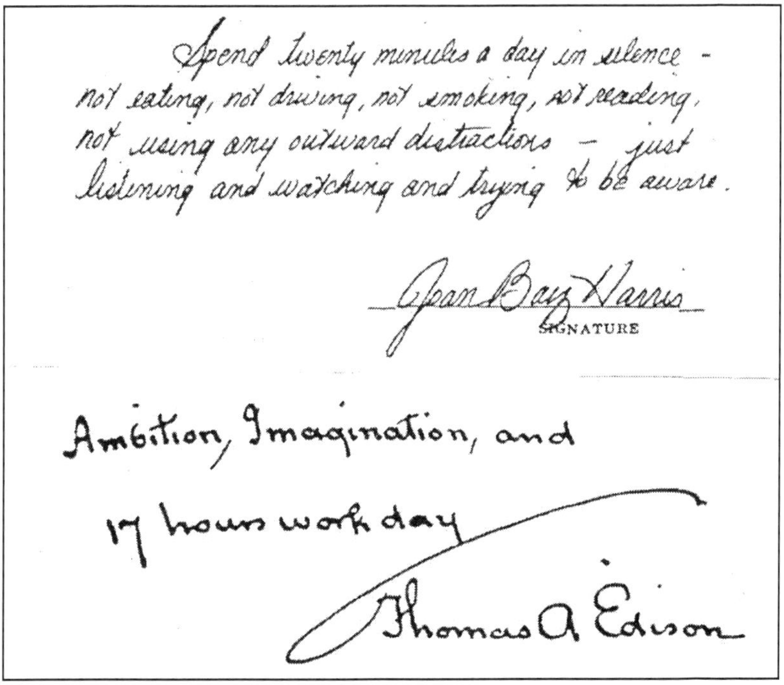
Spend twenty minutes a day in silence - not eating, not drinking, not smoking, not reading, not using any outward distractions - just listening and watching and trying to be aware.
Joan Baez Harris
SIGNATURE
Ambition, Imagination, and
17 hours work day
Thomas A. Edison

Specimen "C-1" (Mahatma Ghandi)

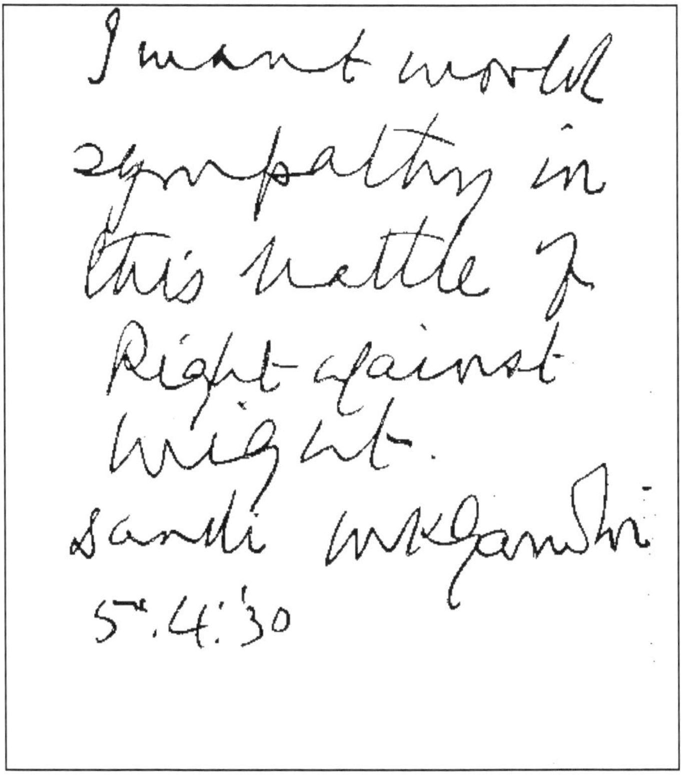
I want world
sympathy in
this battle of
Right against
Might.
Dandi M K Gandhi
5.4.'30

Note, in specimen "C-1" above, the strong self-control (convex t-bars) over his anger and temper (t-bars to right of stem). In the slower and more careful writing below, temper is present while self-control is not evident.

Specimen "C-2" Gandhi

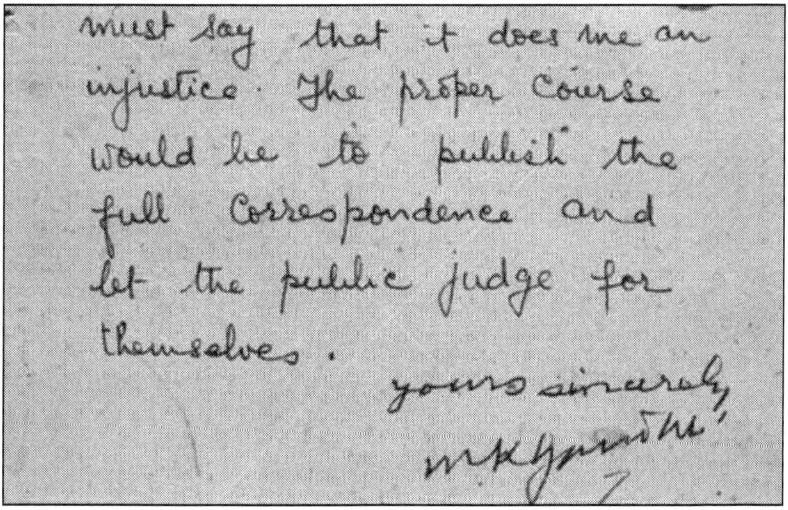
must say that it does me an injustice. The proper course would be to publish the full correspondence and let the public judge for themselves.

yours sincerely,

M K Gandhi

Specimen "D" (actual size)
(Albert Einstein)

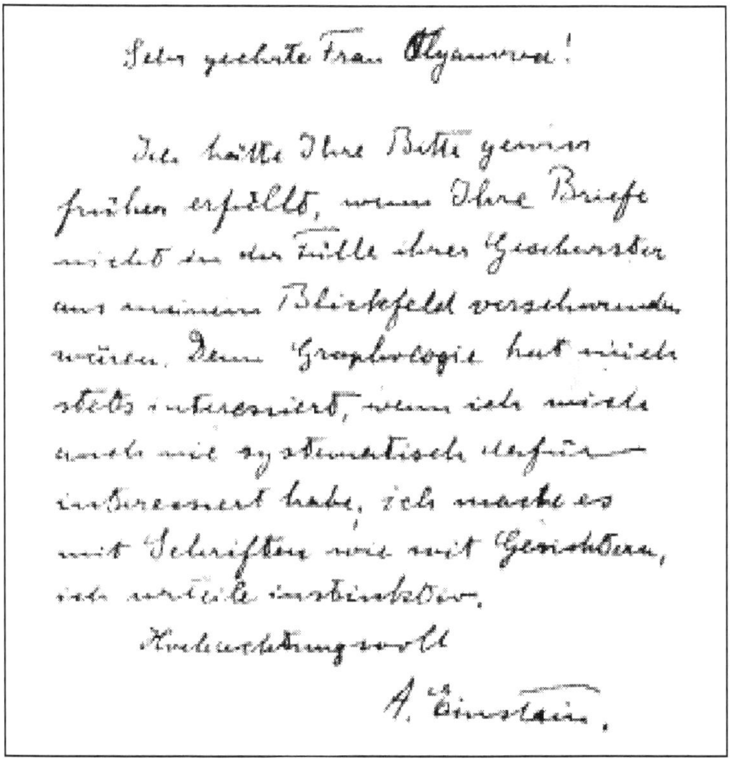

Sehr geehrte Frau Olyanova!

Ich hätte Ihre Bitte gewiss
früher erfüllt, wenn Ihre Briefe
nicht in der Fülle ihrer Geschäfte
aus meinem Blickfeld verschwunden
wären. Denn Graphologie hat mich
stets interessiert, wenn ich mich
auch nie systematisch dafür
interessiert habe, ich mache es
mit Schriften wie mit Gesichtern,
ich urteile instinktiv.

Hochachtungsvoll

A. Einstein.

Specimen "E" (Mother Teresa)

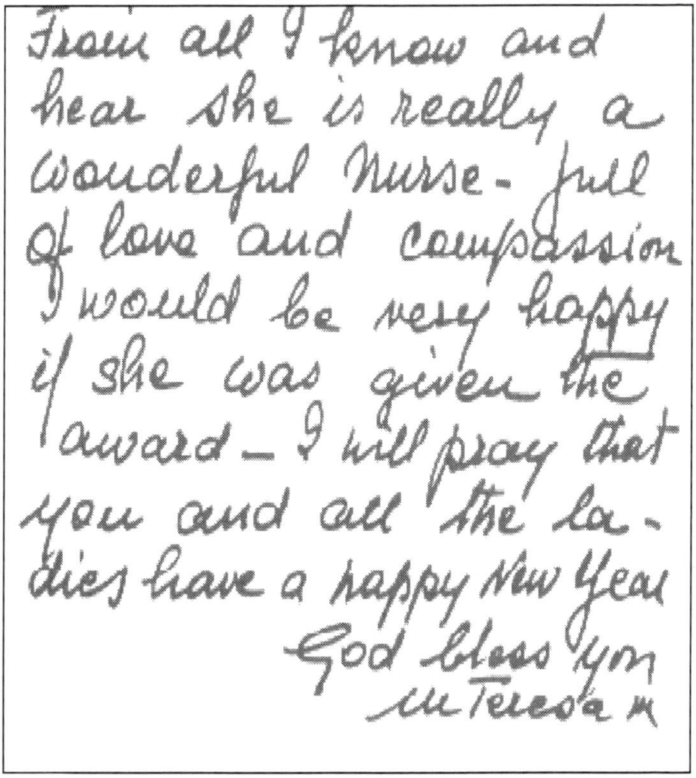

From all I know and hear she is really a wonderful Nurse - full of love and compassion I would be very happy if she was given the award - I will pray that you and all the ladies have a happy New Year

God bless you
M Teresa M

Specimen "F-1" (Charles Dickens)

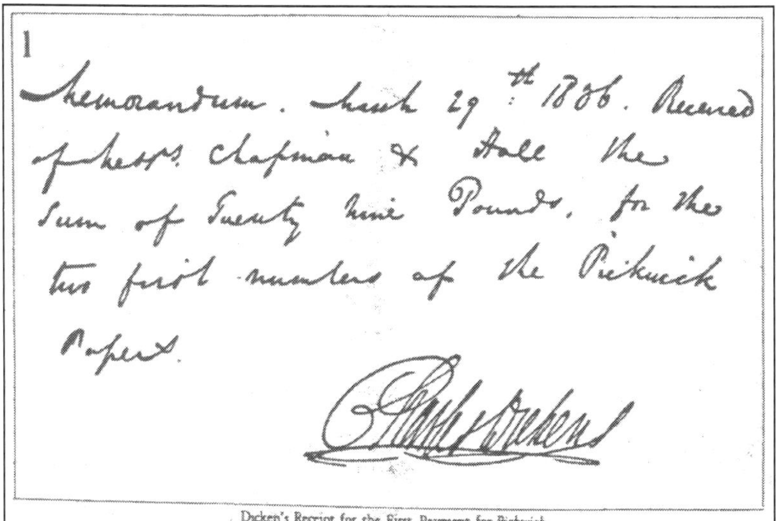

1

Memorandum. March 29th 1836. Received of Mess.rs Chapman & Hall the sum of Twenty nine Pounds, for the two first numbers of the Pickwick Papers.

Charles Dickens

Dicken's Receipt for the First Payment for *Pickwick*.

Specimen "F-2" (Charles Dickens)

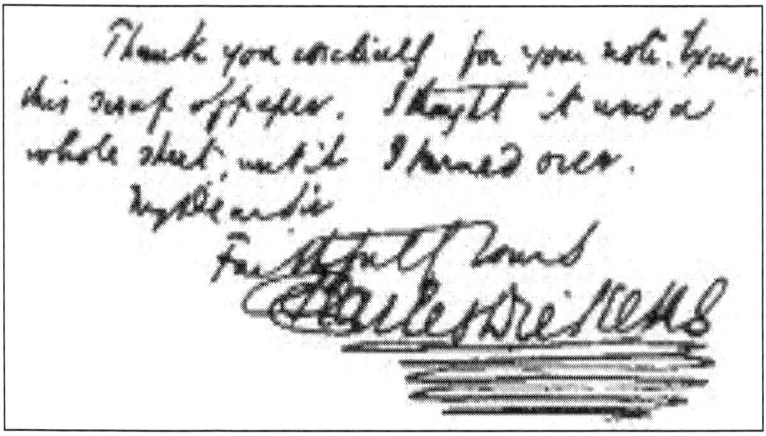

Thank you cordially for your note. [illegible] this scrap of paper. I thought it was a whole sheet, until I turned over.

My dear Sir

Faithfully Yours

Charles Dickens

Specimen "G" Simon Wiesenthal

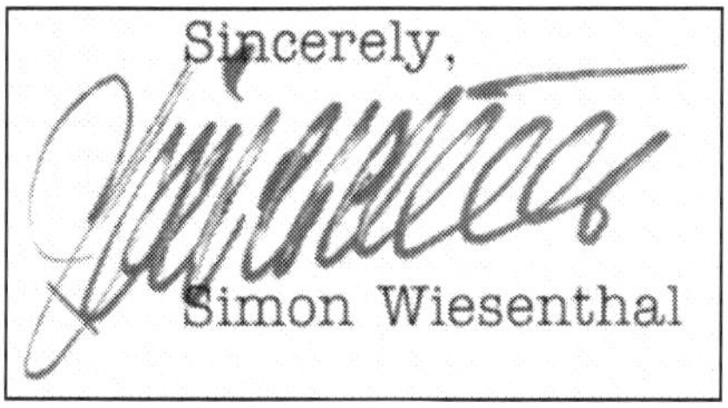

Handwritings and Signatures of Some Presidents

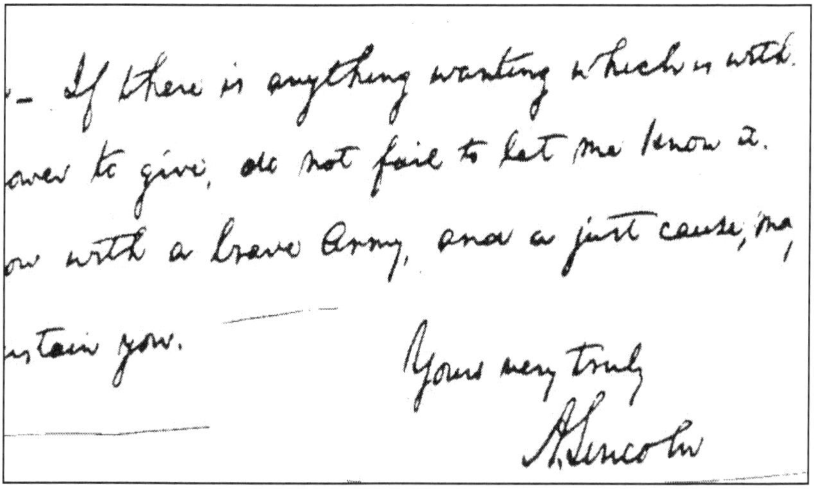
– If there is anything wanting which is with
ower to give, do not fail to let me know it.
ow with a brave Army, and a just cause, ma
stain you.

Yours very truly
A. Lincoln

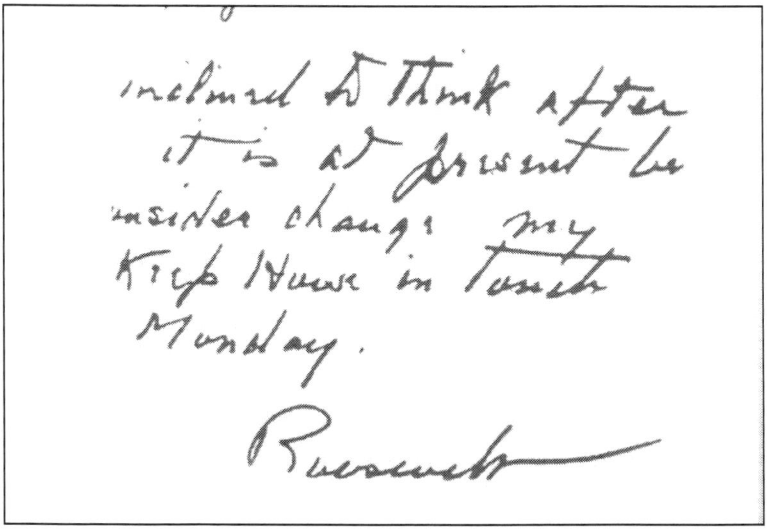
inclined to think after
it is at present be
consider change my
keep House in Town
Monday.

Roosevelt

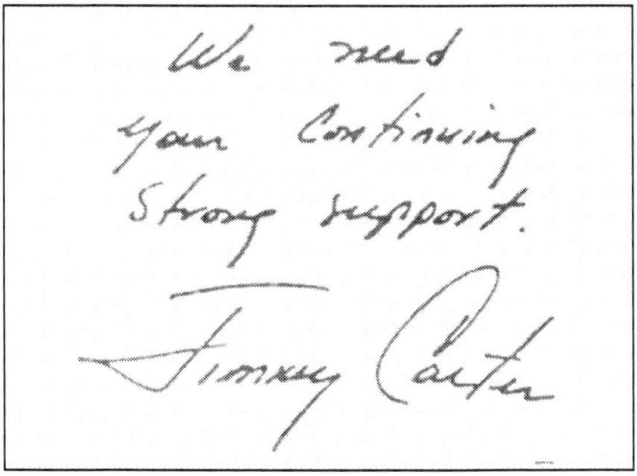
We need
your continuing
strong support.

Jimmy Carter

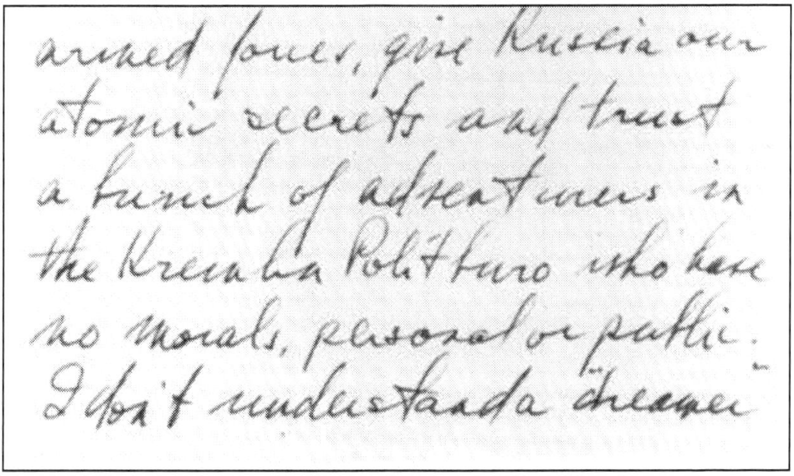

armed forces, give Russia our atomic secrets and trust a bunch of adventurers in the Kremlin Politburo who have no morals, personal or public. I don't understand a "dreamer"

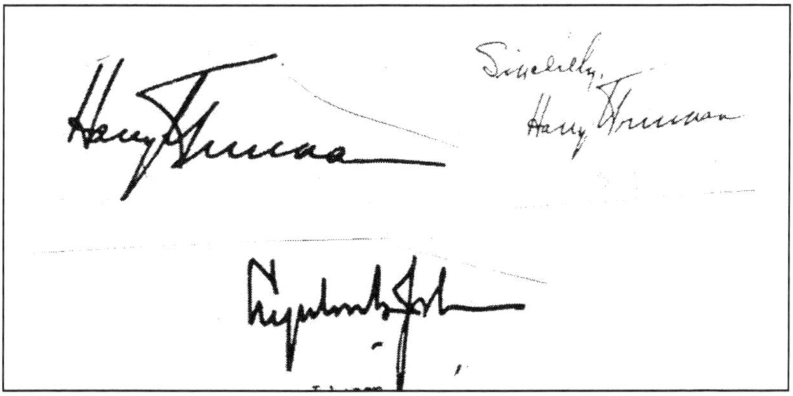

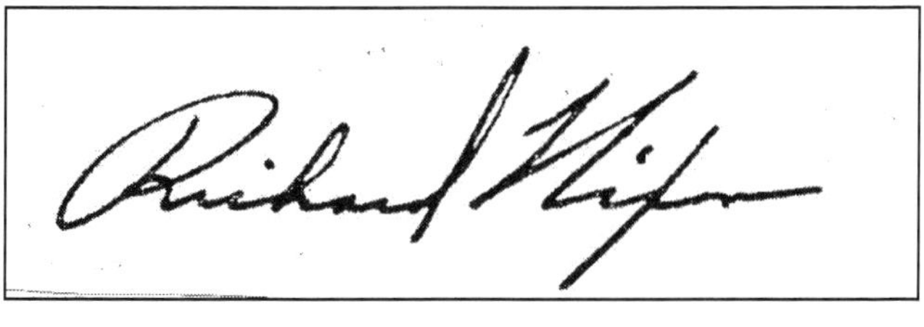

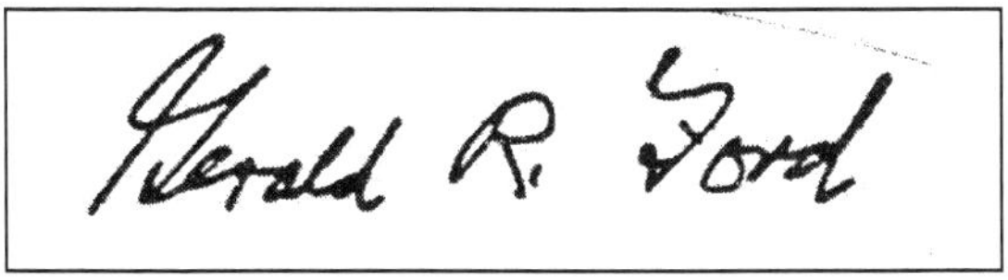

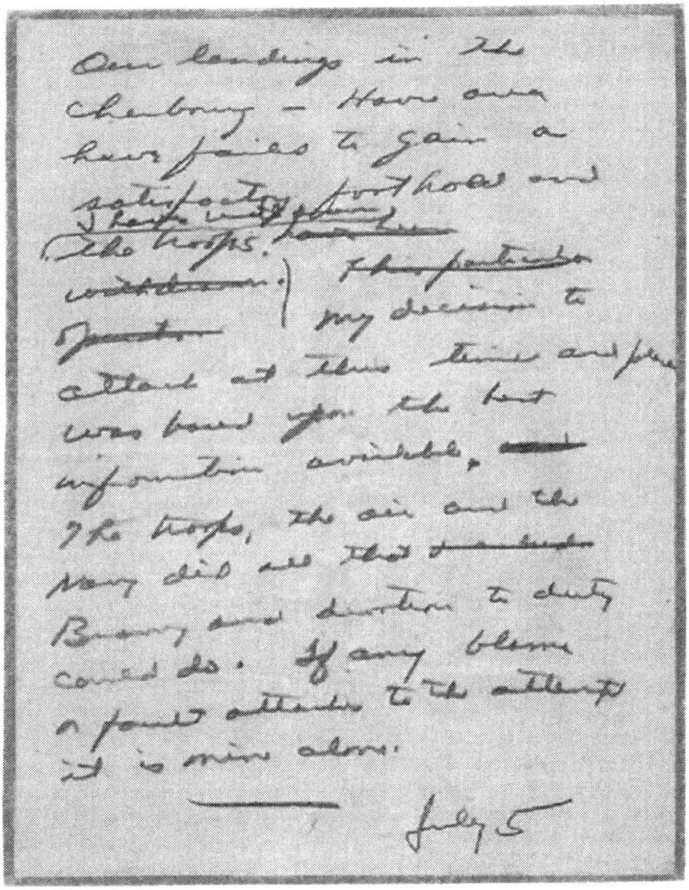

Our landings in the Cherbourg – Havre area have failed to gain a satisfactory foothold and the troops. my decision to attack at this time and place was based upon the best information available. The troops, the air and the Navy did all that Bravery and devotion to duty could do. If any blame or fault attaches to the attempt it is mine alone.

July 5

Dwight Eisenhower

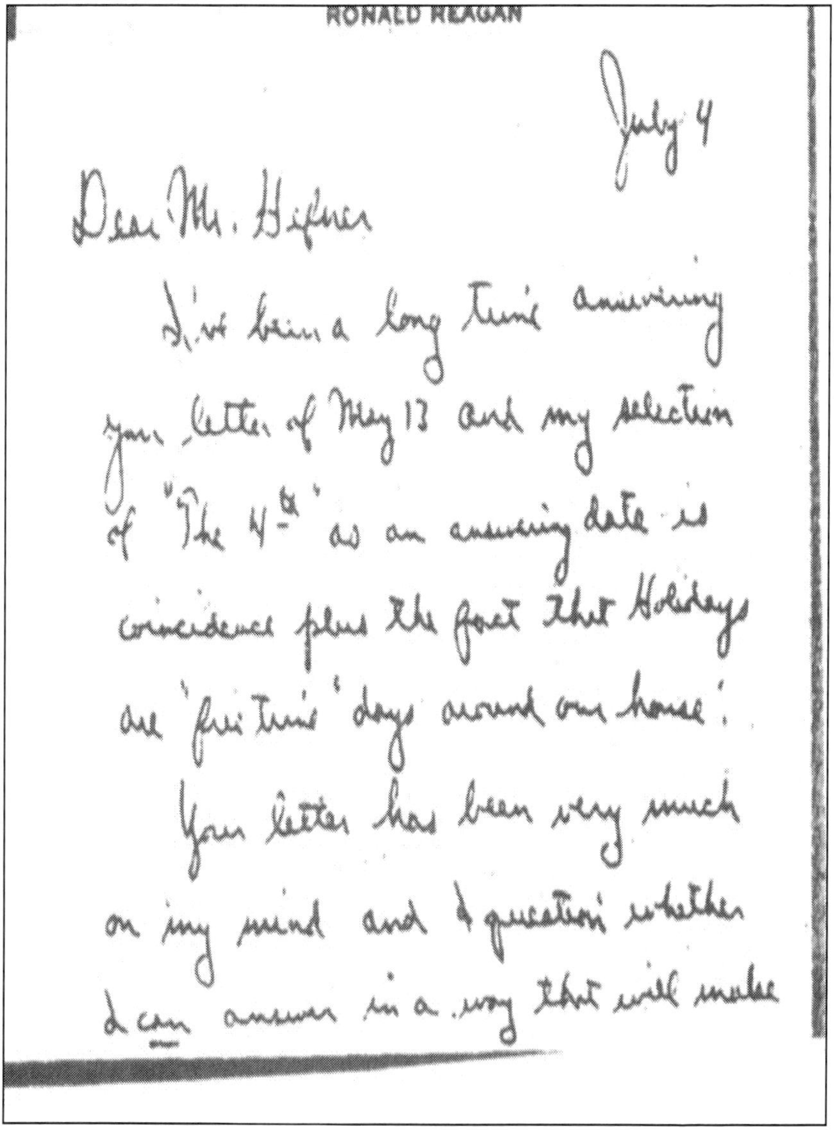

RONALD REAGAN

July 4

Dear Mr. Hefner

It's been a long time answering your letter of May 13 and my selection of "The 4th" as an answering date is coincidence plus the fact that Holidays are 'free time' days around our house.

Your letter has been very much on my mind and I question whether I can answer in a way that will make

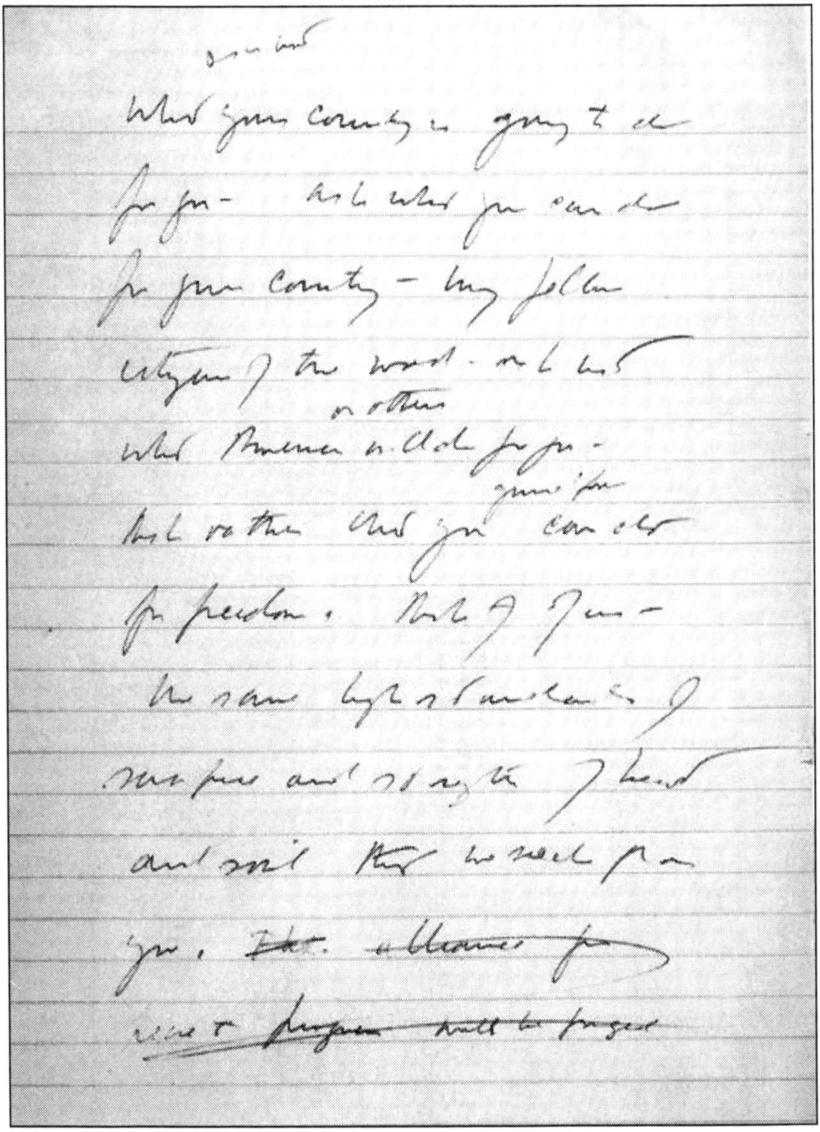
What your country is going to do
for you – ask what you can do
for your country – my fellow
citizens of the world – ask not
what America will do for you –
ask rather what you can do
for freedom.

John F. Kennedy

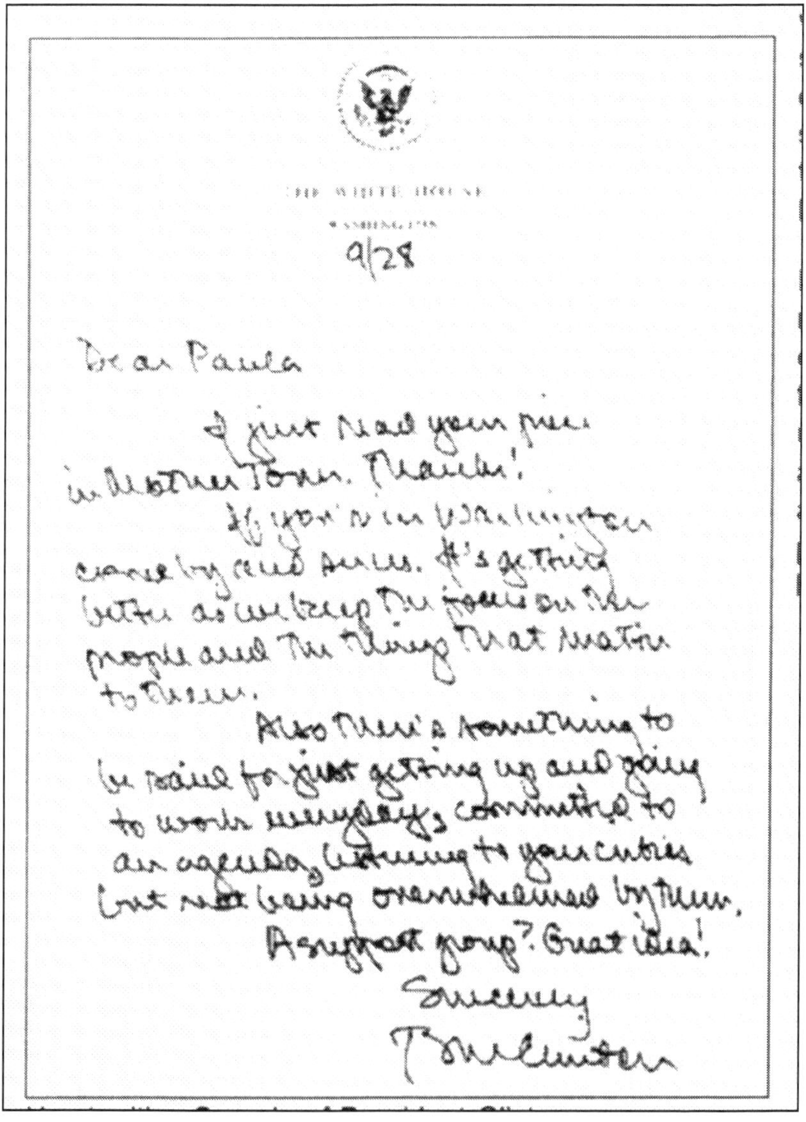

THE WHITE HOUSE
WASHINGTON

9/28

Dear Paula

I just read your piece in Mother Jones. Thanks!

If you're in Washington come by and see us. It's getting better as we keep the focus on the people and the things that matter to them.

Also there's something to be said for just getting up and going to work everyday, committed to an agenda, listening to your critics but not being overwhelmed by them.

A support group? Great idea!

Sincerely
Bill Clinton

Bill Clinton

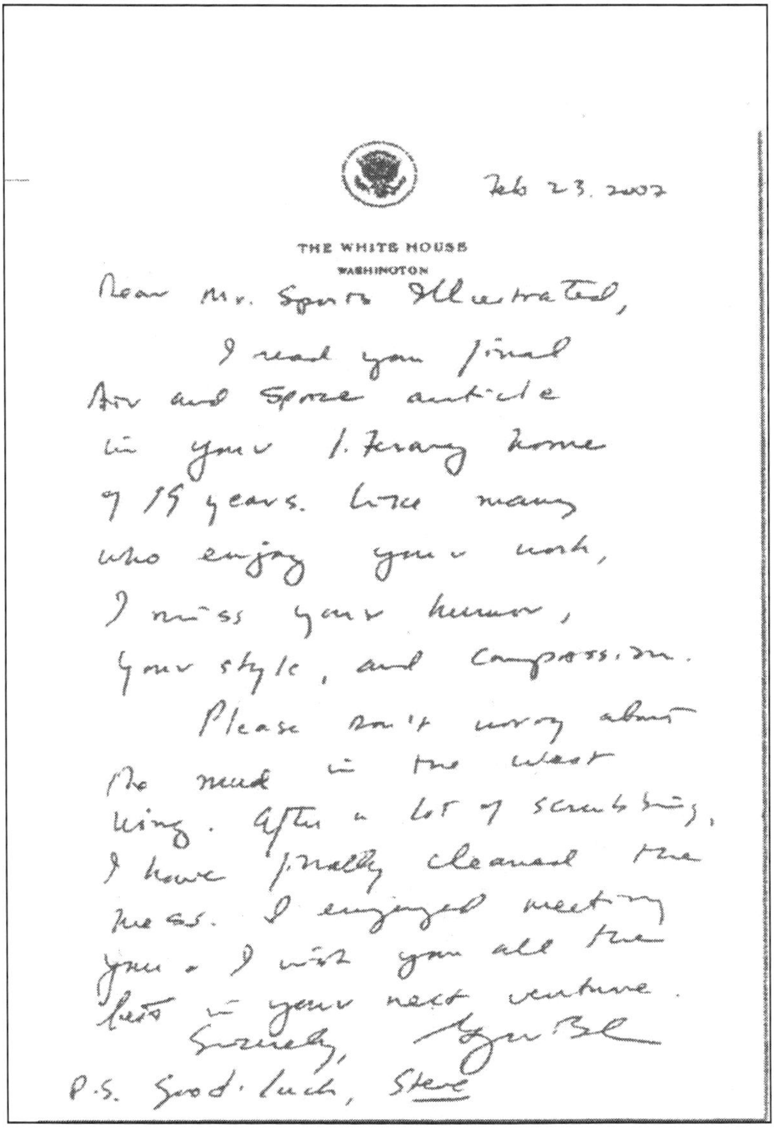

Feb 23, 2007

THE WHITE HOUSE
WASHINGTON

Dear Mr. Sports Illustrated,

I read your final Air and Space article in your literary home of 15 years. Like many who enjoy your work, I miss your humor, your style, and compassion.

Please don't worry about the mud in the West Wing. After a lot of scrubbing, I have finally cleaned the mess. I enjoyed meeting you & I wish you all the best in your next venture.

Sincerely, George Bush

P.S. Good luck, Steve

George W. Bush

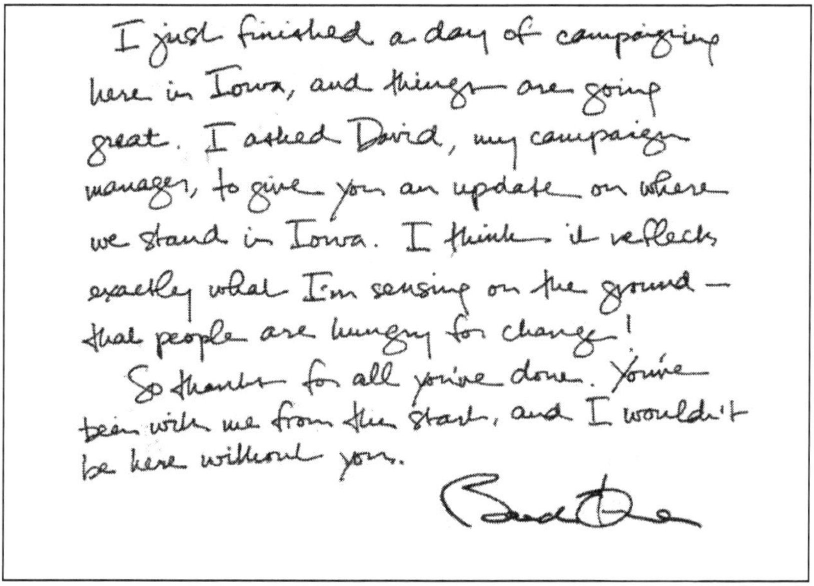
I just finished a day of campaigning here in Iowa, and things are going great. I asked David, my campaign manager, to give you an update on where we stand in Iowa. I think it reflects exactly what I'm sensing on the ground — that people are hungry for change!

So thanks for all you've done. You've been with me from the start, and I wouldn't be here without you.

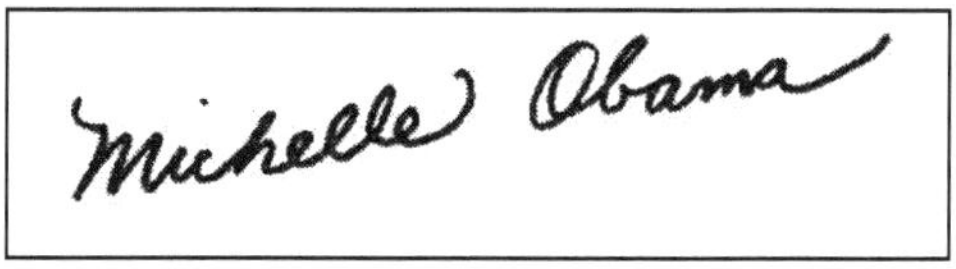

Barack Obama
Michelle Obama

Various Other Politicians (below)

Writers, Musicians, and Scientists

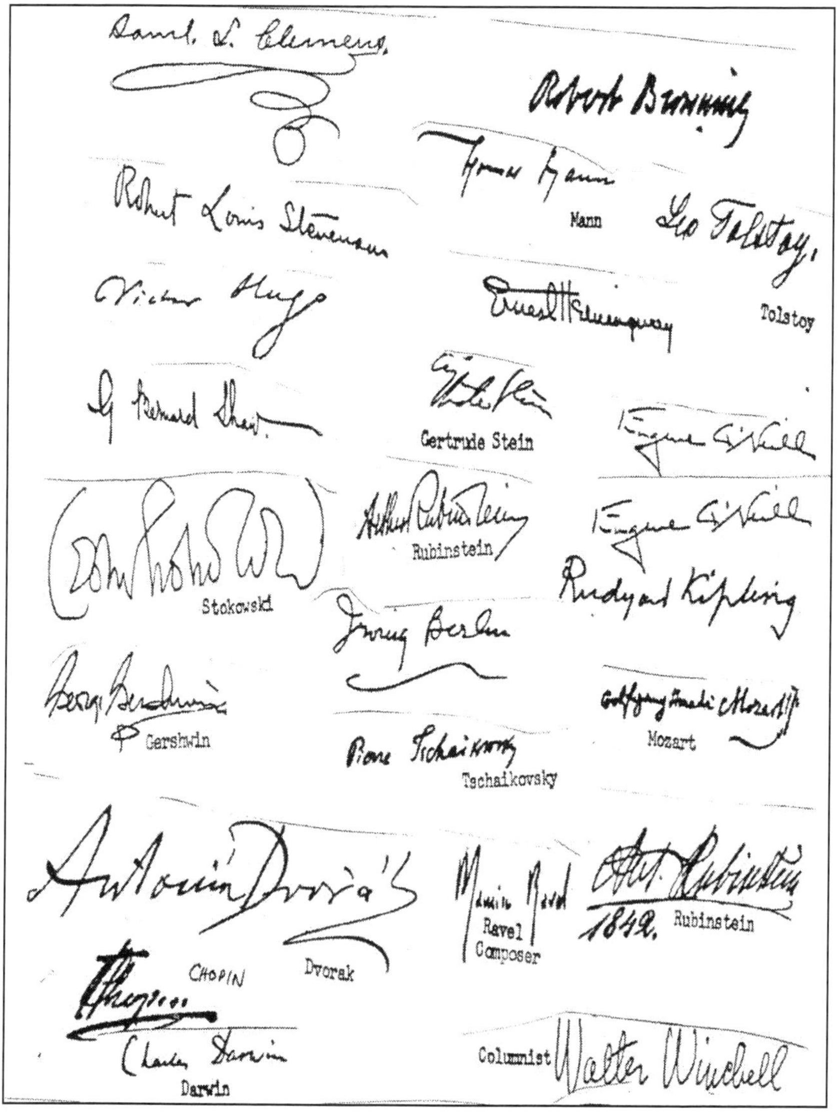

Actors, Artists, Singers, and Dancers – people on stage (signatures reduced 25%)
Note: all (except directors Bergman, Chaplin, and Robinson) have **large** and/or **heavy** writing.

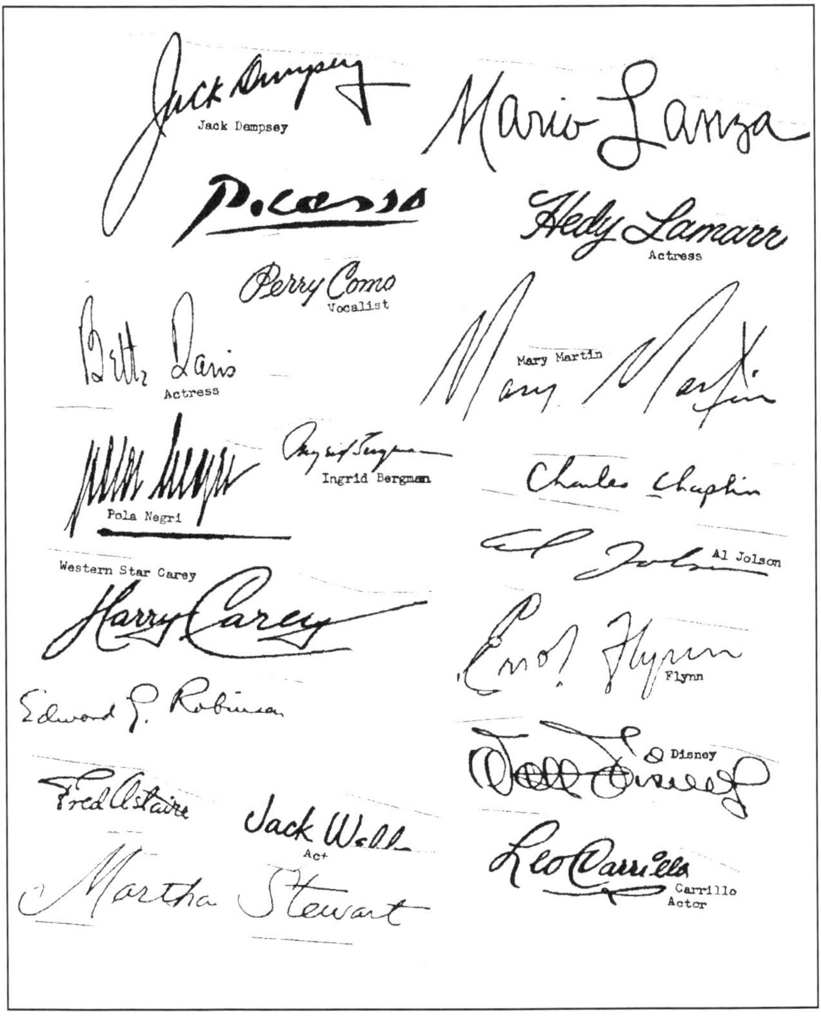

Leaders Who Have Shaken the World in Various Ways

[**Note:** Unfortunately, I have no signatures of those of Asian or Middle Eastern leaders.]

Others Who Greatly Influenced the World in Various Ways (a short list)

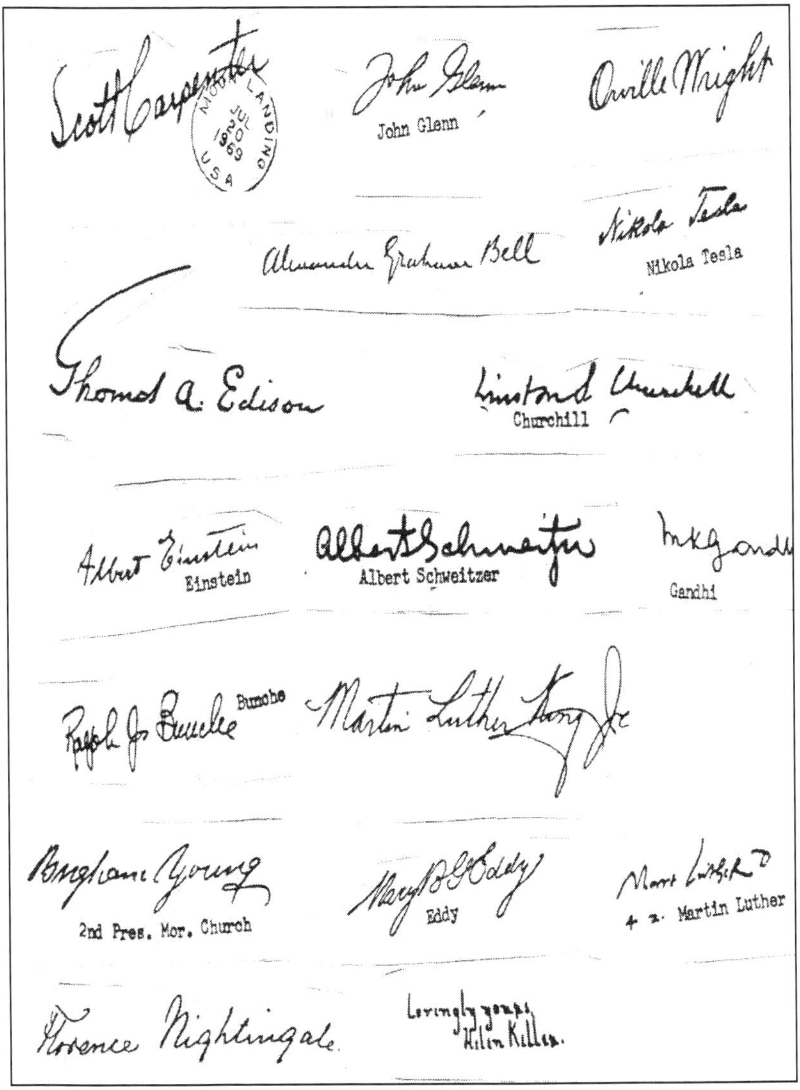

Suggested Reading

Handwriting Analysis in Business: The Use of Graphology in Personnel Selection, by Noel Currer Briggs

Making Vocational Choices by John Holland

Dyslexia---A Beginner's Guide by Nicola Brunswick

Website: Bright Solutions , Inc.

How to Detect and Manage Dyslexia: A Reference and Resource Manual by Philomena Ott

Emotional Intelligence: Why It Can Matter More Than IQ by Daniel Coleman

Do What You Are: Discover the Perfect Career for You Through the Secrets of Personality Type by Barbara Baron Tieger

The Pathfinder: How to Choose or Change Your Career for a Lifetime of Satisfaction and Success by Nick Lore

APPENDIX

Basic Graphology

Brain-writing – The "A," "B," and "C" of It

A **slant** to the right is toward people and the future. To the left, fear of people (getting hurt emotionally), seen in teenage girls as well as adults.

A **slight slant to the right** is considered mentally healthy. It's the writing of a trusting person, responsive to others, willing to risk being hurt.

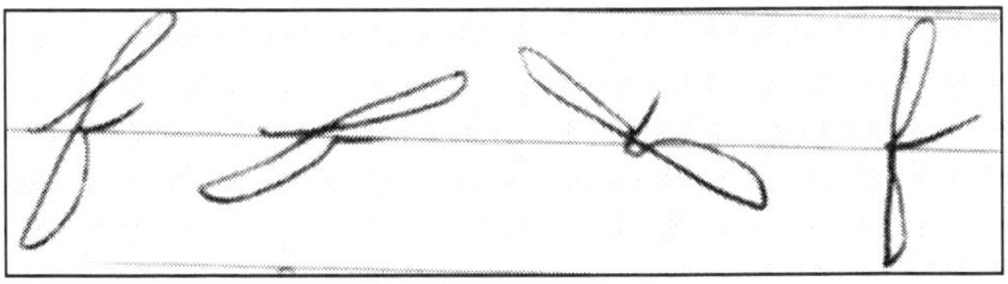

Very far to the right – too impulsive, too hysterical. **Backward slant,** you fear to reach out emotionally. Extremely ***far to the left,*** you'll need some professional help. **Straight up and down?** You're cool, calm, and collected, objective, unemotional.

Lines or words slanting down – pessimism, sadness, depression. If the slant is severe, the writer may need medical help. **Lines slanting upward –** graded from optimism, to seeing with rose-colored glasses, to the extreme of manic.

"A pessimist sees the difficulty in every opportunity;

an optimist sees the opportunity in every difficulty."
– Sir Winston Churchill

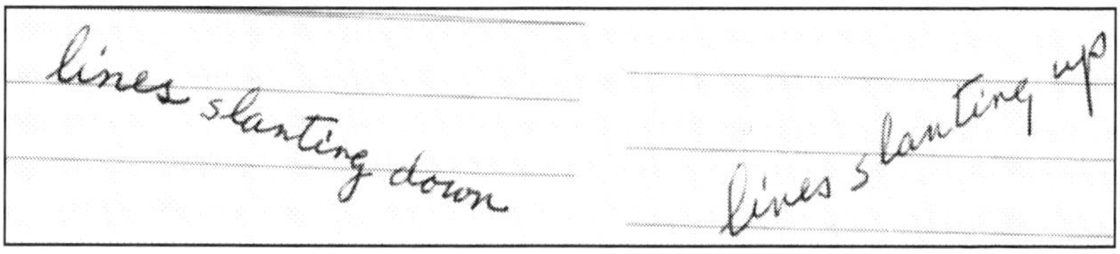

Tiny writing – 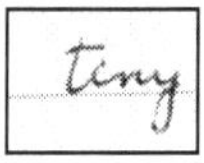

– the absent-minded professor. He concentrates so hard he doesn't see or hear what's around him. (Einstein, researchers.)

Large writing – Aware of one's surroundings and other people (actors, singers, and people who wish to be in the limelight, for example, write in large letters).

The middle-zone letters "m, n. i, e, a, o, r, s, r" represent mundane, everyday life. The **size of the middle zone letters** compared to the upper and lower loops denotes what is either dominant or balanced in the personality make-up.

Almost balanced zones – balanced interests, balanced personality:

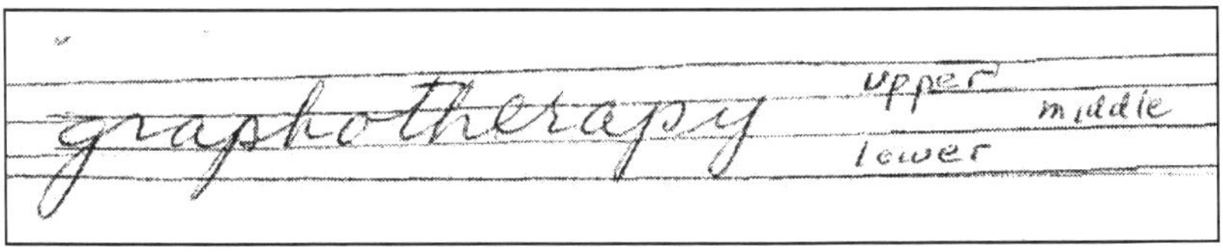

Predominantly Upper Zone – Interest in the abstract, religion, philosophy dominates:

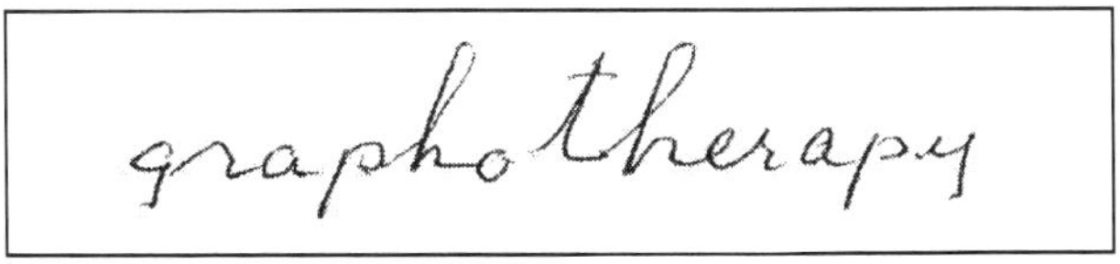

Predominantly Lower Zone – interested in material, physical projects, and sexual activity:

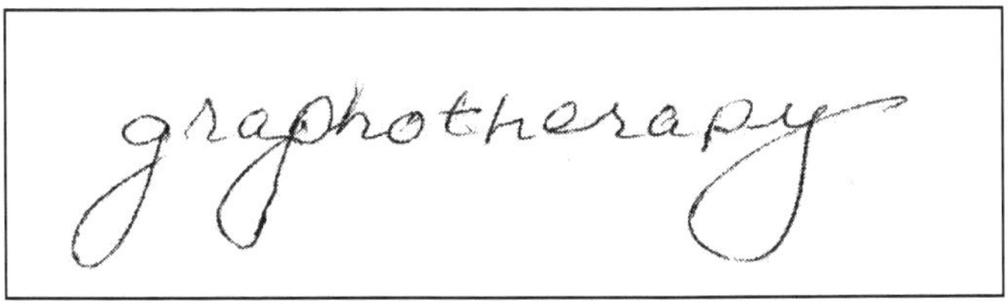

Predominantly Middle Zone – interested mainly in day-to-day living and its requirements.

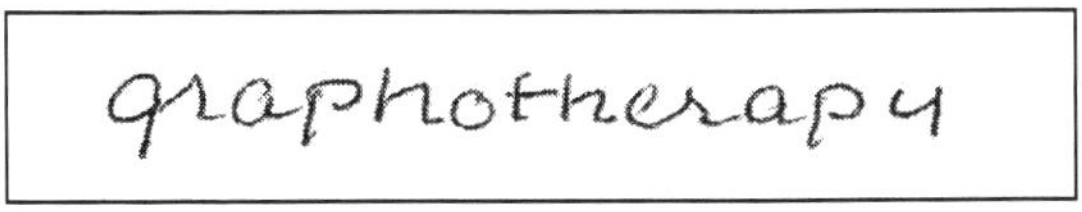

In *all* zones, loops denote imagination. **Loops in the upper zone:** interest in abstract ideas philosophical, spiritual, and psychological, often attended by oversensitivity to criticism. This latter trait can be seen in the loop of a small "d":

Upper loop "l" in various height and width:

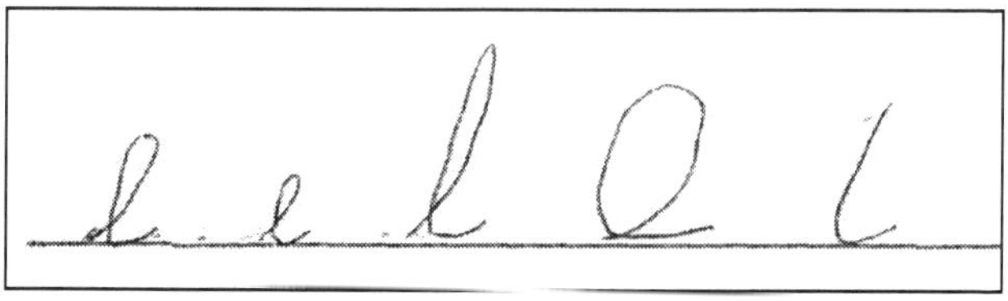

Lower-zone letters and some of their various forms:

Loops in the lower zone denote ideas in the material world (projects) as well as sexual vitality or sexual inhibitions, depending on the length, strength, shape (round, angular) and its direction (down, right or left), completed, or left unfinished. Lower-zone endings may also be without loops, reversed, or hooked, as in the above, each with special meanings.

Loop "e" in middle zone: wide denotes open-mindedness, narrow closed-mindedness:

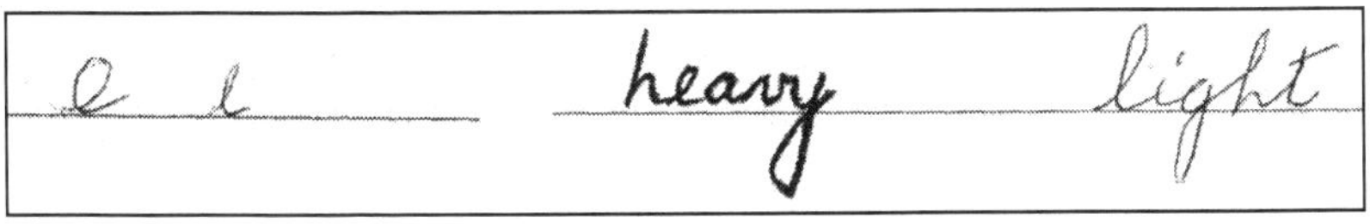

Pressure: thick and/or heavy pressure, where the writing makes indentations onto pages below it, denotes profoundly powerful emotions and feelings held in for a long time before suddenly bursting forth, often seen in artists, musicians, etc. **Thin and/or light pressure** – the writer responds immediately with emotion and then forgets it just as fast.

And now the **baseline**. It represents reality, normality, or society's norms. Is it straight or wavy? If straight, it can denote versatility. If very wavy, it can denote emotional problems. Does it slant up or down, and how much? In other words, are you moody, optimistic, pessimistic, or depressed – and to what degree?

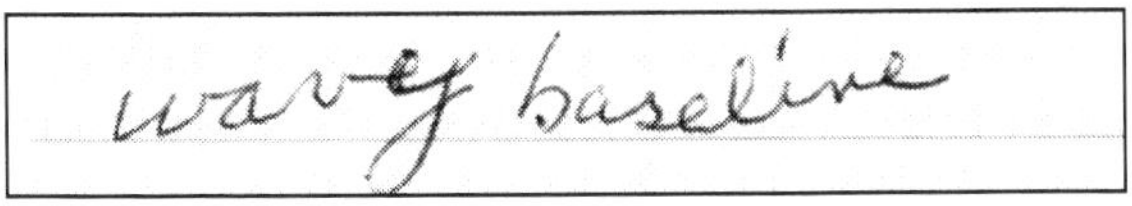

Large left margin and narrow right margin – no ruminating on the past; eagerness to meet people and willingness to embrace the future. **Large right margin and narrow left margin** – fear of people and the future; clinging to the familiar and the past:

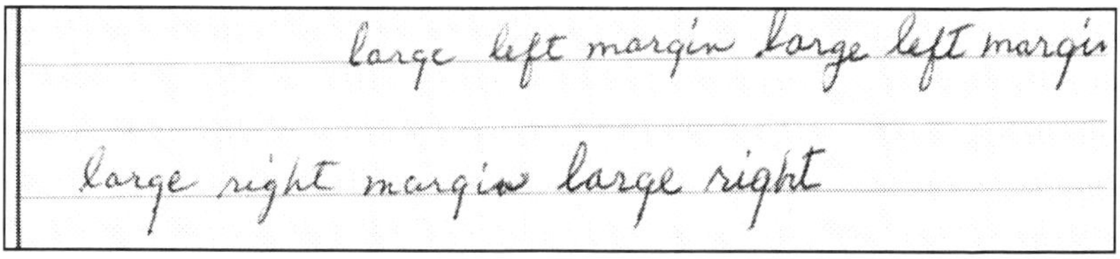

Wide spacing between words – a need for personal space, or more time alone.

Wide spacing between letters – expansive; emotions easily communicated. **Narrow spacing between letters** – emotions held back, suppressed:

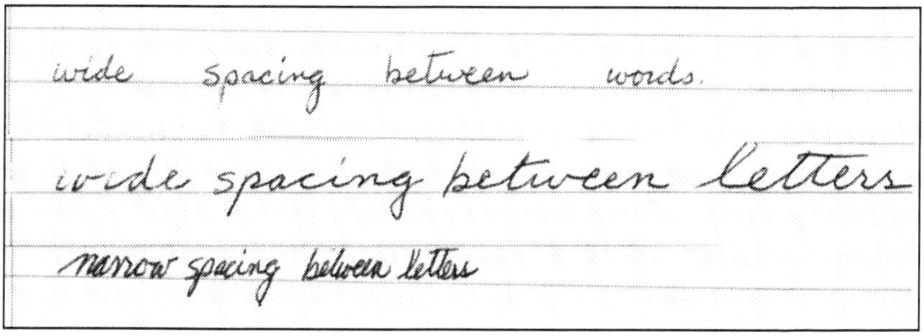

Your "t's" Tell on You: I can tell more from your cursive "t" than any other letter:

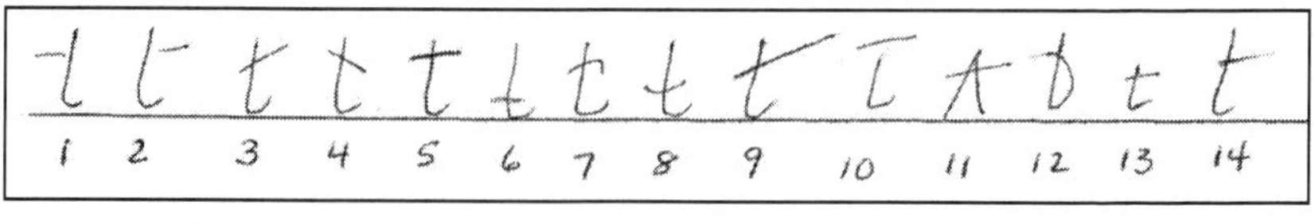

1) Procrastination.
2) Strong irritation to losing temper.
3) Optimism.

4) Pessimism and wanting one's own way.
5) Strong willpower, realistic goal-setting.
6) Weak will, low goal-setting, lack of confidence, low self-esteem.
7) Self-control.
8) A giving-up.
9) Enthusiasm.
10) Daydreaming, visionary goal-setting.
11) Stubbornness.
12) Blaming self.
13) Independent-minded, or not caring what others think.
14) Sarcasm.

Our **thinking processes** show in our "m's" and "n's." The **rounded** "m" in the writing of the genius Thomas Edison is predominantly rounded (slow and logical). The faster **sharp-angled** "m" denotes an analytical and investigative mind. The **inverted** "m" that looks like a "u" is the fastest; the writer understands instantly, comprehensively. However, the fast is not necessarily bright, nor the slow stupid:

How we **communicate** is indicated in the "a' and "o". **Loop on the left** – lying to yourself (rationalizing). **Loop on the right** – secretive. Loops both left and right – possibly not completely honest with others. No loop but closed – reticent. Wide open – very talkative.

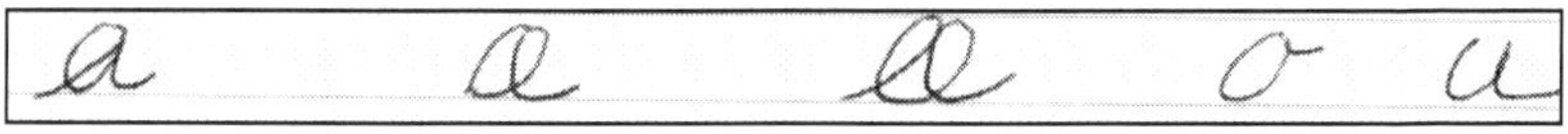

Now, the basic traits necessary for success in achieving what you want in life (realistic goal-setting and determination to carry out the goal) – high "t-bar" with firm and long down-stroke of "g" (shown below) indicating confidence and self-esteem. Lack of those traits are seen in a weak, low, concave t-bar and weak, curved, short down-stroke of the "g" next to it:

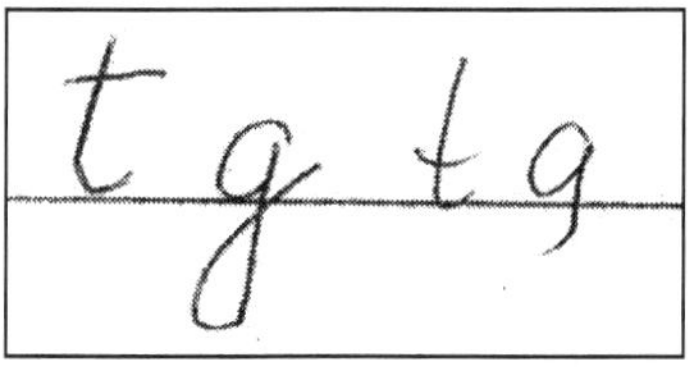

Evidence of integrity: what you want to see in the handwriting of a mate or employee or politician: sincerity, directness and frankness; broad-mindedness; generosity; self-confidence; pride; dignity; ambition and determination; loyalty; caution and self-control.

Some traits reducing its influence: dishonesty; evasiveness; weak willpower; yieldingness; prejudice; shallowness; pride; self-deceit; secrecy; selfishness, procrastination.

Evidence of Lack of Integrity (or dishonesty). Dishonesty is revealed in a **combination of various traits** – for example, loops and hooks in middle-zone letters, together with weak and concave t-bars (weak will), acquisitive hooks, and vanity, just to name a few. There are others and all are needed to be taken into consideration before judging dishonesty.

Finally, you need to be aware that printing does not give as much information as the cursive. What is lacking in printing (especially block-printing, **but is more present in cursive**) is evidence of traits indicated by the following strokes:

SLANT: Enough upstrokes *to evaluate your total emotional make-up.*

BEGINNING STROKES: Straight, curved, long, short (desire to acquire, aggression, resentment, anger, humor.)NO BEGINNING STROKES IN CURSIVE: Direct and to the point in communication

UPPER LOOPS: Wide, narrow, high, low, twisted, or pointed (abstract and philosophical ideas)

LOWER LOOPS: Long, short, wide, narrow, small, large, to right, left, curved or straight (physical and sexual energy, material imagination, completion of tasks, determination)

NO LOWER LOOP IN CURSIVE: Can work alone

MIDDLE ZONE LETTERS: Large, small, tiny (awareness of surroundings and people, or ability to concentrate.) Loops and hooks (rationalizing, secretiveness, deceit, evasiveness)

T-STEMS: High or low (standards and goals set, pride, vanity); looped (sensitivity to criticism)

T-BARS: High, low, floating, right or left of stem, heavy or light pressure, straight, concave or convex (strong, weak will, temper, procrastination, self-control, confidence or low self-esteem)
D-STEMS: High, low, looped or retraced (independent thinking, sensitivity to criticism)

Of course, there's much more to handwriting analysis than this. What I've given you are barely the basics. I have purposely not gone into more detail, especially when **a thorough analysis depends**

a great deal on *evaluation* of various strokes taken together. This requires years of study and years of practice. If you are a beginner, offering more in-depth analysis may only confuse and frustrate you. If you wish to delve more deeply into handwriting analysis, there are various courses available.

Good luck!

24748948R10155

Made in the USA
Charleston, SC
04 December 2013